WINDOWS 98

in easy steps

SPECIAL EDITION

Michael Price

COMPUTER
STEP

In easy steps is an imprint of Computer Step
Southfield Road. Southam
Warwickshire CV47 OFB. England

Tel: 01926 817999 Fax: 01926 817005
http://www.computerstep.com

Reprinted 2000

Notice of Liability

Trademarks

Printed and bound in the United Kingdom

ISBN 1-84078-030-4

Contents

Customising the layout | 117

6

Installing Applications | 141

7

Exchanging Information   159

8

Controlling the printer   179

9

Plus! 98   315

16

Performance tuning   335

17

What's new?

This chapter looks at the evolution of Windows. It identifies and explains the new and changed features to be found in Windows 98, as they appear to Windows 95 users and to users of other systems.

Covers

Chapter One

Evolving Windows

The first operating systems for the IBM PC at its launch in 1981 were the text based CPM and MS-DOS, which featured command line interfaces to the user. Microsoft introduced the Windows graphical interface two years later as an add-on to MS-DOS, and using 16-bit architecture to match the early PC processors. The early versions (1.0 to 3.0) were to a great extent experimental and niche products with limited function. Windows version 3.1, released in 1991, was a very significant milestone, since it marked the point when Windows gained widespread use and established itself as the de facto standard for the graphical user interface. The workgroup version 3.11 followed, adding networking capability but otherwise remaining similar.

Year	91	92	93	94	95	96	97	98	99
3.1x	Windows 3.1	Windows 3.1	Windows 3.11	Windows 3.11	Windows 3.11				
NT/2000			3.1 WindowsNT	3.1 WindowsNT	3.5 WindowsNT	3.51 WindowsNT	4.0 WindowsNT	4.0 WindowsNT	Windows 2000 Professional
95/98						Windows95	Windows95	Windows98	Windows98

At the same time, Microsoft introduced the 32-bit Windows NT, aimed at the corporate environment with improved security and administration support. Lacking support for many Windows games and applications, this system was for businesses and the standard for network servers.

The next major change occurred in 1995 with the release of Windows 95, which set new standards for the user interface and also for the hardware management. As a 32-bit system it also took advantage of the power of the more advanced 386 and 486 PC processors. Windows 95 removed the need for an MS-DOS operating system, by the simple expedient of including the basic function in the Windows system.

...cont'd

OSRs (OEM [Original Equipment Manufacturer] service releases) are updated versions of Windows, for loading onto new PCs.

Windows NT 4.0 picked up the Windows 95 desktop and user interface, but was quickly eclipsed by the release of Windows 98. This moves the standards forward and integrates Internet technology into the operating system. The changes it introduces are more evolutionary than revolutionary, since some of the hardware device support has already appeared in the Windows 95 OSRs, and the interface and Internet features are already familiar to users of Internet Explorer. However, there are significant performance and ease of use benefits, and support for new PC systems and peripherals.

Windows 98 is more reliable than its predecessor, and so may appeal to those users who remained with Windows 3.11 on account of reported problems with Windows 95. However, the PC that runs Windows 3.11 comfortably may need upgrading or replacing to run Windows 98 effectively.

Windows NT remains the system of choice for network servers, but workstation users can switch to Windows 98 or look to Windows NT 5, now known as Windows 2000.

Apple Mac users, who have long enjoyed the benefits of a

fully intuitive graphical user interface, may find themselves tempted by the combination of the power and economy of current Intel based PC compatibles with the mature graphical user interface that Windows 98 can now offer.

If you are currently using Windows 95, the move to Windows 98 is relatively painless, and you will automatically get the benefit of many of the enhancements, especially those that are included "under the bonnet". However, you may need to apply changes to take full advantage of the new environment. The following pages outline the main features, and the subsequent chapters describe them in more detail and tell you how to achieve the maximum benefits.

Requirements

The basic requirements for Windows 98 are not too demanding, by current PC standards. Microsoft quotes the following minimum specifications for the Windows 98 PC:

- Intel 486DX66 or equivalent.

- 16 MB RAM (random access memory).

- Between 120 MB and 295 MB hard disk. Typical is 195 MB.

- CD-ROM drive.

- 3.5" HD floppy drive (optional).

- VGA monitor and graphics adapter.

- Two button mouse.

Setup enforces this requirement and will for example detect a 486-33 processor and refuse to continue. Be warned, however that the specification is what is needed to *install* Windows 98. There is no allowance for applications or data, so you must allow more disk space and memory.

A more realistic minimum is a Pentium 90 PC with 24 MB memory and 512 MB disk space, but many Windows applications, especially those with database or graphics, will demand more resources. You will also need a higher specification SVGA monitor and matching graphics adapter to display Windows applications effectively.

Many specialists will advise you to upgrade to a PC with a Pentium II or a Pentium plus MMX processor and 32 MB memory, and even then they may recommend that you minimise the numbers of concurrent applications. Some features of Windows 98 such as full motion video and 3D graphics may require more memory and a faster processor to operate realistically and avoid jerky or fragmented video and sound operations.

...cont'd

For applications and games that use these functions, the optimum specification could be:

- Intel Pentium II 266MHz.
- 64 MB memory.
- 6.4 GB hard disk.
- 32-speed CD-ROM.
- 1024 x 768 truColour SVGA monitor, with 8 MB 3D graphics adapter.
- Mouse and joystick or gamepad input device.

These PC hardware guidelines apply to the initial Windows 98 and to the later Second Edition (see page 16).

To use all the features of Windows 98, you will need additional hardware, software or services:

For Internet or e-mail:

- 14,400 baud data or data/fax modem (33,600 baud modem recommended).
- Account with ISP (Internet service provider).

For audio applications:

- Soundcard and speakers or headphone.

For DVD video films:

- DVD-ROM drive.
- DVD decoder card or software.

For network connection:

- LAN adapter.
- Network software.

For Web TV:

- PC TV or TV/radio tuner adapter card.

Versions of Windows 98

There are also two Editions of Windows 98: the initial edition and the Second Edition which includes maintenance fixes and replaces IE4 by the newer IE5.

Microsoft supplies two versions of Windows 98, one an upgrade package and the other a full version. There are just a few differences between these – the upgrade version checks for a qualifying product, while the full version does no check but is more expensive. The qualifying products are Windows version 3.0 or higher, Windows for Workgroups version 3.1 or higher, Windows 95, all versions of Windows NT Workstation, or OS/2 version 2.0 or higher.

* Windows 98 CD £161.50

* Windows 98 CD upgrade £85.50

* Windows 98 on HD disks (extra) £15.00

The retail prices are shown in the table. You may find lower prices in PC shops or catalogues, and if you are a student or a teacher, you may be entitled to take advantage of special academic prices for Microsoft products.

If you format your hard drive to start fresh, you'll need the original Windows installation disks as proof of purchase.

You can install the upgrade version of Windows 98 onto a PC of suitable specification that is currently running any version of Windows 3 or Windows 95. It will replace the existing operating system, though you can retain a copy of the original setup just in case you need to undo the installation.

The full version of Windows 98 is intended for a new PC or a newly formatted hard disk or disk partition. Installing this version requires a bootable floppy disk, included with the product.

This version of Windows 98 is used for new PCs with pre-installed software.

Windows 98 vs other systems

If you upgrade from Windows 3.1x to Windows 98, you will find new ways of performing familiar tasks. To start programs, use the Start menu, and locate the Programs folder or other applications folder and click the program you want. These groups correspond to the program groups in Program Manager, except that you can have program folders nested within folders.

Many Windows 3.1x keyboard shortcuts, like Alt+Tab to switch windows and Alt+F4 to end tasks, also work in Windows 98.

The Windows Explorer program is like File Manager with the additional benefit that it displays all your drive connections in one window. You can make changes settings in the Control Panel, and start an MS-DOS prompt to run DOS programs, or select Start and Run programs from the command line.

You can use the Copy and Paste methods that you use in your word processor to copy or move files in Windows Explorer. The taskbar provides an easy way for you to switch between active programs and open windows.

Windows 98 will bring a feeling of deja-vu for Apple Mac users.

If you were previously using the Apple Mac, you will already be used to the level of function that Windows 98 offers. You just need to become used to new locations and different terminology. Your disk drives are not on the desktop, but they are accessible by double-clicking the My Computer icon on the desktop. Windows 98 uses shortcuts to programs and documents, in place of aliases on the Macintosh. Deleted files are moved to the Recycle Bin. You can use long file names, up to 255 characters. You'll notice that the mouse has two or even three buttons, though selecting and most generally used functions rely on the left mouse button. The right button displays a quick menu of common tasks, but you can always perform the functions using the menu bar commands instead. The third (middle) button, or the wheel that appears on some mouse types, is for navigation and special functions.

Windows 98 desktop

The user interface is where differences will most readily become apparent, but the extent of the change depends on which of the desktop options you choose.

1 The menu bar is 3D as used in Microsoft Office.

2 The Address Bar shows the file path or Web page Uniform Resource Locator (URL), and allows you to type in the location you want.

3 Gradient Title Bars add a touch of class, but only when you select hicolour or better (see example on opposite page).

4 The Windows Explorer has navigation buttons like Internet Explorer.

5 The Quick Launch toolbar starts or selects frequently used applications such as Internet Explorer and E-mail.

The Active desktop shows the most changes, though many of the features will be familiar if you previously had Internet Explorer (IE) installed on your copy of Windows 95. Some of the desktop and Windows Explorer changes are shown:

1 Explorer handles files and folders on your hard disk, and Web pages on your Internet access.

2 The Image Logo changes between Windows and IE to remind you when you are connected.

3 The Channel Guide provides a list of Web sites that can automatically send information updates to your hard disk.

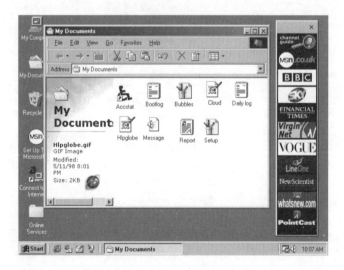

Display can be slow for large bitmap files.

4 The Explorer window displays a description of the selected item – e.g. file, folder or drive item.

5 The Preview Window displays a thumbnail image view of the selected item if it is HTML or one of the graphics file types.

Windows 98 features

Even the initial Setup is easier in Windows 98. The process is clear, and needs little intervention. For upgrades from Windows 95, Setup replicates the original settings and selections, for quicker installation and less user interaction.

Setup tells you what is happening, step by step.

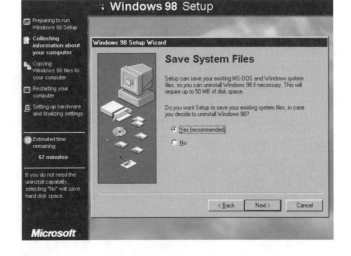

If you convert the file system to FAT32 after you install Windows 98, you cannot uninstall Windows 98 and return to your previous operating system.

Setup will keep a copy of the previous system, so you can revert back if your initial testing proves it necessary to delay implementing Windows 98.

The emergency boot disk (EBD) is created during setup or from the Add/Remove Programs option at any time afterwards. It has a generic real-mode ATAPI CD-ROM driver, so that the CD-ROM drive can be accessed when the PC is started from the EBD. It also supports various backup devices, for use in system recovery, though you cannot use Zip disks unless you add the Zip disk Guest support provided on the program CD.

This driver may not work with all CD-ROM devices. Replace with the DOS device driver supplied with the drive.

For more information, view the associated Web site at www.microsoft. com/ enable/

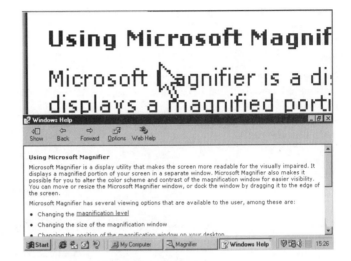

Windows 98 helps people with disabilities, a growing requirement in the light of legislation in Europe and the USA. The Accessibility Configuration Wizard helps adapt the options in Windows for specific needs and preferences. The low-power screen magnifier helps with moderate vision impairment.

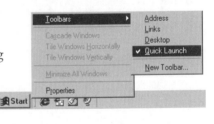

The taskbar has a new Quick Launch toolbar, and you can add further toolbars, including an address bar to directly access Web pages using URLs, or create your own custom toolbars.

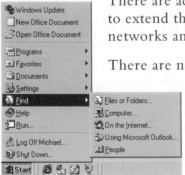

There are additions to the Find command, to extend the scope of searches to include networks and the Internet.

There are new options in the Favorites menu, particularly for Web-related items. You also have the facility to customise this or any of the menus using drag and drop to rearrange the entries.

Integrating the Internet

See Chapter 11, World Wide Web, for more ways in which Windows 98 integrates the Internet.

Windows 98 takes the position that it is part of an Internet-connected world, and it is designed to give access to data in the same way, whether the information is local or on the Internet. It achieves this by using Internet standards such as HTML, and offers the same interface whether the user is accessing the hard disk or the World Wide Web. The Help system for example uses HTML and provides a Web extension for broader or more current data.

To make it easier to access Web sites, Windows 98 uses AutoComplete. This works like AutoType in the Office applications, but handles URL Web site and Web page addresses,

suggesting the address as soon as you have typed in a few characters, and providing a shortcut menu with variations based on URLs that you have viewed previously.

Printing options in the browser are extended to allow functionality which includes background printing of documents, and there are several frame-set printing options to allow you to select which frames you want to print. This allows you to capture the information without the accompanying banner ads.

When you find pages on the Web that interest you and request subscriptions, Windows 98 will check and tell you when they change. It will automatically, or on demand, download copies to your hard disk. You can then disconnect from the Internet and continue to work with the data offline.

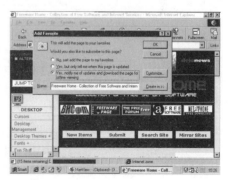

Internet tools

Windows 98 provides a set of tools that can be used over corporate intranets or the Internet. To access the tools:

In addition to the Start menu entries, there are shortcuts to the main Internet tools, Internet Explorer, Outlook Express and Channels, on the desktop and on the quick launch pad.

1 Select Start, Programs, and open the Internet Explorer folder.

2 Choose Internet Explorer or the Internet tool you require.

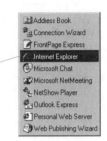

The Windows Address Book keeps track of names, e-mail addresses and other details. The Connection Wizard helps you set up a link to your Internet service provider. Microsoft FrontPage Express is an HTML editor that helps you create the Web pages without having to understand the HTML language.

Internet Explorer Browser allows you to switch to and display Web sites and Web pages. Microsoft Chat lets you enter a chat room on an Internet server and have real-time typed conversations with other people.

Microsoft NetMeeting supports on-line conferences – voice, data or video based. The NetShow player allows you to view live and on-demand NetShow-based broadcasts on the Internet. Outlook Express provides e-mail and newsgroup access.

You can publish Web pages on intranets or the Internet, using Personal Web Server (PWS) and Web Publishing Wizard to create a personal Web site.

Note that PWS will require a separate setup.

Performance

Windows 98 concentrates on reducing wait time, during startup and shutdown and while applications are loading.

Windows 98 system boot remains the same as Windows 95 on older PCs.

On newer PCs with ACPI (Advanced Configuration and Power Interface) fast-boot BIOS support, Windows 98 starts up much more quickly.

The Windows 98 system shut down is also much quicker than Windows 95. This is because Windows 98 does not need to communicate with network servers or hardware adapters during the shutdown process.

Windows 98 allows applications to launch much faster than Windows 95, especially when you have extra memory in the system, and the applications files are rearranged on the disk to ensure that the most used files are located together.

An improved version of the File Allocation Table (FAT) file system allows disks larger than 2 GB to be formatted as a single drive and uses smaller clusters, resulting in more efficient disk access.

Third-party system tools such as PartitionMagic can convert disks in either direction.

There is a Drive Converter utility in the System Tools folder, to convert a partition from FAT to FAT32. It works for drives larger than 512 MB, and converts the disk in place, so you won't have to backup and restore.

Don't convert if you need to access the drive from another operating system that does not support FAT32.

The resource Kit (see page 112) has a tool to tell you the estimated benefit, before you take the plunge. You can expect to gain up to 25% extra disk space, and programs will load 50% faster, on PCs with 2 GB or larger drives.

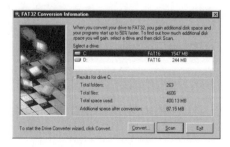

Power Management

Windows 98 has a new Power Management utility that provides a group of power settings, optimised according to the type of PC. This is not just for battery PCs, since you can select Desktop or Portable, or choose Always On for servers, or change the suggested settings for monitor, disk and system unit.

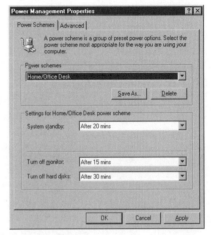

Windows 98 supports the OnNow approach, where the PC appears to be off but responds immediately to user or application requests. The monitor switches to standby mode, and the hard drive will spin-down, reducing both power consumption and noise. For laptop PCs, Windows 98 turns off other devices such as PC Card modems when not in use, to improve the battery life.

Other Advanced Power Management (APM) standards supported include multiple battery management, and modem wake-on-ring, where the system reactivates on receiving an incoming call.

If you are leaving the system for a while, you can manually select the standby mode instead of shutting down, so that it becomes instantly available when you return.

I	Click Start, and then Shutdown.

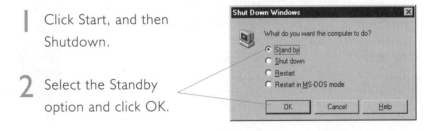

2 Select the Standby option and click OK.

3 Press any key to reactivate the system.

System tools

The Maintenance Wizard system tool schedules tune-up jobs to run automatically on a regular basis, or as required, to check for disk errors and delete unnecessary files. It also tracks file usage to enable programs to load and run faster.

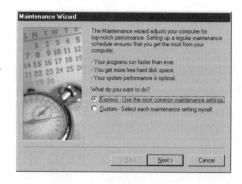

There is a centralised system information utility that gathers system-configuration data that is useful when you need to call on technical support.

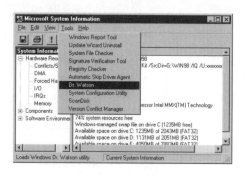

It also acts as a repository where you can find and run the system tools you need to help you diagnose and fix problems on your PC.

Windows 98 has a new backup utility that supports parallel, IDE/ATAPI and SCSI devices, floppy disks and network drives. Amongst other options, it provides for a complete system backup. This can be used in conjunction with the emergency boot disk and with the System Recovery utility to rebuild your system in the event of problems. Boot from the EBD, and restore from your latest full backup without first having to reinstall the operating system and the backup software.

Display features

Windows 98 allows you to change the display resolution and colour-depth without rebooting. You can also set the refresh rate for the monitor.

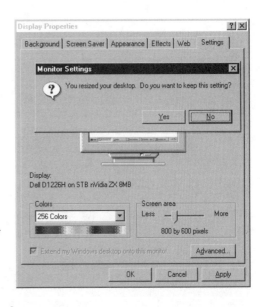

For lower-resolution displays, such as VGA-only monitors or laptop LCD panels, hardware panning may allow you to have a virtual-desktop that is larger than the screen resolution.

You can use more than one monitor with Windows 98, but this requires additional display adapters.

These features were previously included in the Microsoft Plus! add-on for Windows 95. Other features from this that are now part of Windows 98 include full-window drag, font smoothing, large icons and high-colour icons.

A feature that is exclusive to Windows 98 is the built-in capability to display work on more than one monitor. This can be extremely helpful in applications such as desktop publishing and Web-site design. You can add a second display and display adapter to your system, set up the two monitors to different resolutions and colour depths, and assign applications to the most appropriate monitor.

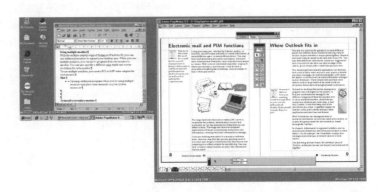

Staying up to date

Windows 98 uses the live update technique to keep your system up to date.

Windows 98 provides support for new types of hardware including Universal Serial Bus (USB), Firewire (IEEE 1394) high-speed serial bus, Advanced Configuration and Power Interface (ACPI), DVD-ROM, Accelerated Graphics Port (AGP) graphics interface, PCMCIA (PC cards), and infrared (IrDA) devices. Web TV for Windows works with a TV/radio tuner card to enable the PC to receive and interact with television and other data distributed over the broadcast network. Windows 98 will get out of date as new devices are announced. There may also be the need for program changes when problems are detected or when new features are developed. Microsoft tackles this requirement through the Windows Update Web site:

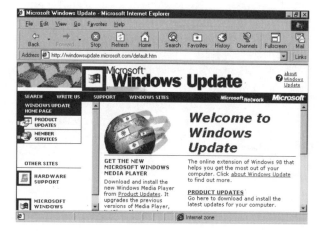

You can download a software tool to give you Critical Update notification of important changes (see page 213).

This will help you keep your system tuned and up-to-date by analysing your setup, and recommending product fixes, updates and new programs, and by providing technical guidance and information. Remember however that the Windows Update facility requires you to connect to the Internet, to install the changes and even to remove the changes that you no longer need.

Microsoft will continue to provide service updates, or new releases such as Windows 98 Second Edition, to provide fixes and new components for new PCs and for users who do not have access to the Internet.

Exploring Windows

This chapter explores the Windows 98 desktop and the components that appear when you start the system, and it reveals the sources of help available on the PC and on the Internet.

Covers

Chapter Two

Starting up

This section assumes that your PC already has Windows 98 installed and ready to use. See Chapter 15 for the steps to install and configure the software.

When you power-up your PC, the system runs for a minute or two and there is quite a lot of disk activity before the system is available for you to use. During this time, the hardware is activated and the logo displays, while behind the scenes Windows 98 checks the status of your system, and loads all the software needed to run the applications and the attachments on your PC. The actual details of the startup process will differ from system to system, but these are the main steps that are followed:

1 Check memory, and load hardware BIOS code.

Press Escape when the logo appears, to see what is happening behind the scenes.

2 Load the Win98 system files, and Win98 logo.

3 Load hardware device drivers, and attach the plug and play devices.

The initial programs are defined in the Startup folder.

4 Log on to the Windows 98 system as a specific user and load up the required startup programs.

For normal operations, you just wait while the system carries out all the work. If necessary however, you can intervene, and choose a different course of action, for example to enter the system BIOS setup, or to start the system in safe mode or in MS-DOS.

Restart the system, wait for the message "Windows 98 starting..." then press F8 to display the startup menu (see page 35).

Welcome to Windows

When Windows starts for the first time, it plays a tune and presents the Welcome to Windows initial task list.

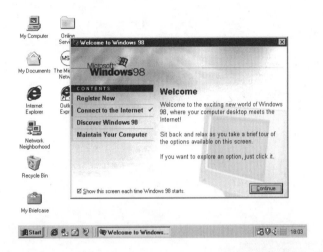

Register Now – to register your copy of Windows 98 in this way requires a modem and telephone line, and it transmits your details to Microsoft, making you eligible for Windows Update. You can register by mail if you wish.

Windows 98 includes access data for 5 services (AOL, AT&T, CompuServe, MSN and Prodigy) but you are not limited to these.

Connect to the Internet – this helps you to specify your Internet Service Provider (ISP) and account details, or to connect to an ISP to obtain a new trial account.

Discover Windows 98 – this has three tutorials, for new users, users of other systems, and Windows 95 users respectively. Note that the tours require files from the Windows 98 CD.

Redisplay the Welcome panel from System Tools in the Start menu.

Maintain your Computer – run the maintenance wizard to set up regular housekeeping tasks.

You don't have to perform all these tasks immediately, since the panel appears each time you start Windows, until you click the box in the bottom-left corner to prevent the display showing each time Windows 98 starts up.

Desktop items

The specific layout of your Windows 98 desktop will depend on the options installed on your system, the changes that you make to customise the machine, and the contents of the desktop at the time it was last shut down. Typically however, you will find these components:

Folders left open when you Shutdown will be reopened when you restart. Programs will not be restarted.

My Computer – a view of the PC that includes drives, printers and the Control Panel

Internet Explorer and Channels – access points for the World Wide Web

My Documents – a folder of your work in process

Outlook Express – your e-mail or diary system

Recycle Bin – intermediate storage for deleted files

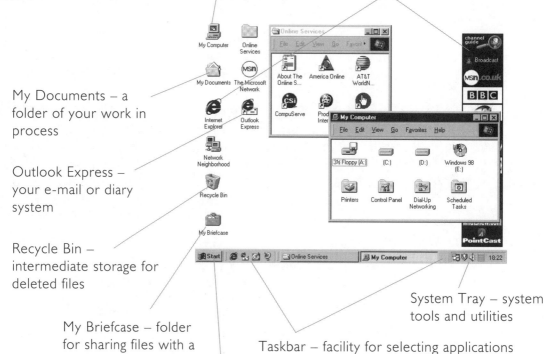

My Briefcase – folder for sharing files with a laptop

Taskbar – facility for selecting applications and tools, with toolbars such as the quick launch bar

System Tray – system tools and utilities

Start Button – the list of application groups and programs

My Computer

If the desktop is obscured, click the Show Desktop icon on the Quick Launch bar, or press Win+M.

To see the devices on your computer:

1 Double-click the My Computer icon on the desktop.

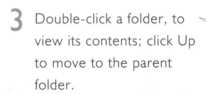

2 Double-click the drive icon to see the files and folders in the root folder.

3 Double-click a folder, to view its contents; click Up to move to the parent folder.

To see the contents of the selected folder in the same window, instead of getting a new window each time:

4 Select View, Folders options, and click the Settings button.

Refer to Windows 98 in easy steps (ISBN 1-874029-70-9) for more general coverage of essential Windows features.

5 Click the option to Open each folder in the same window.

6 Press OK, Close to save the change.

You can reverse this for any particular folder whenever you wish, by holding down the Ctrl key while you open that folder.

As well as drives, you can view and work with the printers defined on your system, the Control Panel device folder, your network connections, and your scheduled tasks.

Channel bar

Something that is quite new to the desktop is the Active Channel bar. These are Web sites that have information specially packaged to match interest areas. If you Subscribe to a channel, updated information will be transferred from the selected Web sites to your hard disk, for you to read offline. Channels are designed to be updated via broadcast TV, but this will require a TV tuner card and possibly a move to the USA.

To close the Channel bar, move the mouse pointer to top of the Channel bar, and click the Close button on the frame that appears around the bar.

Channels are provided by the BBC, Sky, the FT, Virgin, and many other suppliers.

If the Channel bar does not appear on the desktop:

1 Press Start, Settings, Active Desktop, and then select Customize my Desktop.

You can also open Internet Explorer with the channel bar showing: click the Channel icon in the quick launch bar.

2 Choose the Web tab, and click the box 'View my Active Desktop as a web page'.

3 Click the Internet Explorer Channel Bar check box.

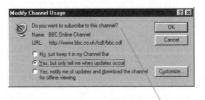

When you select a channel, Internet Explorer starts in full screen mode, and switches to the selected site. You are invited to subscribe to the channel and you can ask to be notified of changes or request downloads to be sent automatically.

There are several thousand channels in all, so you must be very selective.

To find the channel that will suit you, go to the Microsoft Channel Guide Web site which keeps a count of the channels available and offers a search facility.

Start menu

To display the contents of the Start menu, press the Start button on the taskbar. The shortcut entries and folders on the Start menu include several new items and some extensions to older items.

- There's high level access to the Internet. You will also find entries to create or open documents, if you use the Office suite.

- Programs displays the subfolders and application programs. You can now drag and drop entries to customise the menus.

- Favorites allows you to open Web sites that you have previously visited and book-marked. This list is also on the menu bars in My Computer, Network Neighbourhood, Windows Explorer, Control Panel, and even the Recycle Bin.

- Settings has new commands to display and modify the Folder Options and to turn on and customise the Active Desktop.

- Find has new commands to search for documents and Web sites On the Internet, and the People command to consult directory services and address books to locate address details.

- Help and Run commands as in Windows 95.

- Log Off allows you to log off and log on again as a different user.

Find files and folders

The Find command caters for the times when you know that the document is somewhere on the hard disk, but you just can't remember where you saved the file. It supports simple searches by file name or more advanced searches using whatever information you have, date, file type, keywords, etc. To start the Find command:

If you have the Win key, press Win+F to start Find immediately.

1 Press Start, Find, Files or Folders to display the initial panel.

2 Type the file name. Use wild cards (e.g. *.txt, *.doc) if unsure of the name or type.

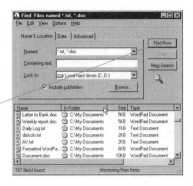

3 Select the drive or browse to the folder that should contain the file, and press Find Now.

You can search all local hard disks with the one Find command.
Select Look In, Local hard drives (C:,D:).

4 You'll get a list of all the files that match.

If you're looking for a document, you can expect a long list. Find will return a list of up to 10,000 files. Beyond that, the search will be terminated.

You can sort the list of results to help locate the file:

5 Click on a header (Name, Folder, Size, Type, or Date Modified) to sort the entries by the values in that column.

6 Click the header again to invert the sequence.

...cont'd

When you have defined a useful search command, save it as a shortcut on the desktop.

There are several methods to reduce the number of files in the list, to save you examining them individually.

1   Add a key word or phrase from the document to the Containing text box. This can be with, or instead of, file names and types.

2   For an exact match, select Options, Case Sensitive. Select it again to remove the option and ignore case.

3   Select the Date tab, enter the range of dates, or the days or months since the files were modified, created or last accessed.

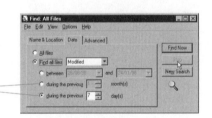

4   Select New Search to clear the criteria on all the tabs, so you can make a fresh list.

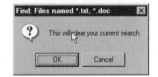

5   Select the Advanced tab and select from the list of file descriptions. These may pick up several related file types e.g. HTM and HTML. Providing a range of file sizes is another way to subdivide a list of matches.

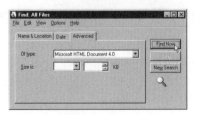

Viewing results

When you have narrowed the results list to a manageable number of files, you can investigate them more closely.

I Highlight a file you want to review and right-click it (or press the Application key).

MDI (multiple document interface) applications handle several documents at once in separate windows.

2 Open the file with the associated application if you want to make changes, or Quick View the contents. You can also Print, Copy etc.

3 Hold down Ctrl and select several files to process at one time. Then right-click the group and select the action. File types that use an MDI application will open together. Other applications like Wordpad will open multiple copies.

You can use Find to look for Internet documents and objects stored in the page cache on your hard disk:

When you select multiple HTML documents, choose 'Open in same window' to see them in the same IE4 session.

4 Select Browse and locate the Temporary Internet Files folder, in the Windows folder.

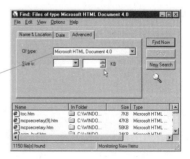

5 Choose the file type, for example HTML documents and press Find Now.

Recent documents

If you are trying to locate a document that you have recently been working with, don't overlook the recent documents list. To open a file from the list:

Not all applications are able to add their files to the Documents list.

1 Click Start and then select Documents. You'll see a list of wordprocessing and image files.

2 Click the name of the document you want to open, and the associated application starts up with that document loaded.

You can right-click a clear part of the taskbar and select

Properties.

To clear the Documents list:

3 Click Start, Settings, Taskbar & Start Menu, and choose the Start Menu Programs tab.

4 Press the Clear button in the Documents menu. This does not delete the files themselves.

If all else fails, look in the Recycle Bin. To restore a deleted file:

Recycle Bin

5 Double-click the Recycle Bin on the desktop to select the file or files you need.

6 Right-click the selection and choose Restore.

Starting programs

If the program you want is not in the Start menu, click Start, Find, Files or Folders, and use the Find utility to locate the program file.

To start a program, locate the appropriate entry in the Start menu. For example, to start Calculator and Wordpad:

1 Press Start, Programs, Accessories and Calculator.

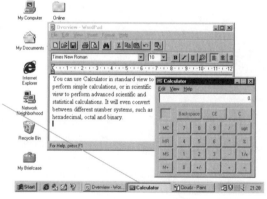

2 Press, Start, Programs, Accessories and then Wordpad.

3 Click the program name on the taskbar to make its window active.

4 Click another name to switch programs.

5 Click the active name to minimise its window and select the next program.

6 Click the minimised name again, to redisplay the window.

To stop running the program, click the Close button on the top right corner of the window, or right-click the taskbar entry and select Close. In either case, you will first be prompted to save any open files.

Components

You can find out what is installed by viewing the Start menu folders Programs and Accessories and its subfolders.

There are many application programs, tools and utilities provided with Windows 98. Not all will be installed on your PC, since the items provided depend on the choices made at Setup, or on the selection already installed for your previous system, and on the attachments fitted to your PC.

The groups available include:

- Accessibility options that make the PC display and keyboard easier to manage.

  > 🗗 Accessibility Wizard
  > 🔍 Magnifier

- Accessories such as Calculator and Wordpad, Briefcase, Paint and other office tools.

  > 🖩 Calculator
  > 📷 Imaging
  > 📝 Notepad
  > 🖌 Paint
  > 📄 WordPad

- The games programs provide light relief, and are particularly useful for providing practice with the mouse and keyboard.

  > 🎴 FreeCell
  > ♣ Hearts
  > 💥 Minesweeper
  > 🃏 Solitaire

- Communications tools link the PC with other users and systems, through cables or the telephone system, and allow you to share data and to conduct meetings electronically.

  > 📶 Dial-Up Networking
  > 🖧 Direct Cable Connection
  > 🖵 HyperTerminal
  > 📡 ISDN Configuration Wizard
  > ☎ Phone Dialer

- Desktop themes add sets of wallpaper, sounds, mouse pointers, screensavers and icons to personalise your PC.

- Internet tools allow you to create pages on the Internet, to access the pages that other users have created, and generally to treat the Internet as an extension of your system.

  > 📖 Address Book
  > 🔗 Connection Wizard
  > 📝 FrontPage Express
  > 🌐 Internet Explorer
  > 😊 Microsoft Chat
  > 🎦 Microsoft NetMeeting
  > 🎬 NetShow Player
  > 📧 Outlook Express
  > 🌍 Personal Web Server
  > 🌏 Web Publishing Wizard

- E-mail messaging, newsgroup and address book management features are also provided to support your use of the Internet.

Many of the 3D and multimedia features are designed to enhance the performance of games on the PC.

- Windows provides support for Western European languages and additional support is available for the Baltic, Central European, Cyrillic, Greek or Turkish languages.

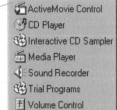

- There are many multimedia tools, to support soundcards, CD and DVD drives and video players, and special features to speed up screen display and add interesting effects.

- There are some pre-defined on-line services to support your Internet and e-mail, but you can connect to any service using the wizard.

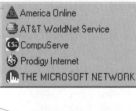

- System Tools, ranging from Backup utility to the System Monitor, provide the facilities to maintain your system and keep it working at peak efficiency.

- Features to support Web TV will be added if you have the TV tuner adapter required.

The full version of the Resource Kit provides many more utilities and information files.

- There are applications and utilities like Notepad that are automatically installed without you having to specifically request them.

- The Windows 98 Resource Kit sampler on the Windows 98 CD provides some very useful tools including WinDiff for comparing files and folders, and TweakUI for changing system settings.

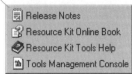

- Other utilities on the CD include network tools, old MS-DOS and Windows 95 commands.

Adding components

If the component you want is not installed, you can add it from the Control Panel:

You can also open the Control Panel from the My Computer folder.

1 Press the Start button, choose the settings option and click Control Panel.

2 Double-click the Add/Remove Programs option and select the Windows Setup tab.

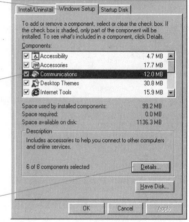

3 Click the component you want to add (or clear the box to remove a component).

4 To add or remove parts of the component, click Details for a list of the individual items.

The installed system device files take over 100 MB hard disk space, so you may prefer to free this space and use the CD-ROM when devices change.

If you installed your copy of Windows from a CD-ROM, you will be prompted to insert it. Pre-installed systems may have the necessary setup files stored on the hard disk.

The ResKit utilities have a setup program of their own in the ResKit folder in the Tools folder on the Windows 98 CD-ROM (see page 112).

The other utilities can be copied if required from their respective folders within the \tools folder.

Taskbar and toolbars

As well as the Start button and the icons for active programs and open windows, the taskbar contains the Launchpad and the system tray.

The launchpad is intended for shortcuts to any programs that you use often, but Internet programs are the default entries:

Internet Explorer, the Internet browser

Outlook Express, the e-mail program

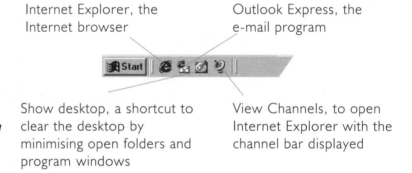

Show desktop, a shortcut to clear the desktop by minimising open folders and program windows

View Channels, to open Internet Explorer with the channel bar displayed

The system tray has icons for resident tools and utilities, usually installed at startup time. The entries depend on the hardware installed, but typical entries include:

The task scheduler utility

The Virus checking program

The Resource meter to check the level of activity

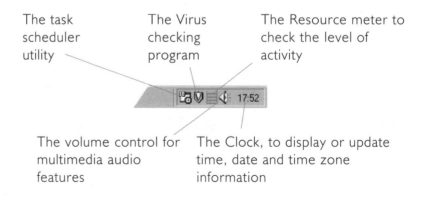

The volume control for multimedia audio features

The Clock, to display or update time, date and time zone information

You can add other toolbars to the taskbar, including the Address bar, the Links bar and the Desktop bar (the desktop icons in a toolbar), or you can create your own.

... cont'd

You can add your own toolbar to the taskbar, to supplement the standard toolbars. The easiest way is to create a folder of shortcuts, then convert this to a toolbar.

1 Create a new folder on the hard disk, and create or copy shortcuts into it.

2 Right-click the taskbar, select Toolbars and choose New Toolbar.

3 Enter the path to the folder of shortcuts that you created.

This makes the folder into a toolbar on your taskbar. The folder title and icon text are included so you will have to scroll the toolbar by clicking the arrows to see the rest of the entries.

You can change the way that the shortcuts are displayed in the toolbar, and use it as an alternative to the desktop.

A single click on a toolbar icon will start the application. A second click may start a second copy or may switch you to the current copy (as with the Internet Explorer on the quick launch bar).

When you right-click the taskbar, you will find that the new toolbar has been added to the list. However, this is not a permanent addition. If you ever de-select the toolbar it is dropped from the list, and you must repeat the above, from step 2 onwards, to redisplay your toolbar on the taskbar.

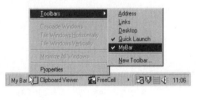

Getting help

When questions or problems arise using Windows 98, you have a number of options available for getting more information and advice.

If you have turned off this panel, you can find it again in System Tools on the Start menu.

The Welcome to Windows 98 panel appears automatically when you start Windows 98 (see page 31). This provides introductory tutorials at various levels to suit new or experienced users.

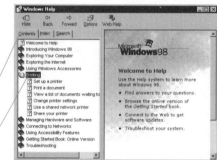

For everyday, general help requirements:

1 Click the Start button, select Help and choose the Contents tab.

For help and guidance in solving specific problems, select the Troubleshooting chapter.

2 Double-click a chapter heading to display the list of sections.

3 Double-click a section heading to open it.

If you are connected to the Internet, you can use Support Online to review current technical information and search the Microsoft Knowledge Base.

1 Press the Web Help button and click Support Online.

If necessary, your browser is started and connected to the Internet. The Microsoft Support page is displayed for you to enter searches.

Exploring the CD

The Windows Setup CD contains more than just the install program files.

Before looking more closely at the contents of your Windows 98 system, it may be worth taking a few minutes to explore the Windows CD.

1 Insert the CD while Windows 98 is active.

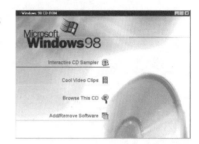

To avoid the AutoRun, hold down the Shift key while inserting the disc. Then right-click the drive icon and select explore.

2 The AutoRun program automatically displays a menu of the contents.

The Interactive CD Sampler tells you about the other software available from Microsoft, divided into four different areas.

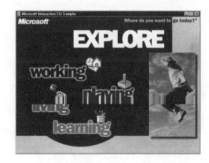

- Working.

- Playing.

- Living.

- Learning.

Cool video clips demonstrate the multimedia capabilities of Windows 98, through a series of movie clips that are commercials for other Microsoft products.

You can browse the files and folders on the CD, and transfer some of the additional utilities (see page 112). You can also start up the Add/Remove option if you want to change your selection of Windows 98 components.

Closing down

Alt+F4 is a universal Close that ends the current window or application.

One more thing to do before continuing the exploration of Windows 98, is to make sure that you know how to stop. Closing down the system properly is an essential part of using the system.

1 Close all open windows and end all active programs.

2 Select Start, Shut down and choose the type of shut down.

3 Click OK to action the shut down, or Cancel to return to Windows.

Any folders that are left open will be remembered and reopened the next time you use the system.

Select Restart if you want to refresh the system, for example if unexpected problems arise after you have been running for a long period. Problems can arise with a program and the Windows resources allocated to it, especially if you start and stop applications a number of times.

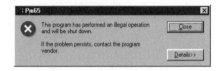

You can Restart the system in the original MS-DOS command line mode. This may be necessary to run an old DOS application, or to run special utilities that cannot operate in the normal protected Windows environment.

If you have finished working with your system and you are ready to switch it off, choose Shut down, and Windows will terminate all running programs and prepare the machine for power-off. If there are active programs which have modified data in memory, you are prompted to save the associated file.

My Computer close-up

This chapter looks at the My Computer folder which provides a graphical representation of the PC and its hardware and software attachments.

Covers

Chapter Three

My Computer

You can also open the folder by left-clicking and pressing Enter, or by right-clicking and selecting Open.

Double-click the My Computer icon on the desktop to open the folder. You will see icons – small images representing the drives on your PC – including the floppy drive, the hard disk, the CD-ROM drive or other removable drives, and any networked drives, plus a number of system folders.

Double-click any icon, for example the C: hard disk, and it will open as a folder, displaying another set of icons, the folders or directories it contains, plus any files that may be in the top level or root folder.

Your folder may appear in Web view (page 52) instead of the classic view shown here.

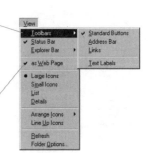

The selected folder may open in the space previously occupied by the My Computer folder, or it may appear as an extra window on the desktop. This depends on the Folder Options that are set. These options also govern the style and content of the folder window. You can make extensive changes to the settings (see page 128). To see the main options:

1 Select View from the menu bar, and click Toolbars to select and display.

Refer to Windows 98 in easy steps (ISBN 1-874029-70-9) for more general coverage of essential Windows features.

2 Display Status bar and Explorer bar (used when connected to the Web).

3 Switch between Classic view and the Web view for folders (see page 52).

4 Choose the size and the organisation for the folder contents (see page 51).

5 Adjust folder and file options (see page 53).

Folder views

The folder normally displays its contents as large icons, but when there are many files in the folder, you won't be able to see many names. You can change what's displayed using the View menu. You can choose:

1 Large Icons, showing the least number of entries in a folder.

2 Small Icons, allowing you to display a large number of items in the folder window.

3 The List view, listing the small icons, organised in columns, to make it easier to locate files.

4 The Details view, providing information about the files and folders, with size, type, location and date of change.

Sort by two fields in turn to get, for example, a list by Size within Type.

You can sort the items in the Details view by clicking on the header, to order by name, type, size or date. Click the header a second time to reverse the sequence.

You can also sort in ascending order by selecting View, Arrange Icons and choosing the field.

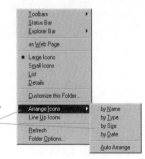

View as Web page

You can create your own style of folder, using the customisation option (see page 129).

The folder windows shown on the preceding pages are all in the style used in Windows 95, but in Windows 98 you can also view the folder in a more pictorial manner. Select View from the menu bar and click As Web Page. The exact form of the window will depend on the size. If there is room, you get extra details about the highlighted entry:

Selected item.

Folder name.

Name and description of the selected item.

Preview (for image items).

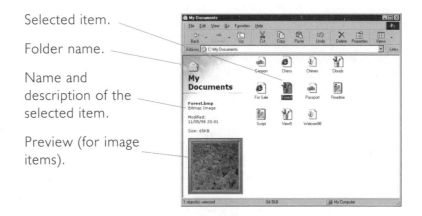

When the Window size is reduced, the display area for the extra information is also reduced, and scroll bars are added. Beyond a certain level of reduction, the details are dropped, and only the folder name remains.

Other features of the folder window apply to classic as well as Web style folders. They include:

Title bar with optional path.

Standard toolbar, with optional text labels.

Folder Address bar.

Links bar for URLs.

Status bar for snapshot data on the selected items.

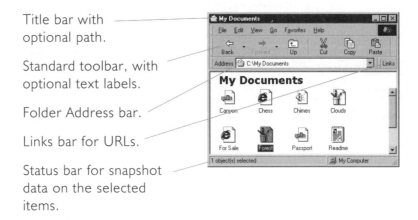

Folder Options

To review or change the settings for folders, when there is no folder open:

1 Press the Start button, select Settings and choose Folder Options from the list displayed.

To review or change the individual settings in an open folder:

2 Select View from the menu bar, choose Folder Options and select the General or View tab.

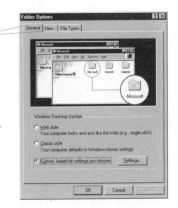

The General tab allows you to select the basic style, either Web or Classic, or to make your own custom selection.

The View tab allows you to apply detailed changes to settings for the current folder or for all folders. The options include:

- Retain individual changes for particular folders.

- Show file extensions for known file types.

- Show file attributes in detail view.

- Display the contents while dragging a window to a new position.

- Show system or hidden files.

File functions

When you double-click a file icon, the action that is taken depends on the type of file – application, data or system.

An application program file such as MSPaint or WordPad will start up ready to process its data files (bitmap images or documents respectively).

Registered data files such as bitmaps or documents will be loaded up for viewing or modification, using the application program specified in the folder options.

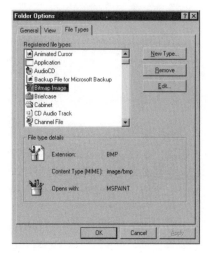

For multimedia file types such as wave, midi or video, the file is loaded up and the appropriate player starts to process the file, playing sounds or displaying motion pictures.

To process unregistered file types:

| Double-click the icon and the Open With dialog displays.

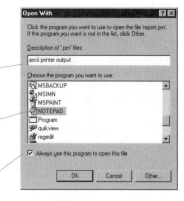

If you clear the box, the application selected is used on this one occasion only, and the file type won't be registered.

2 Enter a description for the file type.

3 Choose which application program can process this type of file.

4 Check the box to register this file type from now on.

...cont'd

The first functions listed when you right-click a file icon depend on the file type, and on the applications that have been installed on your PC. Typically, you will see the following:

1 Open (default action), Print or Quick View for documents and images.

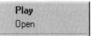

2 Play (the default) and Open without playing for audio and video files.

Hold down Shift for a range of files, or Ctrl for multiple files, and then right-click and select Open in Same Window.

3 Open (the default) to execute, or Quick View for technical information about program files.

4 For applications such as Internet Explorer that handle more than one document at a time, select an additional file and Open in Same Window. You can also Edit the source text.

The functions are also available as buttons on the standard toolbar.

5 Only 'Open with' is offered for unregistered document types.

The other functions on the icon menus are the same for all the file types. You can Send To another location (see page 56), cut and copy the file to another folder, make a short cut, delete or rename the file, and display the file properties (see page 64).

Send To

To send a file or folder to disk:

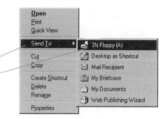

1   Insert the target disk (if removable) and right-click the file or folder you wish to copy.

Sending a file or folder to a disk sends a copy, leaving the original file or folder in place.

2   Select Send To, and then pick the destination.

The target may be a floppy disk, the desktop (as a shortcut), an e-mail message, the My Briefcase or My Documents folder, or the Web publishing wizard.

You can add other destinations, such as a fax or a folder, to the Send To list, by adding shortcuts to the Send To folder, which is in the Windows folder. For example, to add the folder D:\Figures:

1   Select Start, Find and locate the SendTo folder.

2   Double-click the folder icon to open it.

If you send a file to a destination that already has a copy, you can choose to replace it or skip the copy.

3   Select File, New, Shortcut and specify the path and name for the folder.

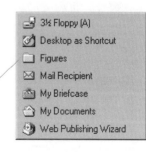

4   Double-click a file or folder icon and select Send To to see the new destination.

My Computer menu

Windows Explorer displays the contents of drives and folders in folder view or in a hierarchical, tree structure view (see page 66).

When you right-click the My Computer icon on the desktop, the quick menu displays all the actions that you can perform, including:

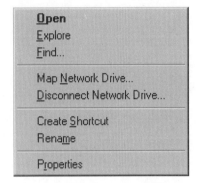

- Open (the default) to display the contents of My Computer in the Windows Explorer folder.

- Explore, to display the folder contents in the other Windows Explorer view.

- Find will launch the Find command with My Computer as the target.

These two commands only appear when some form of networking has been set up on your PC.

- Map drive letters for networked drives on other PCs to which you are connected (see page 291).

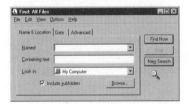

- Disconnect networked drives that you have previously mapped.

- Create a shortcut on the desktop, though this command is hardly necessary, since My Computer is already on the desktop.

- Rename the My Computer icon to something more to your liking.

- Finally, select Properties to display the System Properties.

Mike's Machine

There are at least four ways to open System Properties.

You can also open System Properties from the System option in Control Panel, or by pressing Alt as you double-click My Computer, or by pressing Win+Pause.

System

The Hard Drive

The hard drive icon acts just like a folder.

When you right-click the hard drive icon in My Computer, the quick menu displays the functions that apply to it:

1 Select Open to display the contents of the drive in the Windows Explorer folder view.

2 Choose Explore to see the contents in the Windows Explorer tree structure view.

3 The Find command starts a search for files and folders on the hard drive.

4 Backup begins the archive process, where selected files and folders are copied to another storage device, such as a removable disk or tape.

Windows does check and refuse to run Format if there are any files in use. This will protect the C: drive.

5 The Format command must be treated with care since using it will remove all data on the drive.

There will be an extra Compression property page, for FAT drives, and there may be a Sharing page for networked drives.

6 Create Shortcut places a link to the hard disk on the desktop, not in My Computer.

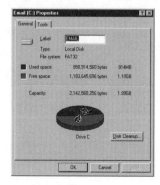

7 Properties displays the space on the disk and allows you to run disk tools (see the next page).

The General disk properties page provides the following data:

- The drive label, or name.

- The drive type.

- The file system type.

- The amount of disk space used.

- The remaining free space.

- The disk capacity.

There are several disk tools available:

You can run these individually, or allow the maintenance wizard to take care of your hard disk and run the tools as needed (see page 329).

- The Cleanup utility to remove unnecessary or outdated files, making more disk space available.

- Scandisk to check for and repair disk errors.

- Backup, to make copies of the drive.

- Defrag, to optimise the data organisation on the disk.

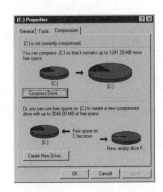

An alternative is to use folder compression such as provided in the Plus 98 package, to compress parts of the information on your disk (see page 321).

For FAT systems, the Compression page provides information about the potential benefits of using disk compression to store extra information, or the actual effects if you do have compression applied (see page 248).

However, using this option would prevent you from using the FAT32 system, which reduces waste space and speeds up file loading.

Removable drives

Right-click the diskette drive to display the quick menu options that apply. You'll see the same options as for the hard drive, with the addition of the Copy Disk command.

Copy Disk is for removable drives only, and allows you to make a complete backup from one disk to another.

To make several copies of the same diskette, use the DOS DiskCopy command instead. It reads the diskette once, and makes as many copies as you want without having to re-read the original.

Format prepares a new diskette, or clears data from an existing diskette.

Use a Full format if you want to make sure that a diskette is valid.

The diskette drive can be the target of files sent from other drives, using the Send To feature (see page 56).

If you Cut or Copy files from another folder, you can Paste them into the floppy drive, from the windows

Explorer folder or tree view.

The diskette drive is not automatically checked when you change diskettes, so Windows and any application with diskette files open will be unaware of the change until disk access is required. If you press F5 at the time of the change, this will prompt Windows 98 to check the drive and detect the change.

The functions offered on the CD-ROM quick menu depend on the type of CD. If it is a data CD, the menu is similar to the hard disk menu, with the Eject command provided in place of the Format command.

You can enable AutoRun for any type of drive, with Registry settings.

Selecting Eject causes the CD-ROM drive to open the disc tray, or to eject the CD caddy, depending on the type of drive, so that you can change discs.

When there is an Autorun.inf present in the root of the data CD, an additional command AutoRun appears on the menu, and it becomes the default action in place of Open. When you insert this type of CD, Windows 98 detects the Autorun.inf file and carries out the instructions that it contains. Normally this will be to execute a front-end program that offers you a menu of actions, such as Install, Demo or Explore contents.

You can change the action taken when an audio CD is detected.

The menu changes again when you insert an audio disc into the CD-ROM drive. The Play command becomes the default, and it automatically runs the CD Player program to start playing the first track of the disc.

The program selected will depend on which particular soundcard you have and which audio software has been installed.

The Properties page for all of these types of CD shows the capacity as fully utilised and there are no maintenance tools, since the drive is read-only.

Control Panel

The Control Panel can be the main point of control for your system, with access to all the devices.

Every hardware and software device in Windows 98 has its own set of Properties pages, and stores its settings and values in the Registry. The Control Panel has icons for each device, defined by .Cpl files in the System folder, to access the properties pages. This allows you to change hardware and software settings from one place within Windows 98, and without having to edit the Registry directly.

For example, you can change settings for:

- Display.

- Internet.

- Keyboard.

- Modem.

- Mouse.

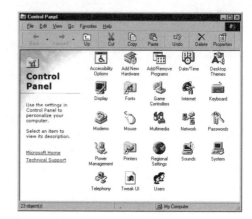

- Printers.

TweakUI is a special utility from the Windows 98 Resource Kit that allows you to change the user interface (see page 112).

- Soundcard.

- Users.

When a new device is added to the system, part of the setup process will include providing the required control file, and adding a new icon to the Control Panel.

There are several ways to open the Control Panel, but the most usual ways are:

You can execute Control.exe from Run, or add it to the Start menu (see page 127).

1 Double-click My Computer and then double-click the Control Panel icon that it contains.

2 Press the Start button and select Settings, Control Panel.

3 Press Win+C (may not work on all PCs).

Printers

You can also access the printer folder from Start, Settings, and there is a shortcut to Printers in Control Panel.

My Computer contains the Printers folder. This holds the Add Printer wizard, and icons for any printers that have been defined on your system. To add a printer:

1 Double-click My Computer and double-click the Printers folder.

2 Double-click Add Printer to start the wizard and build a driver list.

3 Select the make and model of your printer, or click Have Disk if you have a device diskette or CD supplied with the printer.

4 Choose the printer port, make the printer the Windows default and let the system print a sample page.

5 Right-click the printer icon to control the printer and access the properties page.

Check the printer settings. You may find that the paper size defaults to Letter, and Memory to the minimum.

Check the printer properties pages, in particular to see the paper size assigned. It may default to Letter instead of A4. Also check device options such as memory installed and paper trays, since the defaults may not suit your printer.

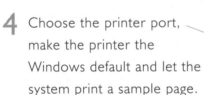

File and folder properties

File and folder options are not the only place where you can affect the actions of files and folders. Some of the characteristics are defined in the properties pages. To display the properties of a file you have several options:

I Right-click the file icon and select Properties from the context menu.

2 Select the icon, press the Application key and select Properties.

3 Press Alt and double-click the icon to display properties immediately.

These options apply to folders as well as files.

The number of properties pages will depend on the file type, but all should have a General page with the main details for the file:

- Icon and long file name.

- File type, location and size.

- MS-DOS name, date created, and dates last modified or accessed.

- File attributes – read-only, archive, hidden or system.

To access folder properties, when the folder is open:

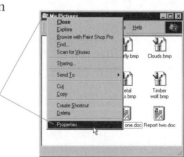

4 Right-click the folder icon on the left of the title bar, and select Properties from the menu.

There are some differences in the general properties for a folder compared to a file:

- There is a count of the files and folders contained.

- There is no track of dates accessed or modified.

- There's a new property check box: Enable thumbnail view.

This must be enabled on a folder by folder basis. With it enabled a new View option appears.

Select View from the menu bar, and select the new Thumbnails option.

This will display every bitmap image in the folder in a small image format, just like the preview displayed for the selected file when you view a folder as a Web page. This applies for most image types, including MIX used by Picture It!

Bitmap preview is another way to view images without opening them *(see page 374).*

The thumbnails are stored in a hidden Thumbs.db file in the folder and updated when you add or remove image files. For this reason, this property cannot be enabled on CD-ROMs or read-only network drives. Non-image files retain their normal icon, but it takes up more space. This view is most suitable for folders with mostly image files.

Windows Explorer

Select Start, Programs, Windows Explorer to display the contents of your PC in a hierarchical view, positioned at the C: drive. This is a two pane window that displays the drives and system folders in a tree

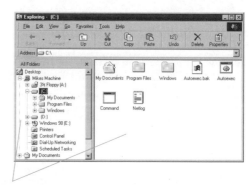

structure on the left, and the contents of the selected drive or folder on the right.

This only works when you start Windows Explorer from the Start menu. You cannot switch from the My Computer folders into the All Folders view since there is no All Folders option.

Hold down the Shift key as you double-click the My Computer icon, and instead of the folder view, you will see the same Windows Explorer tree view, but this time positioned at My Computer.

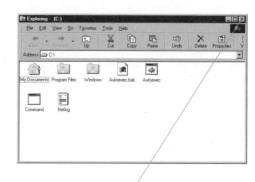

You may find it easier to navigate through your system components with the tree view, but you can switch back to the simpler folder view whenever you wish.

1 Press the Close button on the folders pane, to display the single folder, as in My Computer view.

2 Select View from the menu bar, and then Explorer bar, and select All Folders, to revert to the Explorer view.

File and folder names

The naming conventions for files and folders in Windows 98 are very flexible, but there are some potential pitfalls, especially if you share files on a network with mixed operating systems. So it is worth taking a closer look at the file system. Windows 98 uses virtual file allocation table (VFAT), an enhanced version of file allocation table (FAT) used in MS-DOS. VFAT supports 32-bit file access and allows long file names.

VALIDFIL.NAM $ % ' - _ @ ~ ` ! ( ) ^

MS-DOS and Windows 3.1x file names use upper case letters and numbers, and some special characters. The period is used to separate the 1–8 character name from the 0–3 character extension.

Valid long file.Windows 98.style + . , ; = [ ]

Windows 98 allows up to 255 mixed case characters, with some additional special characters and more than one period in a name. The characters after the last period form the extension, even if there are more than three.

In practice, most file names are much less than the 255 maximum. This is just as well, since the Windows 98 path cannot exceed 260 characters in total. You should avoid over long file names, 20 or 30 characters being a practical limit.

The Windows 98 long file names are also supported by the universal disk format (UDF) used for files stored on DVDs, and by the CD-ROM file system (CDFS). The rules in Windows 2000 and OS/2 Warp are similar, so Windows 98 files can also be stored on network servers managed by these operating systems. However, this does require that you use 32-bit protected mode network drivers. Real-mode drivers, like 16-bit applications, can only work with the short file name.

Naming files

Windows 98 will generate an MS-DOS alias for each long file name.

To preserve compatibility with MS-DOS and Windows 3.1x applications, Windows 98 also generates a standard file name in the 8.3 format. Although known as an alias, it is the primary entry in the directory and carries the file details such as length, first cluster address and creation date.

The rules for creating the alias are straightforward, but they cannot be overridden by the user or the application. Some examples will illustrate the algorithm in action.

```
Alias           Long file name
EXACTLYS.AME    EXACTLYS.AME
INMIXEDC.ASE    InMixedc.ase
WITHSP~1.TXT    With spaces and longer.txt
WITHSP~2.TXT    With spaces and even longer.txt
WITH__~1.TXT    With += and other special characters.txt
```

The alias counter could change when files are moved between folders or to a floppy, if there are already some similarly named files, or if the aliases are generated in a different order.

If the long file name already satisfies the 8.3 rules, the alias would be identical and so there is only one entry in the directory. If it satisfies the rules except for case, there is an alias which is the upper case version of the file name.

Otherwise, the alias is composed of the first six MS-DOS valid characters (blanks ignored) from the name, plus a tilde (~) and a digit. The digit starts at 1, and if the alias name already exists, the digit is incremented until a unique alias is found. The first three characters after the last period form the extension.

To check the alias for a file, right-click the file icon in Windows Explorer and select Properties, General, or issue a Dir from MS-DOS prompt, which will show both alias and long file name.

LFN entries are given attributes RSHV. Because of the Vol attribute, MS-DOS will ignore the entries.

If you want to see the directory entries, you'll need a disk utility such as Norton's DiskEdit. You will see that the LFN entries precede the associated alias. There is one LFN entry for every 13 characters in the long file name.

Name	.Ext	ID
EXACTLYS	AME	File
InMixedc.ase		LFN
INMIXEDC	ASE	File
nd longer.txt		LFN
With spaces a		LFN
WITHSP~1	TXT	File
r.txt		LFN
nd even longe		LFN
With spaces a		LFN
WITHSP~2	TXT	File
t		LFN
characters.tx		LFN
ther special		LFN
With += and o		LFN
WITH__~1	TXT	File

It is useful to explore the folders provided with Windows 98 and the applications you install, to see how these make use of the long file name. Take, for example, the Stationery samples folder installed with Windows 98:

1 The path is already 57 characters long before you add file names.

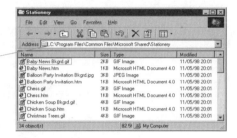

2 The long file name here is 34, making the path\filename 92.

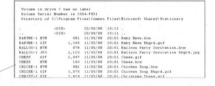

As long as the file type is different, the alias digit does not need to be incremented.

3 The directory listing at the MS-DOS prompt shows the aliases assigned.

Applications such as Word generate a long file name for new files, based on the first line of text in the document. If this would duplicate the name, the last character is turned into a counter. You can of course replace the name offered with a name of your choice.

Use a name with the first three or four letters significant, so that the aliases can be distinguished. For example, "1999 Annual report" would be better than "Annual Report 1999".

Avoid long file names in the root which has a fixed number of directory entries. This is not a problem if you use FAT32 which allows for extendable roots.

MS-DOS prompt

MS-DOS in Windows 98 is aware of long file names, but there are limitations.

When you switch to an MS-DOS prompt, with Windows still operating in the background, you can refer to the long file names from the command prompt. However, long file names must be put in quotation marks, if there are spaces included in the name.

Even then, you may have problems. The keyboard buffer is limited to 127 characters, which in turn limits the file names that can be entered.

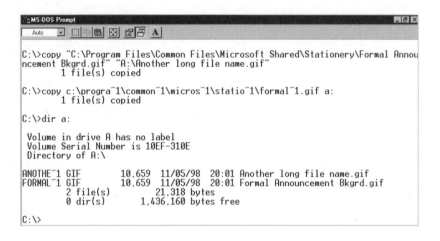

One way to reduce the size is to use the alias in place of the long file or folder names. You must check the aliases however, since it is not easy to predict which alias will be assigned.

You'll find the same effect with floppy disks created in Windows 98 and transported to an MS-DOS or Windows 3.1x system.

Alternatively, you can increase the buffer size to 256, as it is in batch files. To increase the global command-line limit for the keyboard buffer to its maximum add the following line to the Config.sys file:

shell=c:\windows\command.com /u:255

When you switch to MS-DOS Mode, without Windows active, it uses the real-mode FAT file system and long file names created in the Windows are not visible. Only the 8.3 file name aliases will be shown.

Windows 98 Accessories

This chapter forms a ready reference to the application programs, multimedia utilities and games, grouped by category, telling you what each does, how to get started and where to find more information.

Covers

Chapter Four

Accessibility Wizard

If the Accessibility options do not appear on your system, add components from the Windows 98 CD-ROM.

Accessibility options (such as StickyKeys, ShowSounds, and High Contrast) are intended to help users with particular disabilities to work more effectively with their PCs. The name is somewhat of a misnomer, since options such as MouseKeys and ToggleKeys will be of interest to all users. To display the options available:

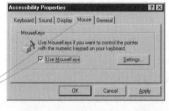

1 Open the Control Panel and select Accessibility Options.

2 Choose the Mouse tab, and click in the box to enable the MouseKeys option and control the mouse pointer using the numeric keypad.

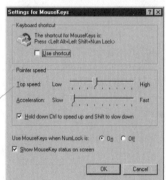

3 Select the Settings button to adjust the pointer speed etc..

4 Select the Keyboard or other tabs and review or enable other options.

The wizard can save parameters to a settings file, to be applied to another PC if you change systems.

An easy way to set up the options is by running the Accessibility Wizard from Accessories, Accessibility in the Start menu. This offers choices for the type of change you need, or the sort of problems you want to solve, and creates a suitable setup.

The settings that Accessibility generates are associated with the particular user Id in use at the time.

Microsoft Magnifier

The Wizard may install a display utility called the Magnifier, to enlarge a portion of your screen in a separate window, with colour and contrast changes if desired.

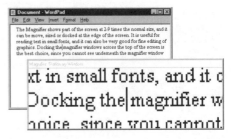

The Magnifier window can be moved or resized. However, you cannot view the part of the display that lies under the magnifier. The best option is to drag the window to an edge of the screen and dock it there. When you do this, the magnifier area is removed from the application screen area so nothing is obscured. To run Magnifier, select it from the Accessibility folder in the Start menu. Right-click the magnifier area to select options:

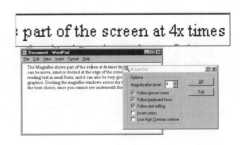

1 Set the magnification level between 2x and 9x.

2 Invert screen colours to their complementary colours.

3 Have the magnified view follow the mouse cursors.

4 Let the view track the keyboard focus.

5 Show the text being entered as you type.

Calculator

You can use your numeric keypad to enter numbers and operators, when Num Lock is on.

The Calculator provides a simple way to carry out calculations on-screen. There are two different views of the calculator. The standard view is used to perform simple calculations:

1 Select Programs, Accessories, Calculator from the Start menu.

2 Enter the first number in the calculation and click the operator key (+ - * /).

3 Enter the remaining numbers and operators, and press = for the result.

The keys include memory, backspace, percentage and square root. To check the purpose of any key, right-click it and then press the What's This? button that appears.

For more complex calculations:

The display is cleared when you switch views, but you can save and recall a value in memory using the MS and MR keys.

4 Click View on the menu bar and then choose Scientific.

You can select the number system (binary, decimal, octal or hexadecimal), use mathematical functions such as sines and logs, or enter statistical data.

5 Enter the data using the Sta and Dat keys, and click a statistics function such as Avg or Standard deviation.

Kodak Imaging

Imaging can input Jpg, Pcx, Xif, Gif and Wif images, as well as Tif, Bmp and Awd.

Kodak Imaging is designed to work with multipage faxed or scanned documents and with various types of image files, saving documents as .Tif or .Bmp images or .Awd faxes. It allows you to view and annotate the documents with text or drawings. There are zoom facilities, and you can rotate the picture through 90 or 180 degree turns. A neat feature is the rubberstamp which allows you to over-print documents with Draft or Date Received etc.

There is a preview facility for quicker display. To preview image documents:

1 Locate the image file using Find, My Computer or Windows Explorer.

2 Right-click the document icon and select Preview.

3 To annotate the document, select File from the menu bar and Open Image for Editing.

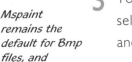

Mspaint remains the default for Bmp files, and Internet Explorer for Gif and Jpeg, unless you explicitly change the files types in Folder Options.

Preview is set as the default viewer for supported file types. To change your default image viewer:

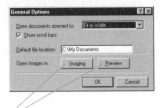

4 Select File from the menu bar and click Tools, General Options.

5 Click the Imaging or the Preview button, to set the default viewer for the supported image file types (tif, awd, wif etc.).

Notepad

Notepad is the Windows text editor used to create or edit plain text files, i.e. files that do not require any text formatting. It is also the default viewer for these type of text files. Since there is no text format, lines of text can be any length and are terminated by the carriage return Enter key. There is a word wrap facility to fit the text to the window width, so that you can view the text without excessive scrolling.

To activate word wrap:

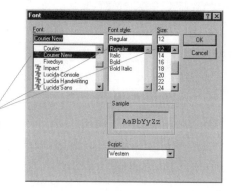

1. Select Edit from the menu bar and click Word Wrap.

2. Select Edit, Word Wrap again to deactivate it.

When you print the test, Word Wrap is ignored. The printer will either truncate lines or split them on a character boundary, depending on the printer type and the page and print settings.

You can change the font and style for the text but the changes you make will be applied to the whole document.

3. Select Edit, Set Font to display the font options.

4. Choose the font, font style and size to apply to all the text in the document.

You can run Notepad from the Start menu under Programs, Accessories, or just double-click the text file to open it in Notepad. It is normally associated with Txt files but you can register other plain text files such as Log or Prn.

Notepad has a time/date option that inserts the current values into the document. You can use this to maintain daily log files:

1 Double-click My Documents on the desktop to open it.

2 Right-click an empty part of the folder and select New, Text Document.

.LOG must be in capitals with a period in front, and at the start of the first line, or else it will be ignored.

3 Name the document Daily Log (or Daily Log.txt if you are displaying file extensions).

When this file is opened, the current time/ date is added at the end of the file, and the typing cursor set ready for you to add the day's entries.

4 Double-click the new file to open Notepad.

5 Add .LOG to the start of the first line and save the document.

Add a shortcut to your Startup folder to open Daily Log using Notepad, and you will see the Daily Log each time you restart Windows.

Paint

Paint works with individual image files in the Windows Bitmap format. With additional graphics filters such as those available in the Office suite, Paint can also read the Internet Gif and Jpg formats. With it you can view or edit a picture, or create your own. There is a range of tools and functions:

Select using a rectangle or a freehand shape.

1 Select parts of the image.

2 Erase, fill, colour or magnify.

3 Draw with pencil, brush or airbrush.

Shapes and text are converted into pixel form and incorporated into the image.

4 Add text, or lines and shapes to the image.

5 Choose colours from the palette or custom colours.

6 You can zoom the image (by 2x to 8x) to make detail changes. A thumbnail image shows you the effects normal size.

There are functions to flip or rotate the image, or the selected part of the image. Resize by a scale factor, to enlarge or reduce the image. Crop or expand the frame size to alter the canvas size but not the image.

...cont'd

You can select and copy the picture, or part of the image, to the Clipboard and then paste the selection into another file such as a WordPad document.

You can also turn a Paint picture into your personal desktop wallpaper, without having to access the display properties to set it up:

1 Save the picture to file but leave the Paint application open.

2 Select File from the menu bar.

Use the wallpaper feature with discretion, and avoid making the desktop difficult to read.

3 Choose Set As Wallpaper (Tiled) or Set As Wallpaper (Centered).

The image is copied as a Bmp file into the Windows folder and will appear as the desktop background.

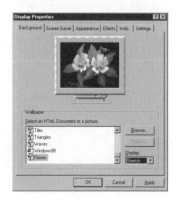

Paint may be registered to work with other image file types, if you have installed additional image filters using the Office suite.

To stretch the image to fill the desktop, you must open the Display Properties and select the Background tab. Use this page also when you wish to remove the background, by selecting the wallpaper named None.

You can run the Paint program from Accessories in the Start menu, or just double-click the bitmap icon in a folder or a document to launch the program.

WordPad

WordPad provides word processing functions that are quite suitable for letters and smaller documents. Output is saved in the .Doc format which is compatible with the Microsoft Word 6 and the Word 95 formats.

The version of WordPad shipped with Windows 98 does not support the Word 97 file format.

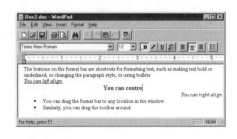

To check the settings for the document:

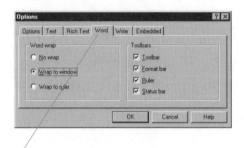

1 Select View from the menu bar and then Options.

2 Click the tab for the Word file format.

You can also choose other file formats such as Write, the predecessor to WordPad, Rich Text Format, useful for exchanging documents over the Internet, or the plain text format, and you can specify separate options for each of the file types. However, when you save the file as plain text, any formats that you have specified will be removed.

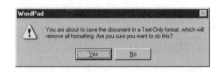

WordPad can be found on the Start menu under Accessories. You can also start WordPad by double-clicking a registered file type. However, if you have another word processor such as Microsoft Word installed, the registration will have been switched to that.

This method of overriding the default open action is available for other types of data file as well as documents.

You may still want to use WordPad for some documents since it will start up more quickly. Hold down the Shift key when you double click the file icon, and then select the extra entry 'Open with' that appears, and locate WordPad in the list of viewer applications.

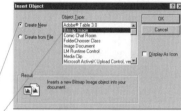

You can cut and paste Paint pictures into WordPad documents. You can also insert Paint images and many other application data types as objects.

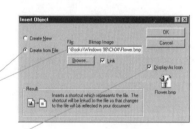

| | Select Insert from the menu bar and then click Object.

2 Click Create New and select the Object type, if desired.

3 Or click Create from File and enter the file name of the item required.

Using a link creates a smaller document, but it is easier to send documents when the data is actually included, and it avoids the effect of accidental changes to the original image.

4 Show the item itself, or a representative icon.

5 You can add the actual file into your document, or just place a link to the data file.

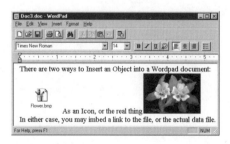

ActiveMovie Control

The ActiveMovie Control is used to play multimedia files of various types, including movies, sounds and songs. These files may be on your hard disk, on a CD-ROM, on a network file or located at an Internet site. Usually, the application or Web page will be responsible for launching the program. However, you can run ActiveMovie Control from the Entertainment folder in the Start menu:

1 Locate the drive and folder for the file you wish to view or process. For examples, see the Cdsamples\Videos folder on the Windows CD.

2 Find the file name that you want. You can search for movies (e.g. Avi or Mpg file types) or for sound files (e.g. Wav). Select a file such as Encarta.mpg.

Hide the controls to maximise the picture size.

3 When the file has loaded, press the Play button.

The Play button changes to a Pause button. Click the slider bar or drag the pointer to reposition the video, Right-click the image to display the functions menu. You can use this menu to switch the counter between duration and frame count, or to manage the video when you hide the controls.

CD Player

Use CD Player to play audio compact discs on the CD-ROM drive. You can listen over headphones plugged into the drive, but with a sound card installed, you can listen over your PC speaker system.

To run CD Player:

1 Insert the music CD into the CD-ROM drive.

2 The CD Player starts and the CD begins playing.

3 Press the Pause key, or the Stop key, fast forward or change tracks, just as you would on a normal CD player.

Select Disc, Edit Play List to enter the title and track details for the CD. They will be remembered when you insert the same CD in future.

4 Select View from the menu bar to display the toolbar, disc and track information, and the status bar.

To close CD Player, click the Close button in the upper-right corner of the display. This normally terminates the CD, but you can leave the CD playing on exit:

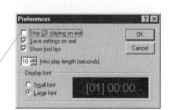

5 Select Options from the menu bar, click Preferences and clear the box.

DVD Player

To play a movie from hard disk or from a DVD disc that is already inserted, run DVD Player from the Entertainments folder in the Start menu.

With DVD (Digital Versatile Disc) Player, you can play DVD discs from a DVD drive connected to your computer, or from DVD files copied to your hard disk.

To run DVD Player with a disc:

1 Insert the DVD movie disc into the DVD drive.

2 The DVD Player starts and the movie begins to play.

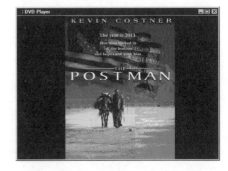

3 Use the controls to Pause , Stop, or Fast forward and back (at 2x or 8x speed).

Windows treats your DVD drive like a CD-ROM drive when you insert audio or data CD.

4 Right-click Play to display commands such as the Go To Previous or Next Chapter.

5 Select Menu to see special features such as trailers, cast list, scenes and biographies.

Media Player

This program is the player used for media clips inserted into documents.

Media Player plays a variety of audio, video, and animation files, including ActiveMovie, Mpeg, Video for Windows, wave sound, midi sequencer and CD Audio files. To start Media Player:

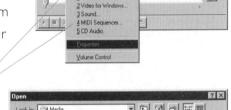

MIDI files (musical instrument digital interface) store a series of commands to instruct the PC sound card which notes to play and which predefined instrument sounds to use. These files are very much smaller than Wave files which contain the complete recorded sounds.

1 Select Media Player from the Entertainment folder on the Start menu.

2 Click Device on the menu bar and select a type e.g. midi.

3 Select File, Open to locate the file you want to play.

4 Open the file, and then press the Play button.

You can copy and paste a media clip into a WordPad document:

Play the multimedia file from within the document by double-clicking its icon or frame.

5 Select Edit from the menu bar and then Copy Object.

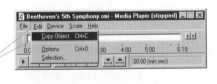

6 Open the document, select a position for the media clip, and Edit, Paste.

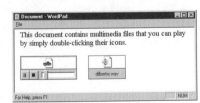

Sound Recorder

To use Sound Recorder, you need a sound card and
speakers. To record live sound, you also need a microphone.
Run Sound Recorder from the Start menu Entertainment
folder. To record from the microphone:

1 Select File from the menu bar
and choose New.

2 To begin recording, click the
Record button.

3 To end recording, click the Stop button, and press File, Save
As to create a Wave file.

You can make changes to your recording, cutting out the
parts you don't want and merging the sounds from other
recordings. You can also apply effects to the recording:

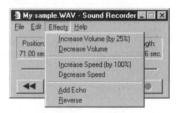

4 Select Effects on the menu bar
to list the options available.

5 Click Add Echo for a
reverberation effect. You can
click a second time, to get an
increased effect.

6 Click Reverse to play the sound
sample backwards.

You can also change the volume levels, and play the sound
clip faster or slower. The changes you make are not made
permanent until you save the file.

Web TV for Windows

Using Web TV for Windows, your computer can display both standard and interactive television broadcasts. You will need a TV tuner card, the hardware to receive and display television broadcasts on your monitor.

With a TV tuner card, you will be able to receive:

If you are upgrading to Windows 98 and already have a tuner card installed, you may need to update the device drivers.

1 Standard television broadcasts.

2 Interactive television broadcasts, which include supplementary information and activities. For example, a cookery program could have recipes to download.

3 Internet content and other data delivered over broadcast networks.

If you have an Internet connection but no TV tuner card, you will be able to receive:

4 TV program listings downloaded from a Web site to Program Guide. This has a search page so you can find programmes with specific actors or in particular categories.

5 Video and other information delivered over the local area network.

Volume Control

If you have a sound card, the Volume Control will adjust the volume and speaker balance when you play audio files. You can access the Volume Control from the individual media players:

ActiveMovie Control and Sound recorder have their own volume control, but these and all the other media players respond to Volume Control run direct.

1 In CD Player select View from the menu bar and choose Volume Control.

2 For DVD Player, click the Volume button on the control bar.

3 With Media Player, select Device, Volume Control.

To run Volume Control direct, there are three different methods available:

4 Click the Volume icon in the system tray to display the master volume slider and mute control.

Click Options, Properties to select volume controls for recording devices and voice.

5 Double-click the Speaker icon to display the full Volume Control.

6 Select the Volume Control from the Entertainment folder on the Start menu.

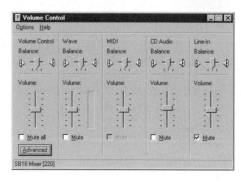

Games

Freecell is a game of patience for one player. The objective in Freecell is to move all the cards to the home cells, at the top right, using the free cells on the top left as place holders. You build a stack of cards for each suit, starting with the Ace and moving in sequence to the King.

It is claimed that every different deal can lead to a winning game, so long as you select the right strategy. The key is to keep your free cells unoccupied as much as possible, and to make empty columns available whenever possible.

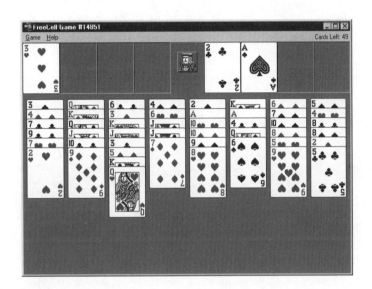

The actions required to play the game include:

1 Right-click a partially obscured card to reveal its contents.

2 Select a card to mark it for moving.

Games are numbered so you can retry a particular game as many times as you wish.

3 Select the destination to complete the move.

4 When only one legal move remains, the title bar flashes as a warning.

...cont'd

Hearts is a game for four players, and the objective is to end up with the lowest score at the end of the series of games. There are three ways to play:

If you are not on a network there is no choice. You play against the computer.

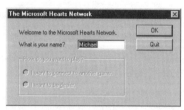

1 Play by yourself against your computer. Click 'I want to be dealer', and then press F2.

2 Start a new game over a network. Click 'I want to be dealer', and wait for other players to join the game.

3 Connect to a game that is already being played over a network. Click 'I want to connect to another game'.

You cannot play a points card in the first trick.

Choose three cards to pass to an opponent, and you will receive three cards from another opponent. To help win:

4 Pass cards with high values, such as aces or face cards.

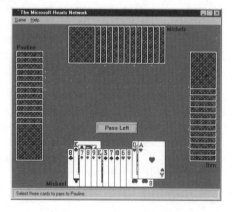

You cannot lead with a heart until a heart has been played on a previous trick.

5 Play your highest cards early in the game.

6 Avoid taking a trick containing hearts or the Queen of spades.

Or take the high risk strategy, take ALL the tricks with hearts and the Queen of spades. This is known as Shooting the Moon. You get zero points and the others get 26 each.

...cont'd

Minesweeper is a game for one person. The aim is to find all the mines as quickly as possible without uncovering any of them. To play the game:

1 Click Game, New. The timer starts when you click the first square.

2 Uncover a square by clicking it. If it contains a mine, you lose.

3 If the square contains a number, it indicates the number of mines in the adjacent eight squares.

4 To mark a square you suspect contains a mine, right-click it.

Look for common groups of the numbers, which may indicate a pattern of mines. For example, the group 2-3-2 at the edge of a set of uncovered squares indicates a row of three mines next to the three numbers.

When you succeed at the beginner's level, try your skill at one of the higher levels:

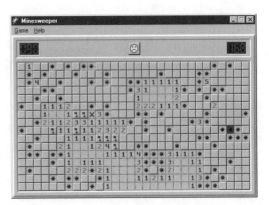

5 Select Game from the menu bar.

Pick Custom to design your own minefield challenge.

6 Choose the level, Intermediate or Advanced.

...cont'd

Known to most UK people as Patience, Solitaire involves you in rearranging all the cards in the deck into the four suits, in ascending order starting with the aces. To play Solitaire:

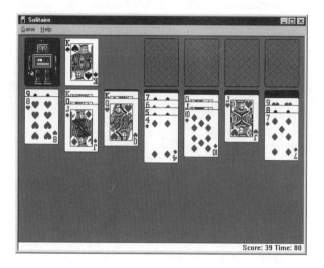

1 Click Game, Deal and the cards are set up in the seven stacks.

2 Click and drag cards to form descending sequences.

3 Double-click aces and other cards to add them to the suit stacks.

You can also set the dealing option (one card or three cards at a time).

4 Make all possible moves on the board before you click the deck to turn over more cards.

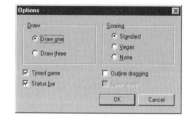

5 Select Games, Options to choose the scoring system.

System Tools

This chapter describes the tools and utilities provided with Windows 98 to handle communications, Internet, hard disk management and other system functions.

Covers

Chapter Five

Dial-Up Networking

To connect to an on-line service such as a bulletin board, use HyperTerminal rather than Dial-Up Networking.

If you have a modem and access to a telephone line, you can connect your PC to another machine known as a server and gain access to shared resources. To define and use the connection:

My Computer

Dial-Up Networking

Make New Connection

1 Double-click My Computer and double-click the Dial-Up Networking folder.

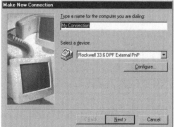

2 Double-click Make New Connection to start the wizard.

3 Follow the on-screen instructions to complete the definition. You will require the telephone number for the server you are connecting to.

Connections to some service providers are made easier because Windows 98 contains specific support to configure the dial-up networking settings.

4 Double-click the new entry in the Dial-up Networking folder.

My Connection

5 Enter the user name or ID provided.

6 Enter the password required, and check the box if you want Windows 98 to remember the password for you.

Click Connect and the modem will begin by dialling the number and making the connection with the other PC.

With Direct Cable Connection (DCC), you can share folders or printers belonging to a nearby PC, without a modem or a network. If the other PC is itself connected to a network, you gain access to that network. DCC is particularly useful when you use a mobile PC and an office PC, so you can combine their resources and keep data contents in sync. To set up a direct cable connection with another PC, you require:

You must use the same type of port on each.

1 An available serial port on each PC, or an available parallel port on each PC.

2 A special direct connection cable, parallel or serial depending on the type of port selected.

3 Direct Cable Connection installed on each PC.

Run DCC from the Communications folder in the Start menu, on the PC that will provide resources for sharing. Select Host, and the wizard will guide you through the steps needed to define the connection.

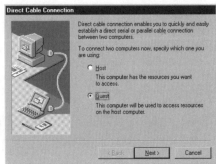

Repeat the process on the PC that will access the folders or printers, this time selecting Guest.

See page 296 for the use of DCC to connect two PCs as a network.

Direct Cable Connection is a convenient method of transferring medium amounts of data, which is too large to fit onto a floppy disk. It is relatively slow, especially with a serial connection, compared to a network adapter, so it may be less satisfactory for large volumes of data transfer.

HyperTerminal

Hyper Terminal uses the same Dialup Adapter as the Direct Cable Connection, Dialup Networking and Internet connections. Only one of these utilities at a time can be active.

HyperTerminal is the tool to use when you want to connect to a bulletin board or information service that isn't running Windows and is not part of the Internet. You will be able to send and receive files, and to explore the indexes and data provided by the service.

As with Dial-up Networking, you will need a modem and telephone line, and the appropriate telephone number. When you connect to the service, HyperTerminal handles the communications as though your PC is a "dumb terminal". To create and use a HyperTerminal connection:

1 Run HyperTerminal from the Communications folder in the Start menu.

To access files and printers on a PC running Windows, use Dial-Up Networking rather than HyperTerminal.

2 Double-click the program and enter the name, phone number and modem for the connection.

3 Save the details for the connection when prompted.

4 Double-click the new icon to start the connection.

5 Instructions for using the service will be displayed. These will vary, depending on the service. Make sure that you note their method for ending the link.

ISDN Configuration wizard

You must have ISDN hardware installed before you can run the ISDN Configuration wizard.

Some analog modems use the ISDN 64Kbps digital connection for the download half of the ISP link, to give an effective rate of 56Kbp.

ISDN (Integrated Services Digital Network) is a high-speed digital telephone service that increases the speed at which you connect to the Internet or to your local area network. It operates at speeds up to 128 kilobits per second (Kbps), which is four times faster than the best analog modems, which operate at 33 Kbps. As well as being faster, the digital service is also more reliable than the analog system. You'll require an ISDN adapter, software, and telephone service, and an ISP which provides connection support for ISDN. To set up your link, run the ISDN Configuration wizard from the Comms folder in the Start menu.

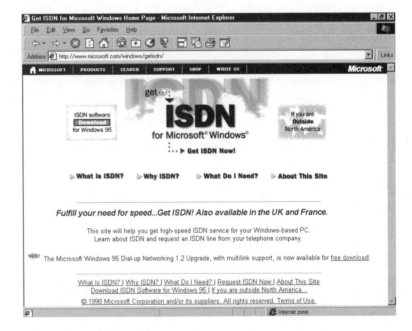

For more information about selecting the right components to set up and use ISDN, you can connect to the Internet and look on the Web at the Microsoft site:

http://www.microsoft.com/windows/getisdn/

Phone Dialer

You require a telephone handset attached to the modem or to the line, unless you have a voice modem and a sound card and microphone.

The modem can be used for simple tasks as well. Using Phone Dialer, you can initiate ordinary voice phone calls from your PC. Dialer displays a number pad, ten memories and a dial button. To dial the phone from the PC:

1 Connect the modem to the PC and the telephone socket, and power it on.

2 Run the utility from the Communications folder in the Start menu.

3 Type in the number that you want, or click the digits using the mouse.

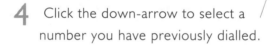

4 Click the down-arrow to select a number you have previously dialled.

You can edit all of your speed-dial buttons at once by clicking Speed Dial on the Edit menu.

5 Click Dial to make the call.

To store frequently dialled numbers:

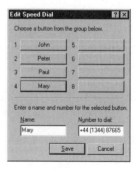

6 Click a spare speed-dial button, fill in the details and click Save (or Save and Dial to use the number immediately.

To dial the number in future, just click the appropriate speed-dial button.

...cont'd

Enter phone numbers as 12345... or in the full form as +44(123)456...

Use the International format if you have a special access number for long distance calls.

There are two formats for entering numbers.

Dialable format contains the numbers just as they are needed, and they are dialled without regard to your location.

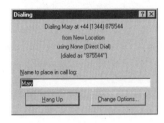

International format specifies the phone number in a format that can be dialled from any location, or using a calling card prefix code. The format is: +cc (ac) nnnnnn where cc is the country code, ac is the area or city code, and nnnnnn is the local part of the phone number.

For example: +44 (123) 5551234.

This is the format you should use if you are working with a mobile PC and visit different locations. To define the dialling requirements for a location:

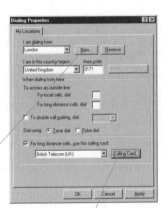

| Select Tools from the Dialer menu bar and click Dialing Properties.

2 Press the New button to create a new location, and enter the name, area code region and dialling rules.

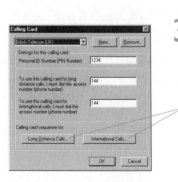

3 Click the box to invoke a calling card and press the button to define or adjust the access codes and number sequences for national and international calls.

5. System Tools | 99

Internet Connection Wizard

If there is currently no connection to the Internet set up on your PC, the Connect to the Internet icon appears on your desktop. Double-click to start the wizard, or select it from the Internet Explorer folder in the Start menu. The wizard offers three connection options:

I Create new Internet account.

Windows 98 has predefined setup information for some of the major Internet services (see page 200).

2 Use existing Internet account.

3 PC already set up for Internet access.

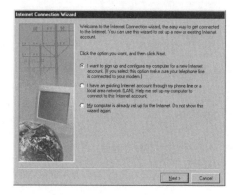

For a new account, the wizard obtains the latest list of Internet service providers from the Microsoft Internet Referral system. Select the name of the ISP you wish to use, to get more information about that ISP.

If you already have an Internet account with an ISP, you can enter the details needed to set up the account on this PC.

This situation also applies where you will be connecting to the Internet through your company's network. You'll need details from your network administrator.

If you already have your Internet connection defined on your computer, using the Dial-up networking utility or the software provided by your ISP, you can instruct the wizard not to display the startup screen in the future.

Backup

The Backup program comes from Seagate, so you'll find more information about backup from the Seagate Web site.

Backup copies selected files from the hard disk to a file, floppy disks, tape drive or other devices on your PC or to another computer on your network. If any of the original files are damaged or lost, you can restore them from the backup.

To start Backup, select it from the System Tools folder in the Start menu. To create and run a backup:

1 Select the option to create a new backup job.

Select Compress to reduce the size of the backup. Images and documents show the best savings.

2 Choose the drives, folders and files that you want to backup. You can specify files that are new or changed since the last backup.

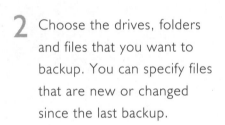

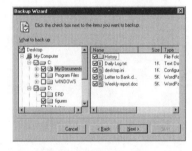

You will not be able to backup files that are currently in use, e.g. open documents.

3 Run the Backup and if desired verify the completed copy. You'll see reports of progress and results, with any problems identified.

When you want to restore one or more files, start Backup and choose the third option, then specify the backup file or disk. The catalog of files in the backup is displayed. You can select all files or individual files and restore them to their original folder's location or a new location if you want to preserve later changes.

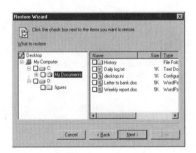

Character Map

Fonts contain up to 256 different characters, so the keyboard is not a good guide to the full character set, especially as there are symbol fonts that are all special characters. To make it easy for you to explore the fonts, Windows 98 includes the Character Map. Run this from the System Tools folder in the Start menu, and you will see the full contents of any font installed on your system.

Highlight a character and press Select, or double-click it, to select it for copying.

1 The holding area for the characters and symbols that you select.

You can select characters from one font at a time.

2 Choose a font from the list.

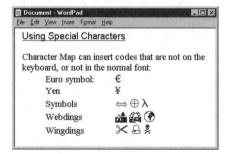

3 Press and hold the left mouse button to enlarge view.

To get the Euro symbol from the keyboard, press Ctrl+Alt+4, or you could press AltGr+4 or Alt+0128.

4 Keyboard entries that generate the current character are shown here.

5 Click Copy to copy the codes to the Clipboard.

6 Paste the symbols and characters into the required position in the document for any Windows program.

If the character does not appear the way you expect, check which font has been assigned for it.

The font type as well as the character code will be inserted into the document. For applications such as Notepad that support only one active font, you will not be able to insert symbols from different fonts. Applications like Wordpad allow you to insert entries from multiple fonts.

Clipboard Viewer

The Clipboard stores the segments of text or images that you cut or copy, and allows you to view or save as well as paste the contents.

To transfer information from one application to another, the most common method is to mark up the item, Cut or Copy it and then Paste it into its new location, for example using Paint and Wordpad. What happens behind the scenes is that the item gets stored temporarily in an area of system memory known as the Clipboard. It will stay there until it is replaced by the next Cut or Copy operation, or until the PC is powered off. This allows you to paste the data as many times as you want.

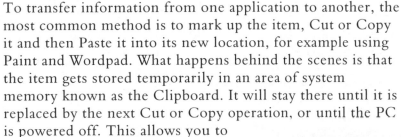

You do not normally need to deal directly with the Clipboard, but Windows 98 does provide a tool for checking the contents.

To cut (move) or copy data from one location to another:

Many applications have Cut, Copy, and Paste buttons on their toolbars, or you can use the equivalent keystrokes Ctrl+X, Ctrl+C and Ctrl+V. Shortcut context menus also offer Cut, Copy and Paste functions.

1 Mark up the source data, select Edit, Cut or Copy to place it in the Clipboard.

2 Run Clipboard Viewer from System Tools in the Start menu to view the contents.

3 To save the contents as a Clp file, choose File, Save As, and enter the file name.

4 Choose File, Open and select the Clp file to restore the contents of the clipboard.

5 Move the typing cursor to the point in the target document where you want to insert the data, and press Paste.

Compression

You can use Compression Agent to compress selected files using the settings you specify. You can save disk space by compressing files, or improve performance by changing the level of compression on your files.

DriveSpace applies a standard level of compression, but you can change the settings to specify the better Hipack compression or the best but slowest Ultrapak compression for selected file classes.

1 Start Compression Agent from System Tools in the Start menu. If there is no compressed drive, the program does not run.

2 Click Settings. Accept the defaults, to Ultrapak files not used for the past month and Hipak the others, or set up your own rules.

3 While the files are being recompressed, the table is updated to show the progressive savings. You can stop at any point, retaining the effects so far completed.

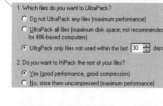

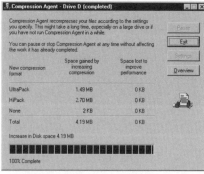

Repeat this process at a later date, to refine the setup and make further space savings or, if you find that the system has slowed down, to restore the performance level.

...cont'd

You can use DriveSpace 3 to compress both hard and floppy disks to create more free space for files. You can also use DriveSpace 3 to configure disk drives that you have already compressed by using DoubleSpace or DriveSpace 3.

You cannot compress drives that use FAT32.

1 Run DriveSpace from the System Folder in the Start menu, and select the drive.

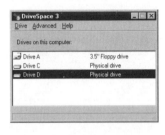

2 You will see a forecast of the potential savings.

3 Press Start, and the drive will be checked for errors, and then all the files will be compressed.

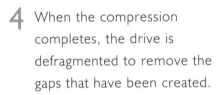

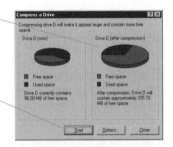

You may need to create a new startup disk, so the utility gives you the opportunity before compressing the drive.

4 When the compression completes, the drive is defragmented to remove the gaps that have been created.

5 The compression results are displayed. These may differ from the forecast, depending on the type of files you have.

6 The compressed drive is still referred to by the same drive letter, but a new drive letter is created for the physical, uncompressed drive.

Disk tools

You can run Disk Cleanup to help you free up space on your hard drive by searching for unnecessary files that you can safely delete.

You can start Disk Cleanup also from the drive Properties page.

1 Start Disk Cleanup from the System folder in the Start menu and select the drive that you want to clean up.

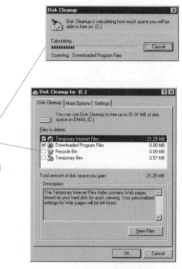

2 Disk Cleanup calculates how much space of various types you will be able to release.

Disk Cleanup works for Zip disks and removable drives also.

3 Review the recommendations for the Temporary Internet Files, the Downloaded Programs, the deleted files and old Temporary files.

4 Click More Options if you want to remove Windows utilities you don't use, uninstall programs you no longer need, or convert your FAT file system to FAT32.

You will be able to adjust the selections before the job runs. You can also cancel the run if it is not a convenient time.

5 Select the Settings tab and click the box to have Disk Cleanup run automatically when this drive runs low on disk space. This option is not available for removable drives.

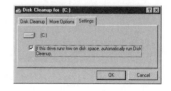

...cont'd

Open the drive Properties, select the Tools tab to run the Defragmenter on that drive.

You use Disk Defragmenter to rearrange files and unused space on your hard disk so that programs run faster.

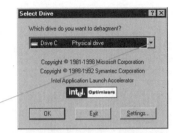

1 Select Disk Defragmenter from System Tools on the Start menu.

2 Click the down arrow to select the drive letter.

If the drive contents change in any way during defrag, e.g. when Windows writes to the swap file, the utility restarts. However, it quickly skips forward over areas already processed.

3 Click Settings to see the defaults, rearrange files and check the disk for errors.

4 Click OK to start the process. The progress bar shows the % complete.

5 Click Show Details to see the process, sector by sector. The legend explains the colour coded movements.

Press Pause at any time to discontinue the procedure, and continue it later.

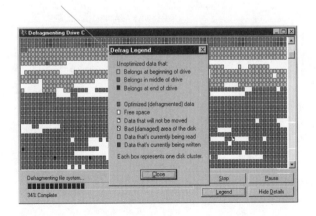

The Drive Converter converts your hard disk from the standard FAT file system to the enhanced FAT32 file system format. This stores data more efficiently, freeing up to 25% of the total disk capacity. In addition, the program files load faster and your PC needs fewer system resources.

Although it is a more efficient file system, there are some compatibility implications that you should consider before converting.

However, once you convert your hard drive to FAT32 format, you cannot return to the FAT16 format unless you repartition, reformat the drive, and restore or reinstall all the applications and data files that it contained.

With FAT32 on the drive, you will not be able to dual boot a previous operating system on your PC. However, if you are on a network, earlier versions of Windows can still gain access to the files and folders on your FAT32 hard drive through the network.

If you convert a removable disk, you will not be able to use that disk with other operating systems that are not FAT32-compatible.

If these issues are not concerns for you, then you can take advantage of the new file system.

1 The conversion Information tool provided with the Windows 98 resource kit tells you the potential benefits.

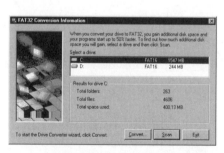

2 Start Drive Converter from System Tools in the Start menu.

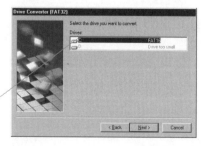

3 Select the drive you wish to convert.

...cont'd

The wizard sets up a schedule to run the disk tools, so you don't have to remember what tasks you have completed.

You can use the Maintenance wizard to make your programs run faster, check your hard disk for problems, and free up hard disk space. By scheduling these utilities to run on a regular basis, you can make sure that your PC is performing at its best.

1 Run the wizard from the System Folder in the Start menu, and select Custom to see the details.

Changing the Startup list here makes it easy to reinstate programs if you change your mind.

2 Select the time period (day, evening, night) for the tasks.

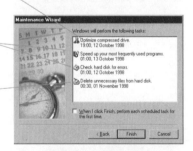

3 A weekly optimise for the compressed drive is suggested.

4 A weekly defragmentation is suggested, with a weekly Scandisk run the day before.

Remember to leave your PC switched on during the times for the scheduled tasks.

5 The Disk Cleanup utility is scheduled monthly.

6 The overall schedule is shown. You can wait for the assigned times, or request the first time to run the tasks immediately.

The next time you run the wizard, it offers the choice of running the tasks immediately or modifying the schedule.

...cont'd

This utility is run to a schedule, through the maintenance wizard.

Use ScanDisk to check your hard disk for logical and physical errors, and to repair the damaged areas. Scan disk should be run before you carry out other disk changes such as defragmentation or conversion to FAT32.

1 Run ScanDisk from the System Folder in the Start menu, and select the drive, or select error checking from the Tools page in the Drive properties.

Click the box to repair errors when they are encountered, or you'll have to repeat the procedure to correct any errors detected.

2 Select Standard to check the logical structure of the FAT area and the folders, and to locate lost sectors etc.

3 Select Thorough to carry out an analysis of the disk surface, to make sure all sectors can be accessed properly.

4 Click Advanced to review the default settings and make any changes you wish.

5 Messages and progress bars show the activity during the scan, and the results are displayed when it completes. A report is made of any errors detected. If you choose Append to Log from the Advanced options, you will build a history of the ScanDisk activities on your PC.

Net Watcher

This utility is not just for Network administrators. You can make use of Net Watcher even if you only share resources with your laptop through the Direct cable Connection.

Net Watcher is for use when your PC acts as the host or server on a network, or when you are sharing resources cooperatively in a peer to peer networking group. With it, you can see who is currently using resources on your PC, add shared folders and disconnect users from your computer or from specific files.

Before you can run Net Watcher, you must have Client for Microsoft Networks installed, and you must enable file and print sharing options.

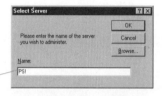

1 Run Net Watcher from System Folder in Start menu. Click the Select Server button, and enter your PC name.

Warn users before you close a file or disconnect, or they may lose data in open files.

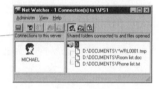

2 Click the Users button to see who is connected to your PC or to disconnect a user.

3 Click the Folders button to check or change the items that are shared.

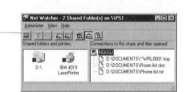

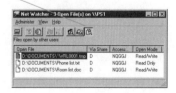

You may see temporary files in your folder, for example the auto recovery files created by Word, which default to the current directory. Users can change this option to use the local disk instead.

4 Click the Files button to examine the status of files. You can see whether the file is open for read-only or for write. You can close a file if you need to work on it yourself.

5 Select View from the menu bar and refresh to update entries.

Resource Kit Tools

Some of the technical data is quite esoteric, but you'll find some of the tools very useful, especially the desktop tools such as ClipTray and TweakUI.

Windows 98 has a Resource Kit available as a separate product, but it includes a substantial part of the kit in the Sampler on the setup CD. To install the Sampler:

1 Insert the setup CD, open the \tools\reskit folder. Double-click the Setup.exe file.

This installs twenty five utilities and information files. The Resource Kit folder is added to the Start menu, and provides shortcuts to the Tools Management Console, the help files and the release notes.

2 View and search the complete text of the book, using Windows Help.

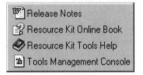

3 Tools Help contains products descriptions and usage notes.

TweakUI will adjust your desktop and Windows setup. WinDiff compares text files in colour. These and other Resource Kit tools are referenced in later chapters, whenever they can provide additional features or ease of use.

4 Tools Management Console acts as the interface to the utilities, organising them by type and alphabetically.

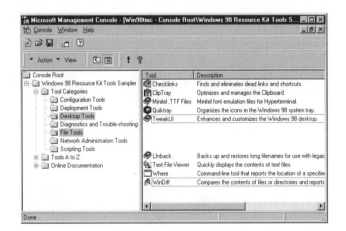

Scheduled tasks

You will find the tasks scheduled by the Maintenance Wizard included in the list of tasks.

Scheduled Tasks allow you to schedule applications and utilities to run at a predefined time. This may be at a time when the PC is unattended, or you may want to make certain that the task does not get forgotten. The Scheduled Tasks utility starts up whenever Windows starts and runs in the background. It places an icon in the system tray to show that it is active.

You can also open the Scheduled Tasks folder from the System Tools folder in the Start menu, or from My Computer.

1 Double-click the icon to open the task list folder.

2 Click Add Scheduled Task, and the wizard lists all the programs in the Start menu folders.

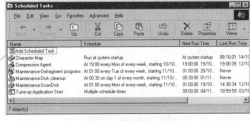

You can control how long a task will run, and specify actions to take when the PC is busy at the scheduled time, or when it is running on battery power.

3 Choose the program, and select the scheduled time for running it (day, evening, night, startup, idle time).

4 To make changes to a scheduled task, right-click it and select Properties and then Settings.

5 To suspend Scheduled Tasks, right-click the icon and select Pause.

System activity

If your PC seems to be running more slowly than usual, the Resource Meter may show you if things really have changed.

The Resource Meter allows you to monitor the state of your PC system by displaying how much of the system resources are available. To run the Resource Meter:

1 Select Resource Meter from the System Tools folder in the start menu.

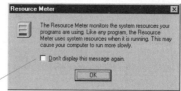

Run the Resource Meter while you are using the system in a normal fashion, and note the type of readings that you get on a typical session.

2 An information box is displayed. Click the box to avoid it being displayed in future.

3 The Resource Meter icon is added to the system tray.

4 If you hover the mouse pointer over the icon, you can view what percentage of the resources are free.

See page 116 for a more detailed view of system activity.

5 Right-click the icon and select details, or just double-click the icon, to display the details as a bar chart. Click OK to close this window.

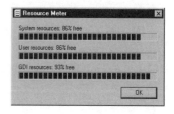

System resources represents the requirements of Windows 98 itself. User resources are taken by applications and the desktop options that you select. GDI resources are graphics functions, and increase with higher resolutions and colour depths, animation effects etc.

System Information has a lot more to offer – it has tools to check the system and help you identify and resolve problems.

System Information collects system configuration data information and displays it in a structured menu. You may be asked to view the tables when you talk to support specialists, to give them the specific details they need.

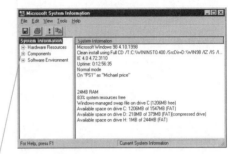

1   Run System Information from the System Tools folder in the Start menu.

2   To expand the display, click the plus signs in the left pane to reveal further subcategories, and then click the item to see its details.

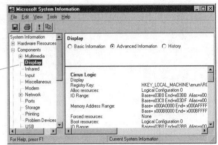

Use Edit, Copy to take selected parts of the system information to the clipboard, to paste it into a document or report.

3   Depending on the topic, you may be offered a choice of basic, advanced, or historical system data.

4   Press File, Save to record the system data as an MSInfo file, or File, Export for a text file, to send the details to another location.

5   Use the Tools menu to access the reporting, checking and analysis tools, usually as directed by your support specialist.

Check various aspects of system activity as they take place.

System Monitor tracks the performance of selected activities on your PC and your network and other links. Each activity is represented by a chart that is updated every 5 seconds.

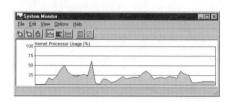

1 Run System Monitor from the System Tools folder in the Start menu.

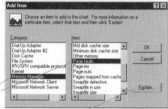

2 Press the toolbar buttons to Add or Remove monitoring for particular items.

3 Click the Category and then click the Item. Press the Explain button for a brief definition of the item.

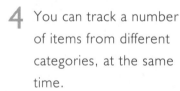

The 'kernel processor usage', the 'memory manager page fault' and the 'file system reads and writes per second' make a useful starting point. Observe the activity as you load or end programs, or open, process and save files.

4 You can track a number of items from different categories, at the same time.

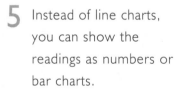
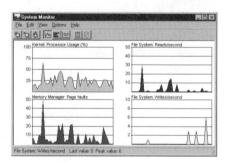

5 Instead of line charts, you can show the readings as numbers or bar charts.

The System Monitor can be used to track the activities on the network or on a communications link. It can even display the system usage for another PC on the network. The advantage is that the effects of System Monitor itself on system usage are minimised.

Customising the layout

You can change the way that Windows 98 appears and the way that it operates, to suit your own preferences.

Covers

Chapter Six

Typical desktop

The way Windows 98 was setup affects the appearance, but what you see on the desktop can be changed.

See Chapter 15 for details of installation and setup for Windows 98.

Your PC may have Windows 98 already pre-installed by the supplier. You may have purchased the Windows 98 upgrade, to setup on existing Windows 95 (or Windows 3.1x) system. If you want to start with a clean slate, you could decide to format your drive before installing the update.

The way Windows 98 is installed affects the contents of the desktop and the folder organisation, but you do not have to settle for the default settings that you inherit with the system. You can make changes and turn things around into the form and layout that suits you best.

To see the type of changes you can make, examine a typical desktop layout, then look at some revised setups, and decide which ideas you like.

The illustrated desktop (opposite) is 1024 x 768 pixels. There are a number of icons displayed in what may be considered a rather small format (depending on the physical size of the monitor), and there are a couple of folders and a channel bar.

Some of the icons are unnecessary, others duplicate shortcuts that are available on the launchpad. There are also icons for documents that have been inadvertently created on the desktop.

The background of the desktop is dressed up with a picture. You may like a picture on your desktop, or you may find that it makes things more difficult to read. In any event, the way in which the 640 x 480 image is tiled to fill the desktop does not enhance the effect.

A shortcut folder has been created on the desktop. This is intended to make applications easier to find, but it puts an extraneous icon on the desktop, and there are better ways to present shortcuts.

The Channels bar may be a distraction, especially since it displays long text messages when the mouse pointer happens to pause a few seconds. And do you still need that welcome screen?

...cont'd

While probably typical, this isn't a recommended desktop, but does illustrate some of the effects you could encounter.

Unless you have a 17" monitor or larger, these icons will appear very small and the titles will be hard to read, especially with the wallpaper.

1 Shortcut folder icon and contents.

2 Bitmap image used as wallpaper, with tiling.

3 Icons that duplicate items on the Quick Launchpad.

4 Misplaced data files, created on the desktop.

5 The (probably superfluous) Welcome Window.

6 Channel bar, also found on Quick Launchpad.

7 Quick Launchpad with Internet and Channel entries.

8 Unsolicited messages pop up near the mouse pointer.

There are many ways to rearrange this desktop, but you must decide what type of setup you want to achieve. For example, you could aim to avoid duplicate entries, or you might decide that desktop clarity is your number one priority.

Clear desktop

A simple answer is to avoid the need for the desktop altogether.

The first alternative is the clear desktop. This will allow you to fill the desktop with application windows yet still be able to get at everything. This is achieved by storing the shortcuts you need on the taskbar, so they are always available. This method uses the Toolbar extensions to the taskbar to hold all your shortcuts.

There are a minimum of icons on the desktop, and all of the shortcuts are on the toolbar added to the taskbar.

See page 138 to position shortcuts on the taskbar or the Start menu.

If you like the idea of a clear desktop but the taskbar approach is too cryptic, you can put everything on the Start menu. You can still make full use of the desktop yet get to all your shortcuts and applications very easily.

2 The shortcuts are added to the Start menu. There is an extra shortcut for a drop down Control Panel.

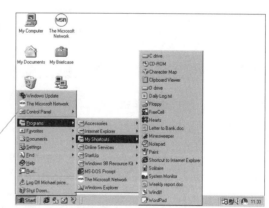

If you are happier using the desktop in the conventional way, you can arrange your shortcuts in groups so they are easier to find, or use subfolders, and you can take advantage of some of the ways Windows 98 provides to let you switch between the application windows and the desktop.

If you do use the desktop, arrange your shortcuts in groups.

3 The shortcuts are grouped together on a much clearer desktop with all the distractions removed.

There is no single best solution, just choose the method that you like best.

To switch back and forth between the desktop and the application windows:

| Press Win+M to reveal desktop, and Alt+Shift+M to restore application windows.

2 Click Show Desktop on the quick launch bar to reveal the desktop, and click it again to restore application windows.

3 Press Win+D, to reveal the desktop, and press Win+D again to restore windows.

Press Win+R to start Run, then type Period, Enter.

4 Press Start, Run, type a Period, Enter to display the desktop in a folder overlaying the application windows.

Check out current setup

Switch the folder view to All Files to see hidden and system files.

Before you make any changes to your setup, take a close look at what you currently have, so you know what needs changing and what you might want to retain. Start by looking at the hard disk organisation. Windows Explorer gives a hierarchical view of the contents of the C: drive. Click the [+] to expand folders to see the subfolders.

The structure created when you make a fresh installation is straightforward, with data, applications and systems folders and subfolders.

1 My Documents folder for data files.

2 Program Files folder for applications folders, Windows components and the Windows resource kit.

3 Recycled folder, the holding area for deleted files and folders.

4 Windows folder for system files, program libraries (DLL files) and the system Registry.

If you are unsure about deleting a file, you can move it to another folder, and delete it later if the system continues unaffected.

5 Root folder (C:) holds system startup files.

From the root folder, you can delete various file types, including Txt, Prv, Log, Old and - - - files. You can also delete Dos files, if you are not planning to use the dual boot facility to go back to your previous operating system. You can delete files from the Windows folder also.

Having Windows setup files on the hard disk avoids the need for the setup CD when you change components or devices.

If your Windows 98 arrived pre-installed by the PC vendor, there will be extra folders for device files, supplier software and data, and other programs such as an office suite. You may also find parts of Windows 98 Setup stored on the hard drive. The actual folders will differ from system to system and supplier to supplier, but these are the type of folders you can expect:

1 Programs and utilities for the sound card and speakers.

2 Backup copies of the key setup files.

You may be able to delete some of these files when you have created the device diskettes required for your system.

3 CD-ROM programs and device drivers.

4 Supplier's programs, data files, on-line guide and diskette images.

5 Mouse programs and device drivers.

6 Additional applications provided with the system, pre-installed in the Program Files and in the Windows folders.

Understanding what is on the hard disk will allow you to decide what you can safely remove if you should find that you need to free up space on the disk.

Detecting setup problems

You should look for some of the setup problems that are often encountered. For example, some machines have the wrong keyboard definition, having the USA layout assigned when there is a UK keyboard attached. To reset the keyboard definition:

Settings on the other tabs, date and time etc., will be changed to match when you restart.

1 Open Control Panel from Settings and double-click Regional Settings.

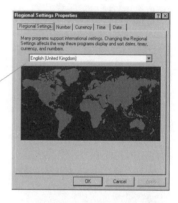

2 Select the zone e.g. English (United Kingdom) setting.

You can add a second keyboard layout if you want to enter text in another language, complete with accented characters.

3 Open the Keyboard in Control Panel and select the Language tab.

4 Check for English (British). Add it if required and make it the default.

Select the keyboard Speed tab to adjust the keyboard delay and the character repeat rate, which control the sensitivity of response when you hold down a key. A test area is provided so you can try out the effects. You can also vary the cursor blink rate.

5 Restart the system to apply the changes.

Display settings

If you have a new type of display adapter or monitor, Windows 98 may not select it correctly and setup will default to the standard display adapter (VGA 16 colour) or standard PCI graphics adapter. The monitor may be set as Unknown monitor. You should try to match the drivers with the equipment actually attached, so that you get the best image and performance available.

To change the adapter settings:

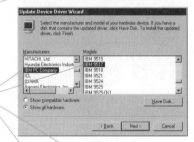

I Right-click a clear part of the desktop and select Properties.

If you cannot find a match, select a standard monitor type that matches the best resolution your monitor can support.

2 Click the Settings tab, and check the display and adapter specified.

3 If changes are needed press Advanced, the Adapter tab and the Change button and select the adapter by make and model.

If the rate is less than 70Hz, you should reduce the screen resolution (the number of pixels), or you will have to put up with display flicker.

4 Press the Monitor tab, and press Change to update the monitor selection.

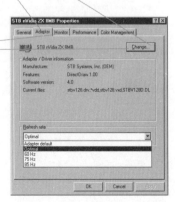

Check the refresh rate that is being used. The Refresh Rate is the number of times per second that the adapter rewrites the data to the monitor. Select Optimum if this choice is given.

Remove unnecessary items

If you don't use desktop themes, removing them saves 30 MB disk space.

Check the components and applications shown in the Start menu, and remove those that you do not need.

1 Select Add/Remove Programs from Control Panel and the Windows Setup tab.

2 Clear the box to remove any item.

You may want to add components that have been missed. The Typical setup for example leaves out the very useful Backup utility.

Windows 98 installed over a previous system will retain a backup of the original system files. When you are satisfied with the new setup, remove that backup.

This makes up to 50 MB disk space available, but does mean that you no longer have the option to uninstall Windows 98.

3 Select Add/Remove Programs from Control Panel and the Install/Uninstall tab.

4 Click Delete Windows 98 Uninstall information, and press Add/Remove.

The Welcome facility remains still available from the System Tools folder in the Start menu.

If you have registered your copy of Windows 98 and finished with the tutorials, clear the check box to prevent display on future restarts.

...cont'd

Press Start menu, Settings options to access the functions needed to change the style and appearance of the desktop, the folders and the Start menu.

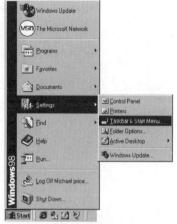

1 Click Start, Settings and then click Taskbar & Start Menu.

2 Choose Taskbar Options and click 'Show small icons in Start menu' to make the menu more consistent and leave room for items at the top.

3 Click Apply to see the effect, and click OK to end, saving the changes.

The other levels already use small icons.

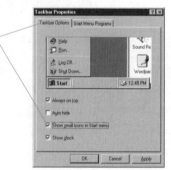

The Taskbar takes over part of the desktop area, but you can still make use of the space.

AutoHide makes the Taskbar disappear until needed, when you merely move the mouse pointer to the bottom line of the screen. This is useful when you have 640 x 480 resolution selected, or when you have increased the height of the Taskbar.

Press Win to display the Start menu and the taskbar. Press Ctrl+Esc instead, if you have no Win key.

Clearing the Always on top options allows application windows to overlay the taskbar. However, this makes it difficult to find the taskbar. It does not appear in the Windows list when you press Alt+Tab, and covering it up takes away some of your options for revealing the desktop and taskbar.

Folder options

You spend a great deal of time working with folders, so Windows provides many options for you to adjust them to your liking.

You can set options for individual folders or set them globally for all folders.

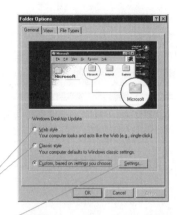

1 Select Folder Options from Settings to specify the characteristics for all folders.

2 Select the Windows 98 Web style or the Windows 95 classic folder view.

3 Press Settings to make your own custom selections.

Switch the active desktop on to display HTML pages or to display the Channel bar.

4 Switch between the Web style desktop, or Classic Windows.

5 Browse folders in the same window, or open a new window whenever you switch to view a new folder.

You can make Windows 98 folders and desktop work the same way as the Internet Explorer, actioning icons with a single click.

6 Change the way you open icons to Single-click, auto select by pointer location, and adjust title underlining.

...cont'd

Change the options for an individual folder.

I Open the folder, and select the View menu.

2 Click Toolbars to choose which of these you wish to display.

3 Select View as Web Page, or deselect for the normal view.

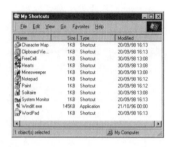

4 Choose icon style - large, small, list or details. You can also sort folder contents by icon name, type, date etc.

This is interesting to try out, but you should restrict its use to keep the system efficient.

You can change the appearance of a folder by selecting Customise this folder from the View menu. The wizard will help you to create or edit a HTML document as a folder background, or to choose a background picture. The third option removes customisation if you have applied any to the folder.

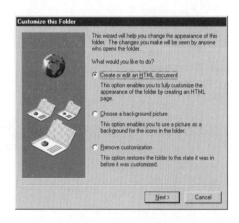

You can also access the Folder Options from the View menu, to make changes for this folder, or replicate the changes to all folders.

File views

The View tab in Folder Options provides advanced settings for files and folders.

This button is greyed out and unavailable if you are using the global Folder Options.

1. Press Like Current Folder to apply all the settings from the View menu (except for toolbar settings) to all the other folders on the PC.

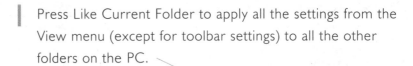

2. Press Reset all folders to return the view settings for the folders to their original values.

When you show all file types take care not to delete system or hidden files.

3. Remember changes to folder settings (or the folder view returns to the defaults on closing).

Display All Files, don't Hide File Extensions and View Details, to see the complete information for the folder contents.

4. Display the full path on the title bar of the folder window, or show file extensions for registered file types, such as DOC.

5. Choose whether to hide the names for system files or for hidden files, or to show all the file names in the folder.

6. Hide icons on the desktop when it is viewed as a Web page.

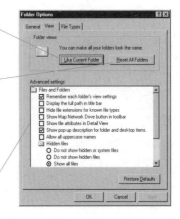

There's also a button to restore the default values for all these file and folder settings.

7. Smooth the edges of screen fonts, and show the contents of the window, rather than just a frame, while dragging the window to a new position.

File types

View and amend the list of registered file types.

When you double-click an icon, Windows checks the file extension against the list of registered file types to select the associated action. Applications usually register their file types and associations during installation. To see the list of registered file types:

1 Select View from Folder Options and click the File Types tab.

Multipurpose Internet Mail Extensions (MIME) define how browsers and mail software handle file attachments.

2 Select a file type such as Text Document to see the registered file extensions, the MIME details and the associated application.

Only one application can be associated with a given file type. To change the application, for example to use WordPad instead of Notepad to open text files, you should:

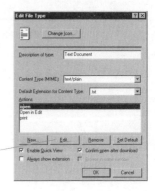

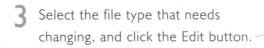

The default action is in bold type.

3 Select the file type that needs changing, and click the Edit button.

4 Select the default entry in the Actions list and click the Edit button.

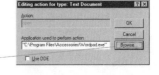

Select Always Show Extension, to distinguish an alternative version of a file, e.g. RTF versions of DOC files.

5 Change the program (use Browse to find the program file) and click OK.

You can also change the settings for other actions, or add new entries to the context menu for the selected file type.

Active desktop

With the Active Desktop feature, the desktop can display Web information saved in the HTML (Hypertext Markup Language) format, and update it each time you connect to the Internet.

1 Right-click the desktop and select Properties, then choose the Web tab.

2 Click New to add Web content to your desktop.

3 There are numerous predefined Web pages that you can use to fill your desktop. You can preview them at the Gallery before you select one as your active desktop.

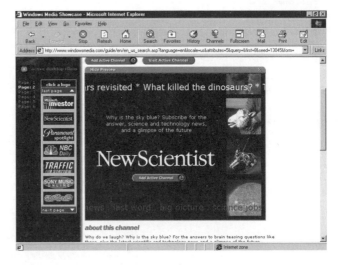

Defining shortcuts

Windows 98 uses Shortcuts to make it easy for you to access files, folders, programs and devices. A shortcut is a small link file that contains a pointer to the document or program file etc... You keep the actual files in their normal location, My Documents or Program Files and their subfolders as appropriate. The shortcuts can be placed on the desktop, in the Start menu or on toolbars such as the quick launch bar on the taskbar, whichever suits you.

To create a shortcut on the desktop:

A quick way to create a shortcut to an application, is to display the Start menu, highlight the relevant entry, right-drag it to the desktop and select Create shortcut here.

1 Use Start, Find to locate the file you want.

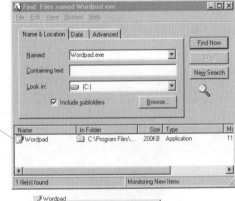

2 Right-click the icon, and drag and drop it on to the desktop.

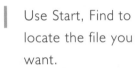

3 Select Create shortcut here.

The shortcut to "Item" is called "Shortcut to Item". You can rename the shortcut, and get Windows to learn to drop the prefix, after several renames.

Alternatively, you can create the shortcut directly on the desktop.

Shortcut to Wordpad.exe

4 Right-click the desktop, select New, Shortcut.

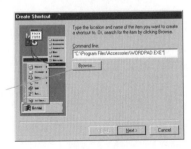

5 Enter the path, or use Browse to locate the document or program file, and select Next, Finish.

Shortcut properties

The actual Shortcut properties displayed depends on the file type of the target file.

Each shortcut has Properties, to locate and describe the target file used to create the shortcut. The information stored depends on the type of file. A document shortcut stores summary, statistics and contents information about the document. An application shortcut is much more limited, but does allow you to choose the icon image you prefer. To display Properties:

1 Right-click the shortcut icon and select Properties from the context menu.

The Change Icon option applies to application shortcuts only.

2 Select the Shortcut tab and press Change Icon to select a new icon.

3 Some applications have several icons that you can choose from.

4 If the application does not offer a suitable icon, click Browse and locate the file C:\Windows\Moricons.dll.

5 You will find other icons in the file C:\Windows\system\Shell32.dll or C:\Windows\System\Pifmgr.dll.

6 Press OK to save the change, and the new icon will be displayed.

If you have chosen the Single-click option, you will have to hold down the Shift key as you select the icon to drag it.

When you create a shortcut on the desktop, you can left-click and drag it to a convenient position, or arrange the icons in groups. If the icons immediately rearrange themselves, you have AutoArrange switched on, and you should switch it off before repositioning the icons. To check its status:

1 Right-click the desktop, select Arrange Icons and view the AutoArrange entry.

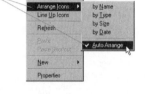

2 Don't select the entry if it is currently disabled (no tick), or all the icons on your desktop will be rearranged.

3 If the option is enabled (ticked) then you should select the entry to disable it.

Rearrange the icons on the desktop to make it easier for you to locate the ones you need. For example:

This is just one of the many different ways you could arrange your desktop. Add a background with colours or lines to emphasise the groups.

System folders etc..

Application programs

Tools and utilities

Documents and pictures

Disk drives

Entertainment (games)

Start menu shortcuts

Shortcuts in the Start menu can be used without having to minimise program windows.

With shortcuts on the desktop, you have to minimise your applications. To avoid this, put your shortcuts into a folder in the Start menu:

1 Select Start, Settings, Taskbar & Start Menu, and choose the Start Menu Programs tab.

2 Click Advanced, select Programs and then select File, New, Folder.

3 Name the folder My Shortcuts.

4 Create your shortcuts in this folder (or copy them from the desktop).

5 Select File, Close and then OK to see your Start menu entries.

The entries you make will automatically be sorted into alphabetical order. You can rearrange entries by dragging them to a new position, or you could consider adding a numeric prefix to the shortcut names, to sequence them into groups.

Alternatively, you can create subfolders in the Start menu to separate the groups.

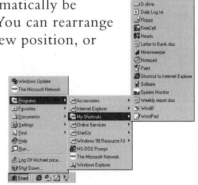

You can use the Start menu to add system folders such as the Control Panel directly to the Start menu by providing the object name when you create a folder.

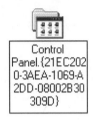

I   Create a new folder on the desktop, and give it the object name:

Control Panel.{21EC2020-3AEA-1069-A2DD-08002B30309D}

2   Right-click the Start button and select Open.

3   Drag the new Control Panel into the Start menu folder, and close the folder.

4   The Control Panel is added to the top of the Start menu, and opens as a drop down menu, instead of the usual folder.

There are object names for other system folders, including Printers, the Recycle Bin and My Computer. You may also be able to add special folders to the Start menu using the resource kit TweakUI, which can create files that represent some of the folders so that they can be added to the Start menu.

Toolbar shortcut

Shortcuts on the taskbar are quickly accessible at all times.

Windows 98 provides an even easier way to access your shortcuts. You can put them right on the taskbar, by creating your own toolbar:

1 Create a My Shortcuts folder with the shortcuts you want.

To add an extra entry, create a shortcut on the desktop, and drag and drop it on the toolbar or the quick launch bar.

2 Right-click the taskbar and select Toolbars, New Toolbar.

3 Locate the folder that contains your shortcuts and select OK.

The toolbar is added to the taskbar but you won't be able to see many entries because of the text.

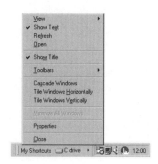

The taskbar may still be crowded and you may need to click the arrow to display further entries. Resize the taskbar to make more room.

4 Right-click the new toolbar and deselect the title and text fields.

5 Left-click and hold the top of the taskbar and drag it to double-height, and you should be able to display the full toolbar and still have room for open windows and applications.

Remind yourself of the name of the shortcut by pausing the mouse pointer over the icon on the toolbar.

Shortcut suggestions

You can create shortcuts from documents and devices as well as applications. Here are some examples of the type of shortcut you might want to use:

1 Shortcuts to the floppy and disk drive icons give you quick access to their files and folders.

Floppy   Hard Disk   CD-ROM

The application associated with the registered file type will start, print the file and then end.

2 With a Printer shortcut you can drag and drop any registered file type onto the printer icon to print the contents using the application (e.g. print DOC files with Word or WordPad).

IBM 4019
LaserPrinter

Select the shortcut properties, and the Program tab, press Advanced and pick the settings that the DOS program requires.

3 MS-DOS Prompt shortcuts can be customised with the program properties to suit particular applications.

MS-DOS   MS-DOS Only

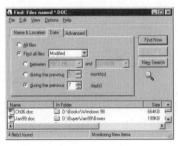

4 Set up and test a Find using parameters that you want to reuse e.g. Find all documents created during the last week.

Select File, Save Search to save the settings on the desktop, and drag the Find icon to your shortcut folder or to the toolbar on the taskbar.

Files named
@.doc

1 Create shortcuts to launch applications such as Word or Excel, or to run any program that you use frequently.

MS Excell   MS Publisher   MS Word

WordPad and Word support document shortcuts. Word also supports document scraps, which contain a copy of the selected paragraph.

2 Highlight a paragraph, right-drag it to the desktop or shortcut folder, and create a document shortcut. This will open the document, and position it at the selected paragraph.

Document   Document
Shortcut 'To...'   Scrap 'To...'

3 Shortcuts to document template DOT files make it easy to create new documents of particular types.

Email   Fax   Letter

If you copy the track id file instead of making a short cut, it will only play if the specific CD is inserted.

Track01.cda   Track01.cda

4 Make a shortcut to a CD track, and it will play that track number when you double-click it as long as there is an audio CD in the drive. You can create playable shortcuts to WAV or MIDI sound files also.

5 Create a shortcut to the report that you are currently working on, and put it in the Startup folder. The report and the associated application will be opened automatically whenever you restart the PC. Don't forget to update the shortcut when you move on to another task.

Installing Applications

This chapter looks at the different types of applications, how to add them to your Windows system and how to manage and access them from the Start menu.

Covers

Chapter Seven

Applications for Windows

Windows 98 provides many tools and utilities, and has quite comprehensive support for communications, especially the Internet. However, it is fundamentally an operating system. Application support for personal and business activities is very limited. You will have to supplement the system with applications that are capable of running with Windows 98 and provide the functions that it is missing. There are various categories of application programs that you can run, including:

1   32-bit Windows applications, designed for PCs using the Intel 486 and Pentium processors or equivalents.

2   16-bit Windows applications, designed for PCs with the Intel 286 or 386 processor.

3   MS-DOS applications designed for the original PC with the Intel 8088 or for later processors.

Your primary choice for applications should be 32-bit since these will take better advantage of the capabilities of the processor, but not all such applications will work effectively under Windows 98, since they may not follow the implicit standards it sets for various common processes that you normally take for granted, such as the method of selecting and opening files, or the printing procedure.

There are some particular categories of 32-bit application that by definition provide better OS compatibility:

Applications that are described as "Windows-compatible" are equivalent to the 16-bit applications.

4   Designed for Windows 95, and the more recent Designed for Windows 98 (and by implication for NT and Windows 2000).

Designed for

Microsoft®
Windows NT®
Windows®98

Designed for Windows 95/8

The logo can be awarded to hardware as well as software products, though of course the criteria relate to features such as plug and play and power management.

Recognising that the level of compatibility with the operating system and between applications was crucial, Microsoft set up a process for assessing products, and awarding the right to display the logo on the packaging. Applications are tested by an independent testing firm (VeriTest) not by Microsoft itself.

Applications with the Windows 95 designation should run without problem on Windows 98. However, applications supporting the Windows 98 and Windows NT joint standard have to meet a more rigorous specification. You can find more details of the logo process and lists of the applications and other products from the Web site:

This protects the programs from one another, and prevents them corrupting system memory.

http://www.microsoft.com/windows/thirdparty/winlogo/

The Windows 98 applications use the Registry to track their configuration details, and they support the long file names. Their programs run in a private memory space to protect applications from one another, and they are controlled through pre-emptive multitasking and multithread scheduling which allows the operating system to manage resources efficiently.

Older programs can interfere with each other's memory space, and are more liable to affect the system integrity.

Windows 3.1x and 16-bit applications are more restricted, using the MS-DOS 8.3 file names, running in the same shared memory space and relying on cooperative multitasking and resource management.

MS-DOS applications may implicitly take advantage of Windows 98 features, depending on the way they are run. Windows 98 runs well-behaved programs in MS-DOS prompt sessions, so you can have more than one MS-DOS program running while the Windows applications continue to run. More demanding applications may require you to start particular system TSRs or device drivers, or to set up specific configuration settings.

DOS utilities are the most demanding. For these it would be wiser to look for a Windows 98 upgrade or replacement.

If the MS-DOS program places too many demands on the system, or insists on direct access to hardware, it may only be allowed to run on its own, in MS-DOS mode without Windows and with no other applications active.

AutoRun installation

This method applies to Windows 98/ 95 applications provided on CDs.

The procedure for installing Windows 98 applications that are supplied on CDs is simply to insert the disc and follow the on-screen instructions.

Windows 98 detects the change of disc and searches the new CD for an AutoRun.ini which specifies the action to take. Installation CDs are specified to run the Setup program, or an interface program that provides details of and access to the Setup program.

For example, to install the retail version of Paint Shop Pro:

1 Insert the CD into the drive.

2 Click Install to start the setup.

3 AutoRun displays an initial screen, with the Install option, plus What's New? and Music Credits.

Windows may put new items at the end of the list initially, but when you next restart, you should find them sorted into position.

4 Press Next several times to accept the default selections and copy the files.

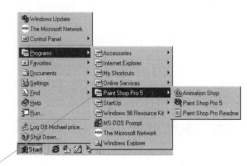

5 The folder, with entries for the Animation Shop and Paint Shop Pro, is added to the Start menu, Programs.

Install Programs wizard

This is also the method to use when you have disabled AutoRun, or if the application comes on diskette or Zip disk.

If the application CD does not use AutoRun, you can use the Install Programs Wizard instead. To install Geoff Hamilton's 3D Garden Designer:

1 Click Start, Settings, Control Panel and double-click Add/Remove Programs.

If you've added Control Panel to the Start menu (see page 137) just click the Add/Remove program entry.

2 Choose the Install/Uninstall tab and click the Install button to start the Install Program Wizard.

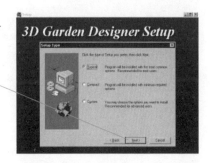

3 Insert the CD (or the first of the floppy disks) into the drive, and then click Next.

The wizard searches the root folder for the Setup.exe or Install.exe program. If the correct program is different, or if it is stored in a folder, you can search for the program using Browse, and Open the file to add it to the command line.

4 Press Finish to begin the actual setup for the application.

5 Follow the setup instructions to complete the installation and add it to the Start menu.

After setup

Setup may be fully automatic, or it may leave some tasks for you to perform.

When the application setup has finished, there may be some tasks for you to complete:

1 You may be offered the chance to view documents such as a Readme file, or perhaps an on-line manual. This is not essential at this time, since the material will be available for reference later.

Registering the application makes sure that you get news of
updates and new versions.

2 Some applications may offer you the option to fill in your details to register on-line or via a printed form.

3 Some applications may require you to restart the PC for the setup changes or Registry updates to take effect.

4 The setup may leave the program folder open on the desktop. Close this, or it will be open next time you restart.

5 If the application is not automatically added to the Start menu, you can create your own shortcuts in the menu.

Run to install

This is the way to install 16-bit Windows 3.1x programs. It is also a quick way to start any Setup, when you know the install program name and path.

You install Windows 3.1x applications using the Run command on the Start menu to execute the setup program directly from the installation disk. Before starting however, you should save copies of the system files (Autoexec.bat, Config.sys) in a backup folder. Then:

1 Insert the CD or the first floppy disk into the drive.

2 Press Start, Run and type the setup path and program name, or select Browse to locate the file and enter the name as the Run command.

3 Press OK to run the program, and follow the setup instructions to transfer the program files.

Running an old version of an application may cause problems that can only be resolved by updating to a later release.

After completing the installation, check what changes have been made to the system files. Look for the addition of real-mode drivers such as Share.exe or Smartdrv.exe. These are not required under Windows 98 and should be removed.

The application may apply updates to Windows files, but Windows 98 intercepts the changes. Program Manager updates and automatically converts them to Start menu shortcuts. Windows 98 also transfers Win.ini and System.ini entries into the Registry.

If you find any compatibility problems when installing or running one of these applications, check with the application supplier for details of any workaround procedure or upgrade.

Often however, you will find that a new version has been produced that is Windows 95 or Windows 98 compatible, and this will be the supported version.

Shareware Installs

Shareware programs from the Internet or from magazine cover CDs, often use compressed file formats.

With programs that you download from the Internet you will find a wide range of installation processes. Some will follow the complete standard for Windows 98 but others may be less rigorous. You will find that most applications are stored and transferred in a compressed format, either as a data file (ZIP or ARJ) or as self-expanding or self-installing EXE files.

Similar comments apply to the applications that you find on magazine cover disks, which generally feature shareware programs or demo versions of commercial applications.

To install Ulead COOL 3D titling software:

1 Select Start, Run and type the full file name e.g. D:\u3d20t.exe, then press OK.

2 The files are unpacked to a temporary folder.

3 The Setup program executes, the program files are copied, and the application is added to the Start menu.

Note how Ulead creates two levels of menu, for the company and then for the application, in the hope that you will add more of their programs to your PC.

...cont'd

You may have more work to do with the Shareware and Freeware programs.

There are many Shareware utilities, including PKzip, Winzip and ZipMagic, which can expand compressed files.

If the application is supplied as a ZIP or ARJ file, you need to expand the file into a folder before starting the installation.

To install the NoteTab Pro text editor:

1 Expand the Notetbpr.zip file using a Zip utility such as the Plus 98 Compressed Folder tool (see page 321).

2 Run the Setup.exe program to install the application.

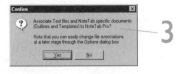

3 You can associate text files and NoteTab files with the new editor.

4 The application is added to the Start menu. Click NoteTab Pro to run the application.

Applications like the smaller utilities and single function programs may include no setup at all, but just the relevant program files for you to manually expand into a suitable folder on your hard disk. Look for the setup instructions in a text file such as Readme.txt or Readme.1st in the expanded folder. There will be no Start menu entries, but you can add your own shortcuts to run the application.

Installing MS-DOS programs

These usually have an installation program on the first floppy disk, and you run this in an MS-DOS session. The cautions (page 147) about changes to the system start up files are even more relevant for MS-DOS application installations, so backup these files before any install. To install Lemmings:

1 Search for the setup program on the diskette. In this case, it is Install.exe.

2 Select Start, Programs, MS-DOS Prompt, and run the program e.g. a:\install.exe.

3 Provide the config details requested.

4 Allow setup to complete, and type Exit to terminate the session.

5 Double-click the program file Vgalemmi.exe in the Lemmings folder to start it in an MS-DOS session. When you supply the config details it automatically switches to a full screen session, which is necessary to display the game's images.

...cont'd

You may need to install the program with nothing else active in the system, not even Windows itself.

Some programs may not work correctly in an MS-DOS session. If problems arise, or if the supplier recommends, you may have to install the application from MS-DOS mode, without Windows active.

To install an application using MS-DOS mode:

1 Select Start, Shutdown and Restart in MS-DOS mode, and then press OK.

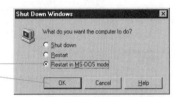

2 Any active Windows program will be ended. You are prompted to save the file if there is any changed data in an open document.

There's no Browse in DOS so type DIR/P/S to see all the files on the diskette, a page at a time.

3 When the PC restarts in plain MS-DOS mode, enter the install command and follow the installation instructions that appear.

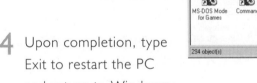

4 Upon completion, type Exit to restart the PC and return to Windows.

The Windows folder contains other PIF files set for MS-DOS prompt and some for running MS-DOS games in MS-DOS mode. See Configuring MS-DOS for the properties.

You'll find that a PIF file (MS-DOS shortcut) has been added to the Windows folder. Copy this to the desktop or a Start menu folder, to allow you to Exit to Dos without having to explicitly select Shutdown.

Configuring MS-DOS

Many MS-DOS programs run without reconfiguration, since the settings for the more popular MS-DOS applications are stored in Windows.

If your application fails to start or doesn't run as it should, you can modify the default MS-DOS settings to control the way it interacts with Windows.

To display the properties for the application:

There are standard MS-DOS settings for the program file Vgalemmi.exe, but the Batch file named Lemmings has MS-DOS mode set.

1 Right-click the program file or its shortcut and select Properties.

2 Click the box to Close on exit, so that the session closes when the program ends.

3 Select the Screen tab, and check the Full-screen option if the application has problems with the windowed view.

This may have caused a slight performance penalty but it is more reliable.

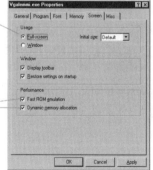

4 If there are problems writing to the screen, or if the application has problems when you switch to Windows and back, clear the Fast ROM and Dynamic memory boxes.

With Lemmings, there are still some display problems, and so it seems that MS-DOS mode may really be needed for proper function, as the Batch file properties suggest.

There are several levels to preventing interactions between Windows and the MS-DOS applications.

To change the mode in which MS-DOS applications execute:

1 Select the Program tab and press the Advanced button.

2 The first level is to prevent the application from detecting Windows and automatically terminating.

3 You can let Windows make the decision and suggest MS-DOS mode when it appears to be necessary.

You'll have the warning message every time, or you can clear the option and switch without a message. You'll still be warned about open files.

4 If there are still problems, select MS-DOS mode but keep the standard system files.

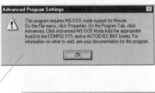

5 If the application needs particular system drivers, select to specify a new MS-DOS configuration. When you select this for the Lemmings.bat shortcut, you get some specific advice.

6 You can add or delete statements in the Config.sys or the Autoexec.bat, to create a set of system files that are unique to that particular application. In the Lemmings example, Mouse.exe must be added to the Autoexec.bat.

Memory Management

The most complex operation in MS-DOS was setting up the memory management characteristics, to get as much memory as possible of the various types required, and arranging for the applications and device drives to be loaded into the right segment of memory.

The techniques available for MS-DOS mode applications are similar, but things are made simple in Windows 98, because you can define individual configurations for specific applications, so that you no longer have to balance off the needs of one application against another.

For MS-DOS applications that run in an MS-DOS prompt, the defaults that Windows provides, effectively unlimited for many types of memory, should be sufficient. However, you can set specific values if you wish, when you do need to adjust memory settings:

Check the application manual to find the setup requirements, then make a suitable change.

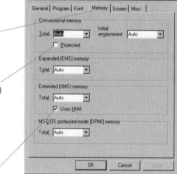

1 Open the program Properties and select the Memory tab.

2 Click Protected if the application appears to cause Windows errors.

3 Use the HMA to increase the amount of conventional memory available.

4 Set values for conventional, expanded, extended or DPMI memory. Leave the value as Auto if you are unsure of the best level.

5 Select OK to save the changes and try out the new configuration.

Uninstalling applications

You need to uninstall applications when you want to transfer the licence from one PC to another or when you no longer use the application and want to release the disk space it uses. The applications add information to the Registry and the Start menu, put libraries and other files in the Windows or Windows\System folders, and may add file associations or entries on the context menus. This makes removal potentially very complex. Windows 98 requires applications to include uninstall features to allow you to remove the program and its associated folders and the settings it added to the Registry and elsewhere. To remove a Windows 98 application such as Paint Shop Pro:

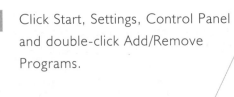

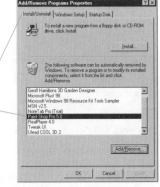

1 Click Start, Settings, Control Panel and double-click Add/Remove Programs.

Only those applications that have a compatible uninstall program appear in the list.

2 Choose the Install/Uninstall tab, and locate the entry for the application in the list of products.

You may also use Add/ Remove to add extra parts of the application. See page 262 Office 2000 installation

3 Click Add/Remove to start the Install/Shield Wizard, which guides you through the automatic uninstall.

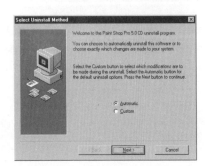

The application may also include an Uninstall option in the Start folder entries. For Windows 95 and Windows 3.1x applications that are not compatible with the Windows 98 Add/Remove feature, this will be the normal method of removal.

Uninstalling other programs

Hold down Shift as you press Delete to permanently delete the folder and contents.

Applications may place information scattered through the system. Depending on the type of program, there could be:

- Program and data folders

- Library and system files

- Start menu entries

- Context menu entries

- File and folder associations

- Registry entries

Unless the application uses the Windows 98 uninstall feature or provides its own uninstall program, you will have to manually remove as many of these as you can. To minimise the difficulties this may cause:

There's no easy way to remove unwanted entries from the Registry, but the system tools can check for invalid entries.

1 Find shortcut entries for the application, open the Properties and press the Target button to locate the original file.

2 Identify the application folder and open it in Explorer.

3 Check for data files or folders that you may wish to keep, and transfer these to a storage folder or backup system.

4 Close the folder then select it and press Delete, Yes to transfer the contents to the recycle bin.

Organising the Start Menu

If your PC is used by more than one person, make sure that you are logged on using your user name.

When you install an application, the installation process creates a new item in the Start menu. You are usually offered a choice of folder, but the default will be to add a program or folder entry into the Programs folder.

After installation, you can remove, resequence or rename the entries. To customise entries in Start menu folders:

1 Right-click an unused part of the taskbar, click Properties, select the Start Menu Programs tab.

2 Click the Advanced button to display the Start menu in Windows Explorer. This limits the display to the Start menu.

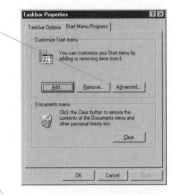

The changes you make to the shortcuts and folders will be reflected directly in the Start menu.

3 Select the Programs folder and locate the entries that you wish to modify.

4 Remove unnecessary entries such as the supplier/product level added by Ulead.

Create a new subfolder to contain an associated group of entries or drag and drop program shortcuts from one folder to another.

Windows sorts the folder and shortcut names in alphanumeric order. To sequence the shortcuts and folders the way you want, rename or add a prefix. Special characters come first, then numbers and then letters.

...cont'd

You can add shortcuts to MS-DOS applications that run in MS-DOS prompt sessions or even those that run in MS-DOS mode. In the latter case, this will cause Windows to shut down before the application starts.

To add a shortcut (Windows or MS-DOS) to an existing folder in the Start menu:

HOT TIP

Select New, Folder to add another menu level.

1   Select the folder in the left pane.

2   Right-click the folder space and select New, Shortcut.

3   Type the path and name, or use Browse to find the application file.

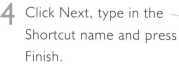

4   Click Next, type in the Shortcut name and press Finish.

HOT TIP

You will get the warning message when you select an MS-DOS mode shortcut - unless you turn off that option.

5   Close Explorer and the new entries will appear in the Start menu.

6   The shortcut appears in the selected folder in the Start menu. Note that there is no distinction between the MS-DOS prompt, MS-DOS mode and Windows types of shortcut.

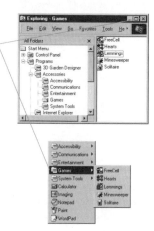

Exchanging Information

This chapter explores the ways in which Windows 98 enables applications to share and update, in particular the facilities offered through Clipboard and resource kit utilities that enhance Clipboard. The roles of OLE, ActiveX and related technologies are also discussed.

Covers

Chapter Eight

Sharing Information

The term Document is used in its generic Windows sense to represent any format information whether textual report, image, spreadsheet or presentation.

The most significant aspect of the Windows environment is the way it allows applications to interchange information. It supports this capability in several ways and at different levels.

Documents in Windows applications can contain objects of more than one type, so a Word document for example can contain bitmaps and spreadsheet information. Such documents are referred to as compound documents. The Clipboard can be used to help build these, since it can handle all the types of data that you find in Windows applications, and will pass the data to the applications in the format that the application expects and is able to process. The data is exchanged through the Clipboard, using copy and paste operations. The transferred data can become part of the new document, or remain as a data object and retain its original identity.

There are several shortcomings in using the Clipboard. It can handle only one item at a time, making it hard to assemble collections of extracts. Any item added to the Clipboard can be reused to add it to other documents, but only until the next piece of data arrives in the Clipboard, and the contents are lost when the system shuts down. Saving clipboard contents provides a very limited solution, and there are many third party products designed to enhance its operations, beginning with the utilities that are included in the resource kit.

The Windows help system with its Internet URLs provides an example of ActiveX in operation.

The Clipboard does not provide support for maintaining the compound document, except implicitly when you use it to rebuild the document, copying and pasting new versions of the transferred objects whenever they change.

Windows does provide control over data exchanges and update, with technologies such as Dynamic Data Exchange (DDE), Object Linking and Embedding (OLE) and the underlying Component Object Model (COM). These have been extended into Distributed Component Object Model (DCOM) for sharing across networks, and ActiveX for sharing over the Internet.

Using the Clipboard

The Clipboard is the easiest way to transfer information, whether it is from one application to another or from one part of a document to another. However, you still have a number of options and alternatives to choose from, and these will vary depending on which application acts as the source and which as the target for the information. To help illustrate these options, the following sections trace some of the paths that a piece of data may take as it passes through the Clipboard.

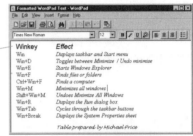

1 Load WordPad and open the source document.

The example document contains text with a variety of font types and effects, put into columns using tabs.

2 Click Edit, Select All and Edit, Copy to transfer the text to the Clipboard.

3 View the contents of the Clipboard using the Clipboard Viewer (see page 103 for details of this).

Styles that are greyed-out are not applicable to the current data object in the Clipboard.

4 Click Display from the menu bar and select a style to see its format.

Normally, Auto is the best option, but you can view the contents of the clipboard in any of the available styles, in this case Auto, Text, Picture and OEM Text.

Text to text

The text in the Clipboard can be pasted into another part of the same WordPad document, or it can be inserted into another WordPad document.

I Load a second copy of WordPad and open the target document, to start a new document.

With the default option, the text appears exactly as in the source document with all of the font formatting and tabs.

2 Select Edit, Paste to add the text to the target document. The text becomes part of the document and you can make changes to it.

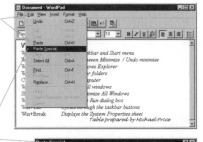

3 To try a different method, select Edit, Undo to remove the copy and then select Edit, Paste Special.

Choose the type of object, for example Metafile.

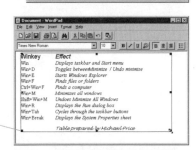

5 Move the pointer to one of the picture handles and when the double arrow appears, click and drag to resize the picture.

With this format, the text is inserted as a picture. You can reposition or resize it, but the text that it contains cannot be directly modified or altered. This is useful when you want to avoid the inserted text being accidentally modified.

Another way to insert the text yet keep it separate from the rest of the document is to choose the WordPad object format, which appears as a separate item like a picture, but can still be modified if desired.

The Icon acts as a place holder in the document.

1 Select Edit, Paste Special, pick WordPad Document and click to Display as Icon.

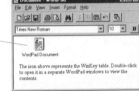

2 Double-click the icon to open the inserted text object in a separate WordPad window.

The text can be changed, but the object remains a separate element in the document.

3 If you make any changes, select File and then choose Update Document to change the object, or Save Copy As to create a new document.

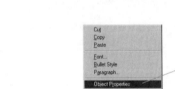

4 Right-click the icon and select Object Properties. Click the View tab and click the Change Icon button.

5 Choose a different Icon image if you wish. You can also change the icon title displayed in the target document.

The Clipboard also provides the data in Rich text format. This provides the data with all the format and style options intact, and allows WordPad to edit the data in the normal fashion.

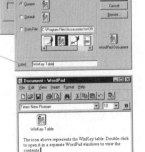

Text to paint

The same WordPad data is still in the Clipboard and can be transferred to the Paint application.

1 Load the Paint program and select Edit, Paste to add the text to the new image file.

The text appears exactly as it did in WordPad, but it is in bitmap format and it cannot be edited as text.

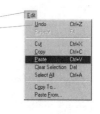

2 Select Edit, Undo to remove the text so that you can try a different method. There is no Edit, Paste Special, but Paint does have an equivalent operation.

Drag the Text toolbar out of the way if it covers the menu bar, or the start point for the text box.

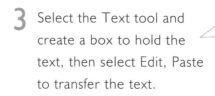

3 Select the Text tool and create a box to hold the text, then select Edit, Paste to transfer the text.

When it is entered as text, the data loses its formatting.

4 If you get a message box saying Not enough room to paste text, enlarge the text box and try again.

You can reposition parts of the text, insert tabs and change the font size or style. However, only one font can be used and any changes will apply to the whole selection.

5 Click outside the text box when changes are finished, and the text is converted to a bitmap which cannot be edited.

Cut and paste images

The process for moving image data through the Clipboard is similar to that for text, although the specific options offered will differ.

1 Load Paint and open the image that you wish to copy from.

Use Free-Form Select for irregular shapes.

2 Click the Select tool and mark the area of the image to extract.

3 Click Edit, Copy to transfer the image data to the Clipboard.

4 Load the clipboard Viewer to see the contents in the default Auto format.

The Auto display is in Picture (metafile) format.

In this example, you will see the contents of the Clipboard stretched to fill the Viewer window, whatever size it is, and without regard to the original proportions. However, the image itself is unchanged.

5 Click Display to see the options. Picture is the default, but if you select Bitmap you will see the image the size and shape you expect.

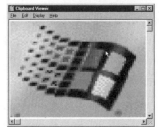

The Display option you select changes the way the image is presented in the Clipboard Viewer but does not influence the way it will be transferred to another application.

Add Image to text

1 Load WordPad and open the target document that is to receive the image from the Clipboard.

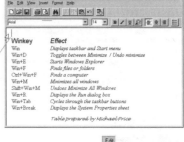

2 Position the typing cursor at the point where the image should be inserted, adding a blank line if necessary.

3 Select Edit, Paste to add the image to the document. It is inserted as a bitmap.

4 Right-click the image and select Bitmap Image Object, and Edit. The Paint tools and menus replace the WordPad items.

5 Click outside the image area to return to the WordPad setup.

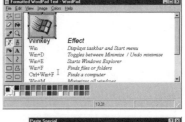

6 If you select Open instead, Paint opens in a separate window. Then you can modify the image and save it back into the document or as a separate file.

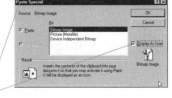

As an alternative, you can select Paste, Special to copy the image from the Clipboard. Then you can click Display as Icon, to insert the image into the document with an Icon to mark the spot. Double click the Icon to view or change the image in Paint.

Paste to Notepad

Notepad has only the one Paste option, does not support text formatting, and has no support for image data of any type. To copy text information from the Clipboard:

1 Load Notepad and select Edit, Paste to insert the Clipboard contents.

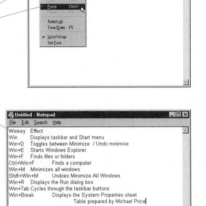

2 The data is inserted as plain text, with no formatting.

You can edit the data and change the font type or style, but any changes that you make apply not only to the whole insert but also to the rest of the document.

When you have image data in the Clipboard, you'll find that Notepad takes no interest:

3 Load Notepad and (attempt to) check Edit, Paste.

Notice that the Paste function is disabled, since there is no data that Notepad is designed to handle.

At the other end of the spectrum, you will find that word processing applications have extra Paste options to match their additional capabilities. For example, there is the Hypertext Link option in Word to handle Internet addresses.

Shortcuts and paste

Use the menu bar, toolbar, or keyboard shortcuts to define Clipboard actions.

There are several ways to specify the actions you want when you are transferring information to and from the Clipboard:

Action	Keyboard	Menu bar	Button
Move to Clipboard	Ctrl+X	Edit, Cut	✂
Copy to Clipboard	Ctrl+C	Edit, Copy	📋
Copy from Clipboard	Ctrl+V	Edit, Paste	📋
Undo last action	Ctrl+Z	Edit, Undo	↺

Graphics programs like Paint provide selection tools to help you mark the part of the image you want to transfer. To select an area of text:

1 Move the mouse pointer to the start of the data, press and hold the left button.

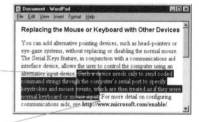

You can also use the keyboard directly in place of the mouse – using the keypad keys to simulate the mouse movements – with the accessibility mouse keys feature.

2 Drag the pointer to the end point and release.

All the text between the start and end characters is highlighted and selected, not just the rectangular area you have dragged across.

It is often more precise to select text with the keyboard. Move the typing cursor to the start point, press and hold the Shift key, then move the cursor using the arrow keys to highlight the required data, and release the Shift key.

...cont'd

You do not always need the Clipboard to copy or move data between applications.

You can copy information within an application or between applications using the drag and drop method. This differs from the clipboard method since the data does not get saved and cannot be used for repeat copies. There are also limitations, since not all applications support the process. WordPad does, but Paint and Notepad do not. To copy information with drag and drop, follow these steps:

1 Run WordPad and open the source document, containing the text that you want to copy.

2 Load a second copy of WordPad and open the target document.

3 Highlight the text you want to copy.

4 Click and Drag the selection.

A No Entry symbol is displayed as the selection moves over areas where text cannot be inserted.

Notice that the mouse pointer changes as you drag and, as you cross over to the other document, a plus sign [+] is added. This indicates Copy to a different window, rather than Move, the default when you Drag within the same document.

Hold down Ctrl before releasing the button, if you want to Copy a selection in the same document.

5 Position the text in the target location in the document, using the vertical bar to see where the text will appear.

6 Release the mouse button and the copy completes.

MS-DOS Clipboard

You can share data with MS-DOS applications as well. To transfer data from a DOS application to a Windows application:

Press Alt+Enter to toggle between MS-DOS window and full-screen.

1   Switch the DOS application to a window, if it is currently full screen.

2   Click the Mark button on the toolbar, or click the MS-DOS icon at the top left to open the Control menu and then click Edit, Mark.

Mark using the keyboard, by holding down Shift and using the arrow keys.

A blinking cursor appears in the upper-left corner of the DOS window, to show that you are in the marking mode.

3   Click the start location, hold down the left mouse button, and drag a box around the text or graphics to be copied.

4   Click the Copy button on the toolbar. Or press Enter, or click Edit, Copy.

The selection is copied to the Clipboard. You can copy the data into the document for the Windows application as normal. You can also copy data from a Windows or DOS application via the Clipboard into the MS-DOS application. However, any formatting will be lost.

5   Click the Paste button on the toolbar. The contents of the Clipboard are inserted into the DOS document.

Clip captures

Clip is one of the programs provided in the full version of the Windows 98 resource kit. It is an MS-DOS command-line utility that copies text from the STDIN stream to the Windows 98 Clipboard. You can then paste the data directly into any MS-DOS or Windows application.

Run any MS-DOS program or command that prints text to STDOUT and pipe the results through Clip. Clip reads from STDIN and copies the text to the Clipboard.

Example: dir | clip

1 dir d:\design shows the listing on screen.

2 dir d:\design | clip sends the list to the Clipboard.

Paste the text into a document which you can then print.

Use a mono-spaced font such as Courier New to preserve alignment.

Example: clip < file

3 clip < readme.txt.

This puts a copy of the contents of the specified text file into the Clipboard, ready to Paste into a document.

ClipTray

ClipTray is one of the desktop tools in the Windows 98 resource kit sampler. It allows you to store pieces of text and copy them as needed into text documents via the Clipboard. It is useful whenever you have lists of information – code or macro samples, quotes, names and telephone numbers, or any text that is used repeatedly.

1. Run ClipTray from the Tools Management Console in the Resource Kit folder, and its icon is added to the system tray.

2. Right-click the icon to display the menu of current entries, and options to add more.

3. Click on a ClipTray entry to copy it to the Clipboard.

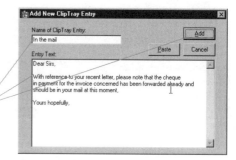

4. To create a new item, right-click the icon and press Add, then enter the title and the text, and click Add.

5. Create any further items, and then press Close to finish.

...cont'd

It is highly advised that you do not manually modify your ClipTray text files. Also, always make a backup copy of the file when you have made changes to it.

To make changes to existing items, right-click the icon, select Options, Edit, and choose the appropriate entry. You can Edit to change the contents or Delete entries that are no longer needed.

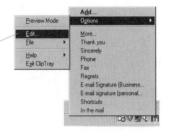

To change the order of ClipTray entries:

1 Right-click the icon, choose More, select the entry and click Move Up or Move Down to reposition it in the list.

The number of entries that fit on the menu varies with the resolution.

2 Move the slider to change the number of items shown on the menu.

This will allow you to group related items such as alternative e-mail signatures so that they are easier to find. The More option also allows you to access extra entries if you have more than will fit on the menu list. An alternative is to use more than one ClipTray text file, for example split by project.

To create a new file, type the name instead of clicking a file, and it will be opened as an empty menu that you can update as required.

To switch to a different file:

3 From the icon menu choose Options, File, Open/Create.

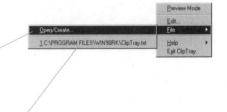

4 Select the file you wish to use, and click Open. The menu will now contain the ClipTray entries from the new file.

Embedded Objects

When you use the Copy and Paste functions to add data from one application into a document created by another dissimilar application, you are building a compound document with embedded objects. Windows uses object linking and embedding (OLE) to manage these compound documents. The application that creates the enveloping document is known as the container or client. The application that supplies and edits the object is referred to as the server, because it supplies OLE services to the client.

When changes are needed, instead of having to edit the data in the originating application and repeating the copy and paste, you can edit the data in situ, without having to exit the client. You just double-click the object and the menus and toolbars change from their normal settings to provide the functions of the server. When you finish making changes, click outside the object area to restore the original client application menus and toolbars.

You can embed information using the copy and paste commands, or by using drag and drop if the application supports it. However, if the object is the whole file, rather than a section of the file, there is another method available, You can Insert the object file, and either embed it or link it in the document. To illustrate how linking and embedding work, imagine a scenario where three users work together on a project and share data across a network.

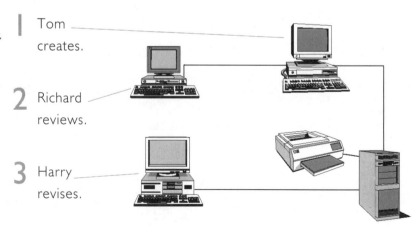

1 Tom creates.

2 Richard reviews.

3 Harry revises.

...cont'd

Use OLE to share image files over the LAN.

1 When the logo has been created and is ready, set up a document to contain the image and associated notes.

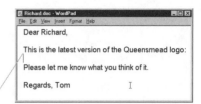

2 Position the typing cursor at the point where the file is to appear.

Press the Browse button to search for the file, if necessary.

3 Click Insert from the menu bar and then Object.

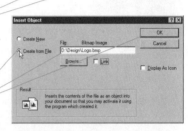

4 Click to Create from File, type the file name and click OK.

The object is inserted into the document. The user with access to this document sees the image exactly as it appears in the original file. By double-clicking the image it can be modified using the same toolbar and palette etc., as you get in Paint.

However, these changes do not affect the original file. Equally, any changes that are made to the original, after it has been inserted, will not be reflected in the document file.

The embedded object is a one way, one time transfer of data between the applications.

Linking Objects

When you link data, the document retains details of the source file. If you choose Icon view, the document contains the OLE details needed to locate and retrieve the data. On the other hand, embedded data is stored in the document, even with icon view, and the OLE details are just to identify the source application.

If changes are allowed, or if the document must be kept up to date, the file should be linked rather than embedded.

To link a file object into a WordPad document:

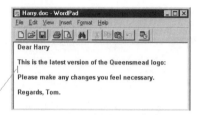

1 Open the document, position the typing cursor, and click Insert, Object.

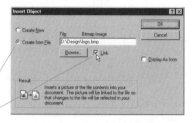

2 Click to Create from file, type the file name and click the Link box, then click OK.

The object is inserted into the document. The user again sees the image as it appears in the original. However, when the image is double-clicked, it opens a separate window for the Paint program with the original image file. Any changes that are made will be saved directly to the original.

Linked objects form a two way dynamic data exchange.

The changes will also affect the copy in the document and the copies in any other document that hold links to the same image file.

Similarly, if changes are made elsewhere to the source file, the changes will appear in this document and every other linked document, when they are next opened.

To see if there are any links defined in the current document:

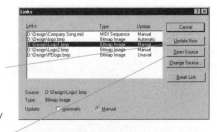

1 Select Edit from the menu bar. If Links is greyed, there are none defined.

2 If Links is available, click it to view and modify the links in the document.

3 Select an entry and click Update Now to refresh the copy in the document.

If you change the name or path of the source document or server application, you must re-establish your links.

4 Click Open Source to view or change the original file.

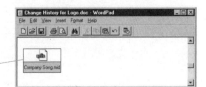

5 You may find other types of links including music files.

6 Click Change source to specify a different path or file name for the selected source file, if the link is marked Unavailable.

The copy remains in the document, but the item is dropped from the Links list.

7 Make updates automatic for the selected link to get the copy refreshed when you open the document.

8 Press Break link if you no longer want updates when the source document is altered.

OLE Registration

You can set up a link between two applications or documents only when both support OLE.

As well as Paint images and Midi files, WordPad can insert data objects and files from any application that supports OLE, including Office 2000 applications such as Excel and PowerPoint and the Office mini applications such as Clip Gallery, Equation and WordArt.

To check which OLE-compatible applications and objects are currently registered on your system:

1 Open the System Information from the System Tools folder in the Start menu.

2 Click the [+] to expand Software Environment, and then expand the OLE Registration branch. They change to [-].

3 Click on INI File to display the OLE objects available.

The example shown has all the Windows 98 components, plus some of the Office applications.

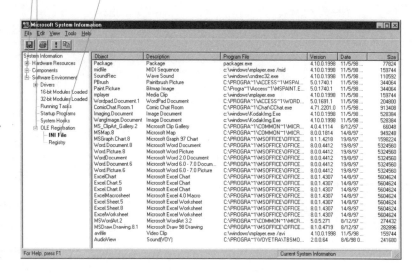

If you have Windows 98 alone installed, you may have very few entries, but each OLE compliant application that you install will add one or more entries to the list.

Controlling the printer

This chapter looks at the Printers folder, and shows you how to add local and network printers, to print from applications or using shortcuts, and to manage print queues and paper changes.

Covers

Chapter Nine

Windows printer

Windows 98 records information about its printers in the special Printer folder. You can access this from the Settings folder in the Start menu, or from My Computer or the Control Panel. The default Windows 98 installation may have no printers defined, since the information must be specific to the equipment that you have attached to your PC, and Windows may not be able to determine this. With a pre-installed system your supplier may have added the printer for you. However, you can easily define your printer, or add extra definitions if you have a choice of printers that you can attach.

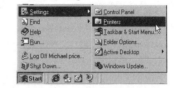

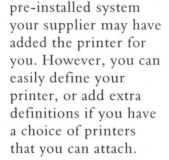

You can add extra definitions that represent different uses of the same printer to save you having to change the properties.

You may also want to add the definitions for printers that are actually attached to other PCs, if you use printers on a network, or if you want to send ready-to-print files to another user.

When you are planning to define a printer, check that you have everything that will be needed to set it up and use it:

*   An available printer port (usually LPT1, though some printers use one of the COM ports).

*   A suitable printer cable, ready-connected between the printer and the chosen port.

*   Printer connected to the power supply and turned on ready for use. This will enable Windows 98 to detect the printer when it starts up.

*   The manufacturer and the model for the printer.

*   A printer-specific device CD or diskette if available.

Plug and Play

You may have to do no more than switch on the printer and system, if the printer and the PC are fully plug and play compliant.

If the system BIOS in your PC supports the Windows plug and play technology, the system can automatically detect many types of hardware attached to your PC, and install the required software drivers and settings without you having to take any part in the operation.

This means that, if your printer is plug and play-compliant, you may just have to turn on the printer and start up the PC into Windows 98, and the installation will take place. Windows will detect that the printer has been added to your computer, and it will display a message box to tell you this. Windows will identify the make and model of the printer.

If the printer drivers for this printer are already on the hard disk (for example with a PC that was pre-installed at the factory, or when you are reinstalling a printer), Windows will be able to re-use the details. Otherwise, you are prompted to insert the Windows 98 CD-ROM. If the particular driver was not included with Windows 98, or if you have received an updated version of the driver, insert the device disk and enter the drive and folder path.

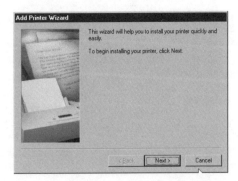

If Windows 98 does not automatically recognise your printer, you need to manually add it to your computer configuration through the Add Printer Wizard.

The following sections look at the steps involved in defining a printer and setting up its properties to match your requirements.

Add Printer

This folder can be found in Control Panel, My Computer or Settings on the Start menu.

To add a new printer definition:

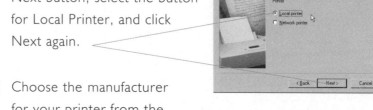

1 Open the Printers folder and double-click Add Printer.

2 When the wizard starts, click Next button, select the button for Local Printer, and click Next again.

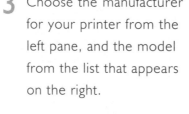

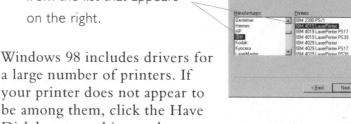

Type the initial letter of the maker's name to position yourself at the right part of the list.

3 Choose the manufacturer for your printer from the left pane, and the model from the list that appears on the right.

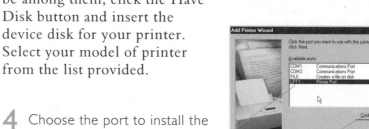

Windows 98 includes drivers for a large number of printers. If your printer does not appear to be among them, click the Have Disk button and insert the device disk for your printer. Select your model of printer from the list provided.

These disks should be provided with the printer, or you may be able to locate copies on the Internet at the manufacturer's site.

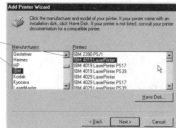

4 Choose the port to install the printer. In most cases, the correct port will be LPT1.

5 Click the Configure Port, for example to have Windows 98 check the status before it prints.

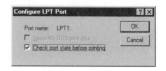

6 Specify a meaningful name for the printer, or accept the default driver name. ———

For a printer that may be used on a network, the name could include the location as well as the type e.g. First Floor Laser.

7 Choose to print a test page, to make sure that everything is working the way you expect, then press Finish.

 If the Windows 98 CAB files have been pre-installed on your hard drive, the CD won't be required.

Windows 98 then installs and configures the printer. Be ready to insert the Windows 98 CD-ROM if requested. The printer driver software and any other files required will be copied onto your hard disk.

An icon for the printer is added to the Printers folder and, assuming this is the first printer installed on your PC, it is made the default printer, as shown by the check mark on the printer icon.

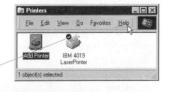

If you did request a test page, it will be generated at this point. The printout will show the printer drivers' names, version numbers and dates, so that you will be able to check that you have the latest level.

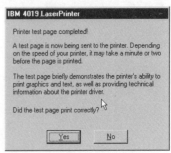

Printers Folder

The Printers folder can contain icons for other printers as well as the Add Printers wizard and the default printer. When you add an additional printer, you will be offered the choice of making it the new default. If you select No at this time, you can change the selection later.

To select another default printer:

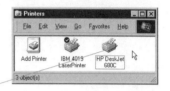

1 Open the Printers folder and right-click the printer icon.

2 From the context menu that is displayed, choose Set as Default.

The check mark moves from the original printer to the selected printer, which now becomes the default.

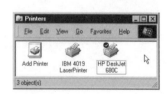

The Printers folder is the central point from which you manage the attached printers and any network printers to which you have access.

The printer devices do not have to be physically attached to the PC or network. They may just be used to generate the correct type of file outputs.

The folder may also contain the icons for other devices that use a printer driver, such as a fax modem, or for software that requires printer definitions, such as postscript printers for Microsoft Publisher or Adobe PageMaker.

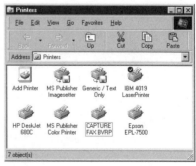

Printer Properties

The printer properties define in detail the functions and operations available for that printer. There are several ways to display the Properties page for a printer:

Hold down the Alt key and double-click the printer to open Properties immediately.

1 Open the Printers folder, right-click the printer and select Properties from the menu.

2 Check the port and the device driver used for the printer.

Increase the time period if you have timeouts while printing large documents.

3 Specify how long Windows should wait before reporting an error.

The Properties pages that are displayed will be specific to the printer type, so each printer may have a different set of tabs and options available.

The default is to download them as soft fonts, which will normally be the quicker option.

4 There may be a choice to print Windows truetype fonts as graphics. This is quicker when the page contains mainly graphics. It is also useful when you overlay text with pictures.

Check the Device features specified in Properties and make sure that the memory size, paper tray options, installed fonts, etc., match the actual configuration of your particular printer.

Network printer

You will find this process very similar to defining your own attached printer.

If your PC is connected to a network, you may be able to share a printer attached to a server or another PC. Before you can use the printer, however, you will have to define the printers involved to your copy of Windows.

Before staring, confirm with your network administrator that the printer is set up for sharing over the network, and that your user id has been assigned authority to access it. You will also require:

*   The printer name and the server or PC name.

*   The manufacturer and the model for the printer.

If possible, connect to the network before adding the printer.

1 Open the Printers folder and double-click Add Printer, and click Next.

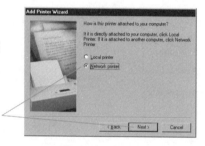

2 Select Network printer and then click Next.

3 Specify the location of the printer on the network. Type in the name of the printer and the PC or server, using the UNC (Universal Naming Convention) path, for example: \\Dell\Lexmark

If you are not sure of the address, click Browse to display all the PCs on the network that have shared printers. Click the plus sign next to a PC in the list to show the shared printers attached.

4 Click the button to say if you want to print from MS-DOS applications, then click Next.

You must assign a printer port for MS-DOS programs, even though the printer is not actually attached. Windows 98 intercepts the data and transfers it to the network printer.

...cont'd

If you want to add several printers, local or network, you must run Add Printer for each one in turn.

If you are on line, Windows 98 connects to the printer to determine its make and model, and downloads it (unless there is already a copy). For this Point and Print feature to operate, you must connect to a PC with Windows 98, Windows NT Server, or Novell NetWare.

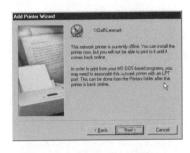

If you are offline, or if Windows cannot download the driver, it asks you to select the device driver for the printer.

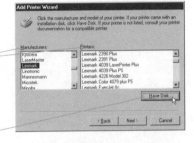

1 Select the make and model as with a local printer.

Another way to add a network printer is to open Network Neighbourhood and browse the PCs shown. When you find a printer to attach, right-click it and select Install. This will open Add Printer but you will be several steps further forward.

2 If Windows 98 does not list the model, press Have Disk.

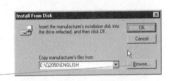

3 Insert the device disk and if necessary Browse to locate the device INF file.

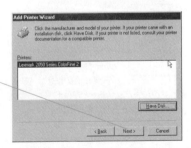

4 Select the model from the list provided, and click Next.

The device driver and any required program files will be copied to the hard disk, and the printer icon is added to the Printers folder, ready for use when you are next on-line to the network.

Application printing

Once you have installed at least one printer, applications on your PC can issue print requests. The printer properties will be adopted for the application, but you can change some parts of the printer configuration from within the application itself. When the job is sent to the printer, you can carry on with other tasks, because Windows 98 has a print spooler that handles the work in the background.

To print from an application such as WordPad:

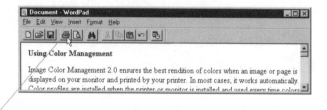

| Print the current document by clicking the Printer button on the toolbar. This sends the job immediately, without giving you an opportunity to change settings.

2 Select File from the menu bar and then select Print.

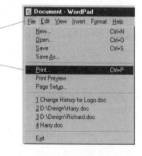

You can print to a file, when you need to send a printer-ready file rather than the document, for example to another user who does not have the application.

This gives you a window that allows you to change settings for that print. The window shows the current printer name and status. You can:

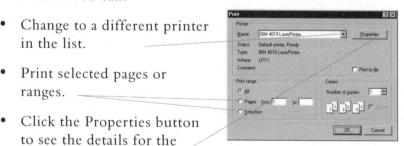

- Change to a different printer in the list.

- Print selected pages or ranges.

- Click the Properties button to see the details for the selected printer.

...cont'd

Changes to the document printer Properties apply to the current application only.

The options that you see will depend on the type of printer you have attached.

On the Properties pages, you can make changes to the selected printer settings for the current document. The changes will not affect any other applications using the printer.

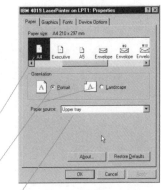

Changes you can make include:

- Select a different paper size.

- Change the paper orientation from portrait to landscape.

- Select a different paper source e.g. manual feed or lower tray.

- Switch to the Graphics tab, and change the printer resolution, adjust the colour dithering effects or vary the Intensity (darkness).

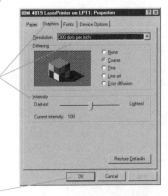

3 Click OK (or Cancel) to close the Properties pages.

4 Click Print to start converting the document to printer data.

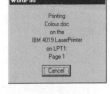

The application does not print the document directly, it just transfers the printer ready data to the Windows print spooler.

When printing begins, an icon is added to the system tray, showing that the Windows print spooler is active, and providing a quick point of access to the printer management functions.

Print Spooler

The Windows 98 print spooler is a 32-bit application that uses the features of pre-emptive and multitasking multithreading to handle the printer with the minimum impact on your on-going activities. You wait only until the document has been prepared and transferred to the spooler, then you can carry on working in the application, or even quit it and start another application.

The print data is stored on the hard disk while it waits its turn. By default, the print spooler starts to send data to the printer as soon as it has received the first page. You can change this so that the spooler does not start printing until the whole document has been sent to the spooler.

To change the spooler properties:

1 Open the Printers folder, right-click the printer icon and select Properties.

You cannot send data direct to the printer if you are sharing the printer with other users.

2 Select the Details tab, and click the Spool Settings button.

3 Change the default settings to wait until the last page is spooled before sending the document to the printer.

4 You can choose to send the print data directly to the printer. This may speed up printing but prevent you working with the application until the printer finishes the job.

Printers like the Lexmark Winwriters that use the PC to process the data require data in RAW form.

5 Choose between enhanced metafile (EMF) printing and RAW spool data formats. EMF returns control back to the application more quickly, but some applications don't support EMF.

The print queue

The application can have more than one job outstanding, and several applications may be using the printer at the same time. This means that a queue of print jobs can build up. To view the status of a particular printer:

1 Double-click the printer icon in the system tray.

2 Right-click the print job, and select Pause to prevent it being printed when its turn arrives.

3 Right-click and select Pause again to reactivate the job.

4 Select Cancel to remove the job from the queue.

The first job (not paused) in the queue is the one currently being printed. Other jobs are waiting for printing, in order of arrival in the queue.

There are some actions that apply to the queue as a whole. To purge all waiting prints:

5 Select Printer, Pause Printing to hold all jobs.

6 Select Printer, Purge Print Documents to clear the queue.

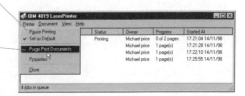

Document printing

You don't have to open the application to print a document.
Simply drop the document onto the printer, or press Print on the context menu. It will automatically run the application, print the document and then close the application for you.

You'll need access to the printer icon. You can use the Printers folder, but it is easier if you create a printer shortcut on the desktop:

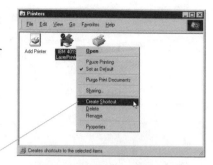

| Open the Printers folder, right-click the printer and select Create shortcut.

2 Click Yes to create the shortcut on your desktop.

To print using drag and drop:

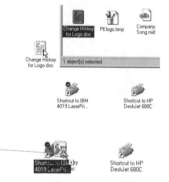

The file type must be registered and the associated application must be installed on your PC.

3 Locate the document icon, drag it to the printer icon and drop it when the icon changes colour.

To print using the context menu:

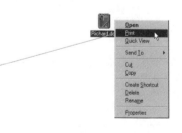

4 Locate the document icon and right-click it then select Print from the context menu that is displayed.

Print uses the default printer. To choose the printer, put shortcuts in the Send To folder:

5 Right-click the document and select Send To, Printer of choice.

Ascii text printer

You may need to print text files that are not associated with any applications. For example, log files or the Prn output produced by an MS-DOS application. If the contents of the file are plain, unformatted text, you can create an Ascii printer for these files by writing a simple batch file. This file should contain a command to copy the text file to the printer port. If you have a sheetfeed printer and want to eject the final page, add a second command to copy a page feed character (usually character code 12) to the printer port.

The text file may also contain codes appropriate to your printer – to skip line, select fonts, emphasise print etc.

1 Create a shortcut to this batch file on the desktop, or in the SendTo folder.

Ascii.bat

You'll find some printer icons in Shell32.dll in the \Windows \system folder.

2 Right-click the shortcut, select Properties, Programs and click Change Icon. Choose a suitable icon, and rename the shortcut.

Shortcut to Ascii.bat

If you want to use this technique with a network printer you must have specified MS-DOS printing, and captured a printer port address for the printer. Use the address selected in place of LPT1 in the batch file.

3 Drag and drop the text files onto the Ascii Printer, or right-click the file and Send To the printer.

Ascii Printer

Web printing

The Internet Web pages displayed by browsers such as Internet Explorer and Netscape Navigator present a unified appearance, for example the Dell UK Web site:

In fact the page is rather more complex than it might appear, because it is built up in a series of separate components called frames. In effect, you are viewing separate pages that have been merged together, usually seamlessly.

This is the part of the page that you click in just before selecting File, Print.

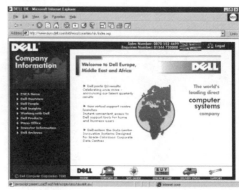

This becomes more evident when you request a print by selecting File, Print. There are several options that apply to the Web page structure, to allow you to:

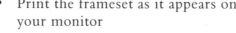

- Print the frameset as it appears on your monitor

- Print the selected frame

- Print all of the frames individually

- Print all linked documents

- Print a table of the links on the page

Links are the addresses or hyperlinks of other Web pages on the same site or on a different site.

In this example, the print consists of eight separate documents, all included into the same Web page, plus numerous hyperlinks to other parts of the Dell Web site.

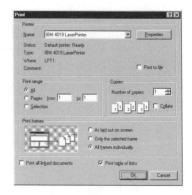

Print and hold

With a mobile PC or with a network printer, you may not always have the printer available at the times you are ready to print. In Windows 98 you can effectively send the documents to the printer, but put the actual printing on hold until the printer is connected. This uses the offline printing feature. To use offline printing:

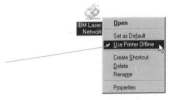

1 Open the Printers folder, right-click the printer and choose Use Printer Offline.

A check mark appears next to the printer icon.

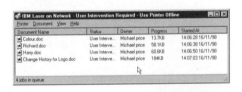

2 The print jobs created from now on will be held in the print queue until you wish to print.

Offline printing is not used with local printers, so for these you must use the Pause option instead.

3 Choose Printer from the menu bar and deselect Use Printer Offline.

With a mobile PC configured for a docking station, Windows 98 selects the appropriate hardware profile at boot time, and initiates offline printing when it detects that you are not connected to the docking station. If you connect to the docking station and restart the PC, offline printing is turned off, and the queued print jobs will be sent to your printer.

You must be using Windows spooling, so this method may not work with printers that provide their own spooling programs. However, these usually have a Pause or Hold feature that can be used instead.

Many printers in one

You may sometimes want to print in draft mode, and other times want proof quality or high resolution graphics printing. You may want to switch between landscape and portrait, or you may have several different paper sources to suit particular types of jobs. You can change Properties between every print job, but a far more effective way is to set up a configuration that you want as a separate printer definition.

To add a new definition:

1 Open the Printers folder and start the Add Printer wizard, and reinstall your printer.

Landscape, Portrait, Draft, Graphics – you must repeat the whole process for each different setup that you require.

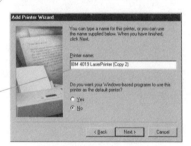

2 Choose to keep the existing device drivers for the printer.

3 Change the name, choosing a name related to the proposed use of the printer.

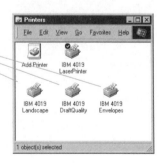

4 Change the printer properties accordingly.

Choose one of these printers within an application, or create shortcuts to print documents by drag and drop, or through the Send To folder.

Be sure to match definitions and actual printer setup. For example, if you choose a printer definition with a different type of paper in the paper tray, make sure that the actual paper in the physical printer has been changed also.

Generic text printer

This may be handy for converting a document into a form suitable for plain text e-mail.

You can use a printer definition to extract text from print data.

1 Open the Printers folder, start the Add Printer wizard, and choose maker Generic and type Generic/ Text Only.

2 Specify the printer port as FILE (create a file on disk).

3 Insert the Windows CD if requested, and the required program files are copied.

4 The new printer icon is added to the Printers folder.

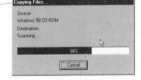

Generic / Text Only

You can drag and drop to this printer, or select it in any application. Note however that some Windows applications may restrict the display of the document to match the capabilities of this printer. This will effectively remove text formatting and graphics from the display (though it doesn't affect the contents of the file). The formatting will be redisplayed when you revert to the standard Windows printer.

You may also switch to a different folder than the \My Documents default.

When you print using this printer you are asked to provide a file name. Change the name from the ★.prn pre-entered.

Delete printer

This applies to local and network printers alike.

If you change printer models, you can Add the new printer, make it the default and leave the old definition in the folder in case you need to revert to your old printer later. However, to remove unnecessary entries from the Printers folder:

1 Open the Printers folder and right-click the printer icon.

2 Select Delete from the menu, and click Yes to confirm the removal.

3 Click Yes if you want to remove the files.

If you are finished with the printer altogether, you can remove the files. If there is a chance that you will reattach the printer, select No. You will be able to Add the printer without the Windows 98 CD-ROM or other device disk.

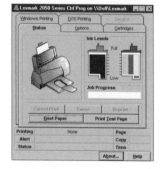

Note that some printers have their own management software, and for these you must also reply No, and use the Uninstall program provided to remove the files.

When the Delete process completes, whether or not the files are removed, the printer icon no longer appears in the Printers folder.

Accessing the Internet

This chapter looks at the functions Windows 98 provides to help you establish an account, connect to the Internet and explore its resources.

Covers

Chapter Ten

Connecting to the Internet

You may be able to connect to the Internet through your company's network if your PC is part of a workgroup. However, if you are like most users you will use a modem and telephone line to dial the Internet service provider (ISP). Windows 98 provides a number of ways to choose and set up the connection. You can:

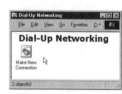

- Run the Internet Connection Wizard to locate and sign up with an ISP, or to configure your PC to use an existing account.

- Use the MSN desktop icon to join the Microsoft Network on-line service with Internet access.

- Open the Online Services folder on the desktop to set up accounts with a selection of ISPs.

You may need to brush up on your TLAs (three letter acronyms) and get used to arcane terminology, to set up your Internet connection. Or you can persuade the wizard to do it all automatically.

- Configure Dial-Up Networking to connect to an ISP by dialling their Point-to-Point Protocol (PPP) or Serial Line IP (SLIP) servers which are connected directly to the Internet.

- Configure TCP/IP and a network adapter to connect to your company's network server which in turn is connected directly to the Internet.

Windows 98 provides support for the communications protocols you'll require to connect to the ISP, including the 32-bit TCP/IP for PPP or SLIP connection. In addition, Windows 98 offers File Transfer Protocol (FTP) and telnet clients, which can be used to browse the Internet and download files from the Internet servers.

To take advantage of the Internet however, you'll need browser software that can navigate between Web sites and display the full graphical contents of the Web pages.

If you want to exchange e-mail with other individuals on the Internet or to receive newsletters through an Internet mailing list you'll require e-mail client software to communicate with the SMTP (simple mail transport protocol client) or POP (post office protocol) e-mail server provided by the ISP.

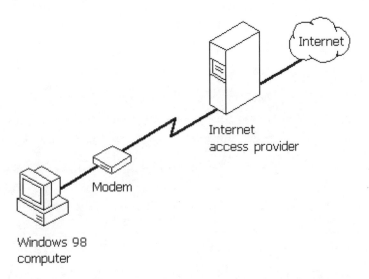

Internet

Internet
access provider

Modem

Windows 98
computer

You may also wish to participate in a newsgroup, an electronic bulletin board where members can post and reply to messages on specified topics. Newsgroups run on servers that support NNTP (net news transport protocol), so you'll need newsreader client software.

There are a number of different browser, e-mail and Internet communications products that can meet these needs. You may find that the ISP you choose provides or recommends a suitable set of programs. However, you will find e-mail, newsreader and browser support already included in Windows 98, with the Internet Explorer and the Outlook Express components and these should work satisfactorily with most ISP services.

The Internet Connection wizard

The Internet Connection wizard in Windows 98 can help you find an ISP and open an account, if you do not already have an account. It can also help you configure your PC and Internet software when you do have an ISP account already, or where you will be accessing the Internet through your company's local area network.

On a new PC, or on a Windows 98 PC where there has been no previous Internet connection defined, you should find three ways to start up the wizard for a new connection:

- One of the entries on the Windows 98 Welcome screen.

- The Connect to the Internet icon on the desktop, a shortcut to Wizconn1.exe.

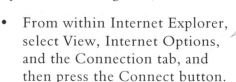

- The Internet Explorer or Outlook Express icons, both of which start the wizard the first time you run them, unless it has already been setup.

These shortcuts to the wizard will be automatically removed when you have made the first connection. However there are still two methods that remain available to start the wizard to reinstall an existing connection or add an extra connection to the Internet. The options remaining are:

You could even Run the program Wizconn1.exe from the Start menu.

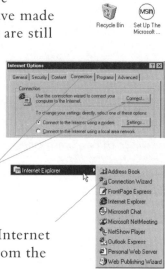

- From within Internet Explorer, select View, Internet Options, and the Connection tab, and then press the Connect button.

- Press Start, Programs, and then Internet Explorer and select the wizard from the shortcut folder.

...cont'd

The modem must be connected to the telephone line, since the wizard dials the referral server to collect data.

Your area could mean the whole of the UK, since most ISPs use a country-wide number with local charge rates.

The ISPs are listed in a different random sequence when you connect to the referral server.

You can also request installation CDs from these ISPs. This saves having to enter credit card details over the network, and you may get more information or software supplied.

Start the Internet Connection wizard and select the option to sign up for a new Internet account.

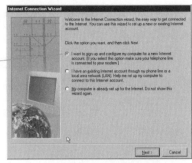

If the IC wizard determines that the modem is not configured, it will run the Install New Modem wizard to configure your modem and request your dialling details, including your location (country and telephone area code).

The model then dials the referral server. This will download a list of ISPs available in your area and registered with Microsoft, e.g:

- Global Internet
- Pipex Dial from Uunet
- Demon Internet Ltd
- The Microsoft network
- Easynet

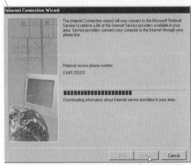

You can review details of the service such as account connection, usage charges, and modem speeds, to help you decide which ISP to use.

Some of the ISPs provide a free trial period, though you are asked to supply a credit card number. When the trial period expires, the quoted charges will be applied, unless you cancel membership.

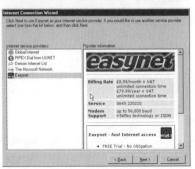

New service

Create a new account using the Internet Connection wizard.

To sign up with one of the Internet providers:

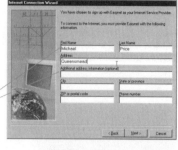

1. Select an ISP (e.g, Easynet) from the referral list and press Next.

2. Enter your personal details and your credit card details when requested, and select the billing option (monthly or yearly).

The user name is also used for e-mail so avoid spaces and punctuation to make the name easy to spell out when you pass on your contact details.

The wizard dials the ISP server, and the sign up continues on-line.

3. Suggest a user name and enter a password. If the name is already in use, you will be prompted to supply another.

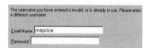

4. You must accept the terms of the agreement to continue the sign on.

This may overwrite settings for an existing connection, but there will still be an entry in the Dial-up Networking folder.

5. Your details are recorded on the server and the account is set up, so you can now press Finish.

The Connection icon is removed from the desktop, and the settings for Internet Explorer and Outlook Express are updated with the particulars of your account. Double-clicking IE or selecting it from the launchpad now initiates your connection so that you can begin surfing the Internet.

Surf the Internet

Account details and passwords may be pre-entered for you, and Windows will record the password if you click in the box.

1 Double-click the Internet Explorer icon, and enter your user name and password in the Dial-up Connection window.

2 Click the Connect button to initiate the connection to the ISP.

The dial-up connection dials the ISP number. It will try up to three times to make the connection, if the line is busy. Then the Easynet security server validates your details and completes the connection.

Many Web pages require a screen resolution of 800 x 600 for effective viewing.

By default you'll see the Easynet home page. Explore the ISP site and other sites by clicking on links or entering Web page URL addresses. The pages you view are downloaded to the hard disk, so you can switch back and forth between pages.

You can see that the connection is active because a dial-up icon is added to the system tray. It shows when data is being transferred by flashing and changing colours. Hold the mouse pointer over the icon to see the data volumes and connection speed.

To end the session, click the Disconnect button, or right-click the dial-up icon and select Disconnect.

To see more details of the connection, double-click the system tray icon. Click Details to see information about the server type and the modem.

Working Offline

The next time that you run Internet Explorer, you could choose to work offline. The pages you viewed previously may still be available.

1 Open Internet Explorer and, when the Dial-up Connection appears, select the Work Offline button.

2 You can also switch IE offline by selecting File from the menu bar and then disconnect.

Even though you are not connected to the Internet, you are still able to view the pages you have accessed previously, as long as they are still in the Internet page cache.

The page cache area is also used to store the pages for subscriptions to Web sites or channels.

3 Click the History button to see the log of pages in the cache.

4 Pause the mouse pointer over the page references (the underlined text).

The hand symbol means the associated page is selectable. With a no-entry symbol it means that the page is not in the cache. When you click on the link for a page in the cache, it will be displayed in the pane on the right.

Note that not all pages can be retained in the cache, and pages that rely on active data from the Internet may display incompletely when you work offline.

Dial-up definition

Examining the entries made by the wizard gives useful insight into the type of settings needed, in case you want to add further services in the future.

To see how the wizard has set up the connection for the new service:

1 Open My computer and double-click Dial-up Networking.

2 Right-click the entry for the service that now appears, and select Properties.

Make sure that the number you are using is charged at the Local rate or the nation Lo-call rate.

3 Select the General tab to see the location, telephone number and modem details used.

4 The Server Types page shows the dial-up server type (in this case PPP), the advanced options (software compression) and the network protocol (TCP/IP).

5 Click the TCP/IP Settings button to see the specific settings for this service.

For most ISPs you will find that the server assigns the IP address for your PC and for the DNS name server.

With Easynet however, there are explicit IP addresses for the client and the server, allocated automatically, and they may change each time you connect.

ISP provided sign up

The ISP you choose may provide a customised set of software equivalent to the connection wizard. This is usually the case with the one month trials that are often included on the cover CDs of PC magazines. The ISP may install additional software or make changes to your installed software. The Dixons FreeServe Internet service provides an example of this, since it customised the Internet Explorer with a distinctive watermark and applies a variety of particular settings.

To install Dixons Freeserve:

1 Insert the Freeserve disc and the setup program will run automatically.

2 Choose to install IE4. For Windows 98 this merely updates the settings for the integrated copy of IE4.

3 When Setup finishes reconfiguring, the system restarts, with a new Freeserve icon on the desktop.

4 Double-click the Freeserve shortcut and the setup program connects to the server.

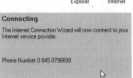

5 Select the option to create a new account, and follow the screen prompts, providing your personal details when requested. You won't be asked for a credit card number.

...cont'd

You get a Domain name in effect from the Account part of the e-mail name.

1 Provide a suggested e-mail name and a password. The names in Freeserve are of the form:

user@account.freeserve.co.uk

2 Provide alternatives if your first choice is already allocated.

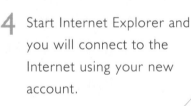

3 When your account is created, the settings are updated, and the PC restarts.

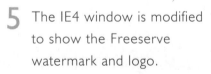

To remove the Freeserve branding from IE4, delete the folder Signup in the Internet Explorer folder in Program Files.

4 Start Internet Explorer and you will connect to the Internet using your new account.

5 The IE4 window is modified to show the Freeserve watermark and logo.

To view the settings, click the Advanced button in the Proxy section.

6 Freeserve uses a proxy server. If you want to use IE with other ISPs, you must turn this off by selecting View, Internet Options, Connections and clearing the box.

Set up existing account

If you choose the option to set up an Internet connection for an existing Internet service in the IC Wizard, it checks whether you will connect to the Internet using an ISP or a LAN, or if your account is with an on-line information service such as MSN or AOL.

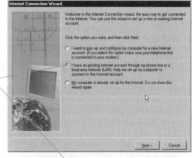

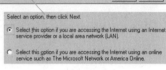

If you are connecting directly, it starts the manual Internet configuration wizard which will:

- Check that your modem is set up properly. If it is not, it runs the Install New Modem wizard to configure your modem.

- Check that your dialling settings are set up properly. If not, it displays the Dialing Properties panel.

- Set up the TCP/IP protocol.

- Set up the Dial-Up Networking connection.

If you are connecting to the Internet over a company network, check with your network administrator for the necessary details. You may need to supply:

- Proxy server information.

- TCP/IP settings.

If you are connecting to the Internet by dialling an ISP, check with the technical support for that service. You will need to obtain information such as the following:

- Telephone number, account ID, and password.

- Mail account information: server types and names, and password.

- TCP/IP settings or IP addresses.

...cont'd

The wizard takes you through all the stages, and requests all the details needed, based on the requirements you select:

1 Specify phone or LAN connection as applicable.

You'd copy an existing connection if it was already set up with special settings that you want to repeat.

2 Choose to create a new dial-up connection.

3 Provide the country, area code and telephone number details for the ISP.

4 Provide the user name (in the form required by the ISP) and the password.

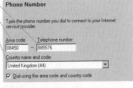

5 You can select Advanced Settings if the defaults are not suitable. This is not usually required.

6 Give a plain English name for the service.

7 Set up your E-mail, News and Directory services at the same time if you wish. You'll require the server names and the account details.

8 Click Finish to set up the accounts ready for connection.

Connect from Dial-up

Drag a shortcut to the service onto the desktop for a quick method of connecting to your alternative ISP.

Only one service at a time can be linked to Internet Explorer, but the Dial-up Networking folder can hold as many network connections as you need, and can be used to start up the links, as well as holding the definitions. This allows you to make use of accounts from more than one ISP, which is particularly useful since it allows for an overlap when you change suppliers.

To start a connection:

1 Open My Computer and double-click Dial-Up Networking.

The user name may be prefixed with a service or country code, when the servers handle traffic for multiple purposes. Your ISP will specify what is needed.

2 Double-click the entry for the service, or select the service and click Connect if you are using Web view.

3 Enter the password if not predefined, and press the Connect button to start dialling the service.

Ignore the time on this panel – it always says 12:45 PM.

After the connection has been completed, Windows 98 displays the Connection Established panel which shows the service name. This is for information only, and you can suppress its display if you click the box. Press Close to remove the panel.

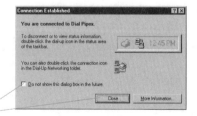

The default IE4 connection is ignored since you are already on-line.

Start your Internet session by running Internet Explorer, FTP, telnet, e-mail or any application that makes use of the Internet connection.

Configure IE

If you have the Second Edition of Windows 98, or if you use Office 2000, you'll have the newer IE5, rather than IE4. IE5 is also available for free download from the Microsoft web site.

Internet Explorer 4 is a separate product with Windows 95, but it has been firmly integrated throughout Windows 98, with the single Explorer view and the Internet aware Start menu, taskbar and desktop. It cannot be separately installed or uninstalled, although the optional components such as FrontPage Express, Microsoft Wallet and VRML viewer can be added or removed as required:

1   Double-click Add/Remove Programs from the Control Panel and select Windows Setup, Internet Tools, and press Details.

2   Add or remove tools as required.

You can also install IE components from the Windows Update on the Internet, and get the latest version or fixes.

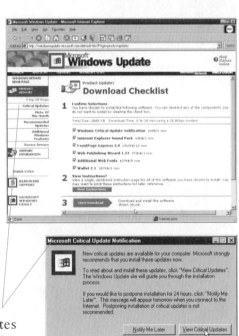

3   Select Start, Windows Update.

4   Choose the items you want and press Download.

Select the Critical Updates notification to be warned when new updates for Windows 98 and its components become available.

Change cache settings

The Web pages you view remain in place after you disconnect, so you can browse them offline. To ensure that the pages remain there, you may need to adjust the cache settings.

When Web pages and other Internet objects are downloaded during an Internet viewing session or as subscriptions and channels, they are stored in the temporary Internet files folder in the Windows folder on your hard disk. The subfolders used to organise these items are hidden, but you can view the files that they contain:

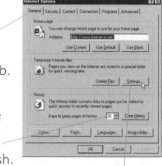

1 Open IE4, click View, Internet Options, and select the General tab.

2 Specify how long you will keep the shortcuts to pages in history. You can also clear the history if you wish.

If you specify to check at start, you'll have to press Refresh to get updated views when you revisit a page during a session.

3 Click the Settings button in the temporary Internet files area.

4 Specify how often Internet Explorer will check for newer versions of stored pages.

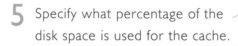

5 Specify what percentage of the disk space is used for the cache.

6 Move the Temporary files folder, if desired.

7 Click View Files to view temporary files, or click View Objects to view downloaded program files.

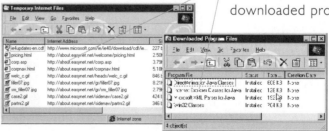

Using IE

Internet Explorer includes a number of features that make it easier to use. For example, Explorer Bars allow you to browse the History or Favorites list:

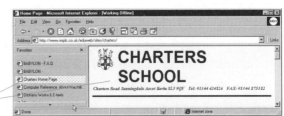

Explorer Bars reduce the area available for displaying page content, so they are best used with higher resolution monitors.

1 Open the bar from the View menu, or click the appropriate toolbar button.

2 Select a link; the referenced page displays in the pane on the right.

The Search bar works similarly, offering search engines and allowing you to enter search criteria to build the list of links. The Channels bar displays a list of subscribed active channels.

AutoComplete completes Internet addresses based on what you have typed so far, using the list of sites previously visited to guess the intention, providing standard prefixes and suffixes to Internet addresses, and correcting syntax errors. Override the suggestions by typing over them. With this feature you can:

The separation characters are // / , ? and +.

- Skip to the adjacent break or separation character in a URL by pressing Ctrl+right-arrow or Ctrl+left-arrow.

- Search your History file by typing the beginning of a URL and pressing the up-arrow or down-arrow key to find the required Web address.

You don't have to type the prefix "http://www." or the suffix ".com".

- Type the middle part of a URL and press Ctrl+Enter to switch to a Web page.

Favorite tips

Add a link for the current Web page to your Favorites list.

1 While the Web page is open, select Favorites, Add to Favorites.

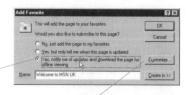

2 Add the name to the list. You can request also to be informed if the page changes.

You can modify the standard actions to control the download, the schedule and the notification.

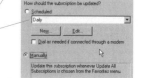

3 Click Customize to change the options.

4 To view offline, request to download this page only, or linked pages also.

If you choose the Manual option, you must request the updates for the subscriptions to refresh the pages.

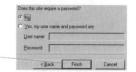

5 Select the e-mail and the scheduling options required.

6 Specify password data if applicable, and then click Finish.

7 To update the pages, select Favorites, Update All Subscriptions.

8 The new contents for changed pages are downloaded to the Internet cache.

Group your Favorites into folders of associated items for quicker access.

1 Select Favorites and click to Organise Favorites, right-click the window background to display the folder menu.

2 Click New to create a folder for a group of Favorites.

3 Drag and drop entries to form related groups or into folders

Use the Favorites thumbnail option to preview all the Web pages in a folder without having to explicitly visit the sites.

4 Open a folder, display its menu, select Properties and click to Enable thumbnail view.

5 Display the folder menu, and select Refresh to update page contents.

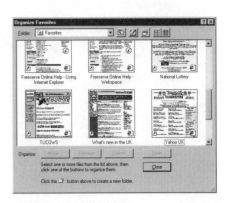

6 Right-click the window background, click View, Thumbnails and all the pages are previewed.

Home page

When you start Internet Explorer, or click the Home button, it displays the Web page specified in the IE properties. The value is defined by the setup program when you define your Internet account, but you can choose your own page:

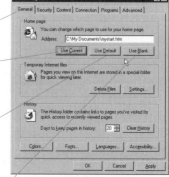

1 Select View, Internet Options and choose the General tab.

2 Click Use Current, to set the active page as the Home page.

3 Click Use Default to restore the page specified at setup, or Use Blank for an empty page (quicker, but not very exciting).

4 Type a URL address to select a particular Web page. You can also choose an HTML page that you have created on the hard drive, or on your own Web space.

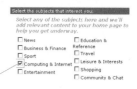

To personalise the MSN home page:

1 Open the page and select the option to personalise the content.

2 Provide your details and select the type of information you want.

3 Click the option to make this your home page.

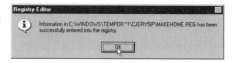

World Wide Web

This chapter looks at working more closely with the Web, using the tools provided in Windows 98 to create your own home pages, upload files, build links and add security.

Covers

Chapter Eleven

Your own Web space

When you sign up with an ISP, you may be given more than access to the Internet and an e-mail address. You could be given your own Web space, in the form of disk space on the ISP server. Typically 20MB in size, this provides you with an area where you can store your own Web pages, and make them available to anyone on the Internet. You can use your Web space to publish anything you like. Home users typically include information about themselves, their hobbies or particular interests. Business users usually give information about their products and services.

Your ISP will expect you to comply with the acceptable use policy that is no doubt included in the terms and conditions for using the service.

There are two stages involved in creating your own corner on the Web: first you must design a Web page, then you must upload it to the server.

Web pages must be written using the hypertext markup language (HTML), which provides the codes used to format the text and images on your Web page.

The easiest way to design a Web page in Windows 98 is using the FrontPage Express utility. This is an HTML editor, but you don't have to know the HTML language to use it. You can include pictures and graphics in your Web pages, using jpeg format (JPG) and gif format (GIF).

To transfer your files to the ISP server you must use file transfer protocol (FTP). There are FTP software products available to allow you to send files, as well as receive them. However, you can also use the Web Publishing Wizard in Windows 98 and it will guide you through the process without you having to know the detailed operations.

Finally, when you have placed your Web pages on the server, you must make sure that others know where to find them, so that they can share the information and perhaps supplement it also.

Create a Web page

You can use the templates supplied (see page 236), or create your own page using the features included in FrontPage Express.

To create a Web page yourself, using Front Page Express.

1 Open FrontPage Express, and it will display an untitled blank document. Select File, Page Properties.

2 Enter the title for your Web page. This will appear on the browser titlebar.

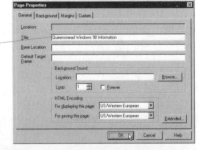

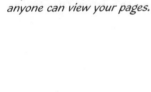

Use standard fonts that you can expect to find on any Windows PC, so you can be sure that anyone can view your pages.

3 Select Heading I in the style bar, then click Centre, and type the heading for your page.

4 Highlight the text and select Format, Font and choose a suitable colour.

5 Type the text for your page. You can use text formatting and change font sizes as desired.

6 To add an e-mail address, highlight the text, press the Hyperlink button, select Mail To, and enter the e-mail address for comments or suggestions.

Extend the page

1 Type in a URL address and FrontPage converts it into a hyperlink.

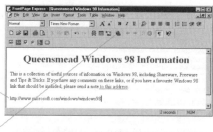

2 You can also type descriptive text, and convert it into a hyperlink using the button.

The default action is to scroll the heading to the left, but you can change the settings.

3 Add motion to your heading by highlighting it and selecting Insert, Marquee.

4 Select Insert, Image to add a picture or graphic to your page. Right-click the image and select properties to adjust size and position.

Be very careful with file names, since many servers are case sensitive. Always use the same method e.g. one initial capital.

5 When you've finished creating the page, save it on your hard disk.

You should name your Web page Index.html or Default.html, so that users who enter your Web site address without a file name will automatically display your Web page. You can add links to the Web page to switch to other Web pages that you create using a different file name. Save all the Web pages and figures in the same folder as the Index.html.

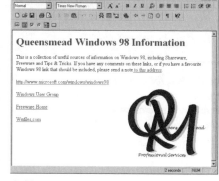

Check it out

You need to view the Web pages that you create, selecting different screen sizes and colour selections, to make sure that the effect you want is retained with various PC setups.

Before you upload the Web page you have created, check to see how it might appear in the browser to users with various types of system.

1 Select a screen size of 640 x 480 using the Display Properties, Settings.

2 Locate the Index.html file in the folder and double-click to open it in IE.

3 Note how the image appears when part of the page is hidden, and look for any overlap between text and graphics.

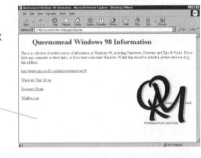

4 Select a screen size of 800 x 600 and re-display the Web page. This is the recommended size for Internet access and is how most viewers will see it.

It may be better to restrict the image to an area of 800 x 600, even for users with higher resolution screens, to preserve the effectiveness of the layout.

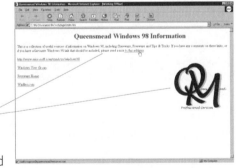

5 Select a screen size of 1024 x 768 and re-display the Web page. Note the differences. Text may be more spread out, and graphics may be placed differently in relation to the text. Too much space can be just as bad as too little.

Uploading

This describes the process for uploading to the Dixons Freeserve ISP. Methods for other services may vary.

1 Before starting the transfer, connect to the ISP. Do not open IE or other Internet applications at this point.

2 Select Web Publishing wizard from the Internet Explorer folder in the Start menu.

3 Enter the folder that contains the files for your Web page. Check the box to include subfolders if required.

You can specify a single file to apply a change. You do not need to specify the individual picture and graphics files referenced.

The wizard skips straight to the FTP transfer the next time it runs, with this name selected.

4 Supply a name for your Web server. You can use this as a reference to speed up transfers in the future.

5 Supply the URL or Internet address you use to access your personal Web pages, and the folder name on your hard disk.

The URL is http://www/ userid.freeserve.co.uk for Freeserve. For other ISPs, it takes a form similar to http://www.servername.com/userid/ .

...cont'd

*The wizard will
check to see if
it can
automatically
detect the
specified server.*

1 Supply the logon details required
for your ISP.

2 If the wizard cannot
automatically detect the service
provider, you'll need to specify
the details, as specified in your
service documentation.

3 Select the service provider, in
this case it will be FTP (file
transfer protocol).

*With the server
defined, the
wizard involves
FTP to transfer
the files.*

4 Select Next, then Finish and the
files start transferring to the ISP
server.

5 The progress bar shows the
transfer taking place, and a
message confirms that files have
been received.

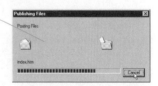

The next time you need to
transfer a file to the FTP server,
the wizard remembers all the
details and move more quickly to
the FTP transfer, without
pausing to check the address.

6 When you display the new page in Internet Explorer, press
the Refresh button to pick up the new version.

Be found on the Web

There's no point in putting pages on the Web if no-one sees them, so you have to take steps to let other Internet users find your pages. If you tell them your Web address, they can simply type this into the address bar of their browser, and it will display your Index.html or Default.html. If somebody else places a hyperlink to your page on their Web site, then when that link is clicked on, the viewer will come to your page.

The best way to ensure that your site receives visitors through the Web is to register it with some of the major Search Engines, such as Yahoo, Infoseek or Excite. Each has a different method of registering, so visit the site and check how to register your URL. To register with Yahoo:

Type Yahoo in the address bar and press Ctrl+Enter.

Anyone can suggest a site to Yahoo, not just the owner.

Make sure you type the details exactly right, so the Yahoo analyst can locate your site to review it.

1 Start Internet Explorer, connect to the Internet and switch to www.yahoo.com.

2 Check to see if your site is already on the Yahoo list.

3 Find the appropriate Yahoo category that your Web site most suitably fits into.

4 From that category, click <u>Suggest a Site</u> link at the bottom of the page and complete the registration form, following the guidelines to ensure that your application is successful.

Registering with other search engines is more mechanistic. You complete a form and the Web site or Web page will be automatically added when the list of requests is next processed.

To register with Excite:

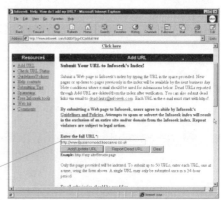

5 Switch to the Excite Web site, and click on Add URL at the end of the page.

6 Enter the URL for your Web site, specify language and location, and select the category that best describes your site.

It will take two weeks before your entry appears in the Excite Index. Registering with Infoseek is quicker, it takes only a couple of days, and there is a link to check the status of the URL.

To register with Infoseek:

Only the specified page will be indexed, but you can send multiple forms, to register up to 50 URLs. You can also submit lists of URLs by e-mail.

7 Switch to the Infoseek Web site, and click on Add URL.

8 Enter the full URL, including the file name of the page you are registering.

9 Click Check URL Status on a later visit to see what has happened with your request. It is worth checking, since a simple spelling errors will void your application.

Raise your profile

There are millions of Web pages on the Internet, so you must set up your registration carefully to maximise the chances of your pages being in the first set of results.

When the search engine locates your page as part of the result, it provides a description based on the text in the page. The Meta tag description field can be used to specify an exact description of your site. This does not display on the Web page, but is just used for search results. You can provide up to 200 characters of text. If your Web page uses JavaScript functions or frames, you need the description tag to guarantee a useful description.

When your site is added to Infoseek's index, all the words on the page are included (except for Comments fields). Meta tag keywords can be used to specify additional keywords or synonyms. They are used in the indexing process but will not display on your page. You can put up to 1000 characters of text. If your page consists mainly of graphics, use the description and keywords tags to define the page.

These notes are based on Infoseek, but apply to any search engine that analyses your Web page contents.

To add Meta description and keywords tags:

1. Open your Web page using FrontPage Express.

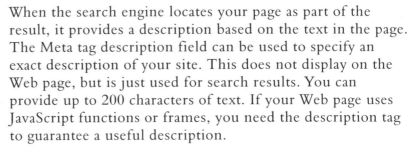

2. Select File, Page Properties and then click the Custom tab.

3. Click Add in the User variables section to create a new entry.

4. Enter the word description in the Name box, put the text of the description in the Value box, and then click OK.

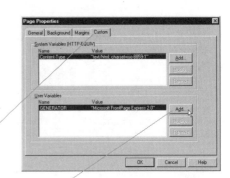

5 Enter the word keywords in the Name box, put keywords or phrases in the Value box, with commas between each item, and then press OK.

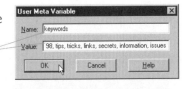

6 The new variables are shown in the list, complete with their values. Press OK again.

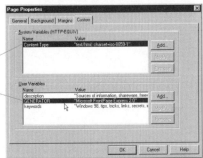

When a URL is submitted, it will automatically be considered for inclusion in the Infoseek Directory. The most relevant, valuable sites are chosen for the Directory. Infoseek Select sites are chosen by the editors from the index based on their editorial value, traffic and the number of links to the sites.

7 The page is redisplayed. The tag fields do not show up, but you can see them if you select View from the menu bar and then click the HTML entry.

The document is displayed in its HTML form.

- Description.

- Generator.

- Keywords.

- Heading.

- Body text.

- Graphic image.

Save the Web page, and upload it to your Web site, using the Web publishing wizard, so that the search engine finds the new tags when it visits your site.

Enhance your pages

FrontPage Express is rather limited in the functions it offers. It excludes features of the full FrontPage editor such as editing frames, image maps, preview In Browser, and other features such as hit counters and other site management features. However, you can still make many enhancements using the functions that are available.

For example, to control the way the text is arranged on the screen:

1 Add a blank line before the text, and select Insert, Table.

2 To make a text box, select I row and I column, set the width to say 500 pixels and press OK.

3 Mark up the text and drag and drop it into the table.

This will position the text in the centre of the screen, and give it the same layout, whatever monitor resolution or window size is set.

4 Click the table and select Table, Table Properties.

5 Set the alignment to Center.

To let visitors know that the information on your Web page is regularly updated, add a time stamp and a descriptive note. Select the position and:

A WebBot is a robot for the Web.

6 Click Insert, WebBot Component (prepackaged FrontPage functions).

...cont'd

7 Select Timestamp, click OK, click Date this page was last edited, and click OK.

8 Add the description before or after the date field 'Last edited date'.

To keep track of visitors, you need a Web counter. There's one in FrontPage 2000, but not in Express, so you can download one of the freeware counters from www.freewarehome.com. You'll also find various freeware Guestbooks on this site. These make it easy for visitors to give you feedback and suggestions about your Web site.

- Scrolling header.

- Text in fixed size table.

- Guest book link.

- Web counter.

- Links and log in table columns.

- Date changed, at the bottom of the page.

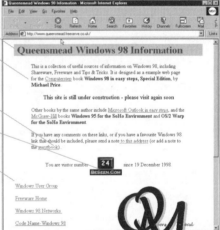

If you want, you can insert the HTML language tags. FrontPage Express acts as an HTML editor, though it does not check the syntax of your markup entries.

For a tutorial that introduces the HTML language, look on the NCSA (National Centre for supercomputing applications) Web site.

Internet security

Connecting your PC to the Internet has major security implications. There is a potential risk to your data, on the hard disk or while it is being transmitted through the network. In addition, you are subjected to a vast amount of information, sometimes involuntarily. It will hardly be a surprise to find many existing and emerging security standards, intended to enhance the privacy of your link, protect your identity on the Internet and protect your PC from potentially damaging code. There is also a demand for functions to restrict the viewing of certain sites.

The security features supported in Windows 98 include security zones, authentication certificates (electronic IDs) and various Internet security protocols.

Internet Explorer security zones divide the Internet into zones with different levels of security, so that you can apply global browser defaults for the content of Web sites, based on your level of trust in that location. There are four predefined zones:

- Sites within your company's proxy server or firewall.

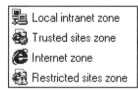

- Sites you know pose no problem.

- Default assignment for Web sites.

- Sites that present a risk or concern.

Use the restricted zone if you are uncertain about a Web site, otherwise leave the default as medium. The trusted zone may be useful for your own Web site, when you are developing it and want to avoid intrusive messages. There is a custom setting for administrators to control the network security for a company LAN.

To add or remove sites in the trusted or restricted zone

Select View, Internet Options from the Internet Explorer menu bar (or click the Internet icon in Control Panel).

...cont'd

You can use a wildcard character (*) as part of the address to add groups.

2 Choose the Security tab, select the trusted or the Restricted zone type, and press Add Sites.

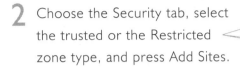

3 Enter the addresses of sites, clicking Add after each.

4 You can limit entries to secure servers (https:// addresses) if you wish.

For sites that use DNS or IP addresses you must be sure to configure both references to the same zone.

5 Select an entry and click remove if it no longer belongs.

6 You can add local Intranet sites in groups by type.

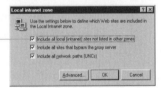

You don't explicitly define Internet sites - they just do not appear in another zone.

The actions that are taken depend on the security level you set for each zone. By default, trusted sites have low security with no warning messages. Intranet and Internet sites have a medium security level, and you are warned before it downloads or opens active material.

Marking a site as restricted will produce many messages and could prevent it being used in any realistic fashion (which is usually the intent!).

Restricted sites get the high security level, which issues messages whenever you send information to the site, or switch from it to another site. If the site is about to download information, or display pages with active content, such as a Java program, these actions are not allowed.

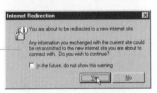

PICS standards

It is unclear how widely supported these standards are, or indeed whether they have any chance of success, given that it is often the younger members of the family who set up the systems anyway.

Parents may want to be sure that children can be blocked from visiting sites that display inappropriate information. Companies may want to block the use of sites that offer no business value to their employees. The Platform for Internet Content Selection (PICS) committee has defined standards for rating Internet content, so you can control access to rated Web sites through Internet Explorer, or use third-party rating bureaus, to control access based on content. To enable:

1 Select View, Internet Options in Internet Explorer and select the Content tab.

2 Click Enable to start the Content Advisor wizard, and supply a password.

This would block many perfectly acceptable, but unrated, sites.

3 You can limit viewing to unrated sights only, and you can allow a supervisor override.

4 Choose levels one to four for each of the categories.

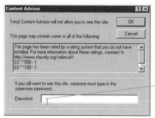

You will need the supervisor password to disable checking.

5 The supervisor password can override the rating if you allowed that option.

6 If you change your mind, you can Disable the ratings checks.

Authentication

You can validate software downloads by 'trusting' some suppliers, rather than checking each certificate.

The authentication certificates are designed to verify the publisher and the integrity of specific items of software code such as Java applets that various sites may offer to download. This helps you decide whether to download the code, and whether to allow it to execute once downloaded, even if you are not familiar with the particular site. The certificates are supported by VeriSign, a certificate authority responsible for issuing and validating digital certificates.

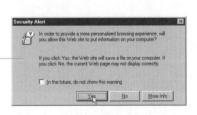

If the software has been digitally signed, Internet Explorer can verify the origin and confirm that it has not been tampered with, and then display the certificate if the software passes the test.

You can choose to automatically accept software from trusted suppliers, once they have been validated, so the checking all takes place without interruption.

Some Web sites use cookie technology to store information on your PC, to provide Web site personalisation features. You can accept automatically, or choose at the time a cookie appears:

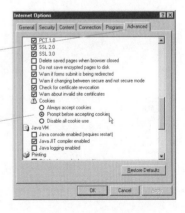

1 Select View, Internet Options in Internet Explorer and select the Advanced tab.

2 Scroll down to locate the Security settings and choose Always accept, Prompt before or Disable use.

3 Click OK to save the settings.

Using a template

Front Page Express will create a Web page for you to complete, using your answers to various questions to set up the framework.

1 Open FrontPage Express from the Internet Explorer folder in the Start menu, and choose File, New.

2 Select the type of Web page you want to create, for example a personal home page.

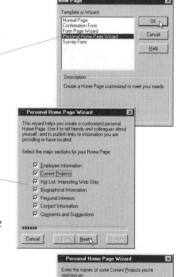

3 Choose the types of personal or business data that you wish to display on the page.

4 Provide a file name and a page title, then select the boxes or fill in the blanks on the succession of panels that are displayed, to complete the initial definition.

A ready-made page will be displayed. This will contain the information you supplied, providing on-page links and headings, but will need lots of changes to replace the prompter text with the actual details you want to show.

It is an excellent starting point, but the page reflects the standard FrontPage style rather than your own ideas of layout and relative importance of items.

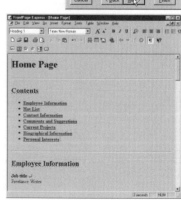

Hard disk management

This chapter covers the ways in which hard disks can be organised to improve the effective capacity or performance or to meet particular requirements, and the use of the tools and facilities provided with Windows 98 or available as add-on products.

Covers

Chapter Twelve

Disk organisation

The hard disk needed to hold Windows 98 and associated applications could be as small as 512MB or less, or could be as large as 16GB. The capacities announced for new hard drives continue to increase, while the cost on a per GB basis continues to fall, in a progression that shows little sign of abating.

- Disk platters.

- Drive arm.

- Drive actuator.

To manage all the disk space on your hard drive you need to organise it to suit your planned uses, but in practice most Windows 98 PCs arrive with the hard drive ready set up, with all the space allocated to a single partition. This may suit many systems, but there are other methods of allocating the space on the disk that might provide you with more efficient or more flexible ways of working. These include:

- Partitioning into application and data.

- Using disk compression.

- Changing file allocation table types.

- Partitioning for multiple operating systems.

To illustrate the options and the potential benefits, the following sections trace the effects in terms of space available on a hard disk drive that undergoes various rearrangements. This will illustrate the steps needed to make the changes and the tools available to carry out the tasks. It will also emphasise the issues involved and the precautions that you must take to prevent losing data.

The test system

The system used as the basis for the disk re-configurations is an older PC with an Intel 486-66 and 24MB memory. Just about minimum specification for Windows 98. It has two hard disks installed. The first is a 1.6GB EIDE drive, the second is a 256MB IDE drive, and the PC contains an IDE hard disk controller.

Hard drive makers specify sizes in millions, not megabytes, and ignore system overhead. The quoted 1,625MB is actually 1,547MB of disk space.

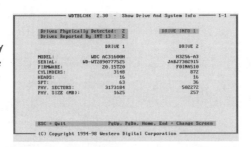

Incidentally, the 256MB drive was original equipment, and the 1.6GB drive was fitted as an upgrade. Because the system BIOS could not handle drives greater than 512MB, the EZ-Drive disk management software is installed on the drive. This means that the PC must always start bootup from the hard drive, even if it switches to a floppy after the disk management code has been loaded.

Using the old, small drive to store the setup files is particularly useful on this PC, since it compensates for the slowness of the x1 speed CD-ROM drive.

As initially setup, these drives are identified by Windows 98 as the C: drive and the D: drive respectively.

- Drive C: contains the system and applications programs and data. It is about 40% utilised.

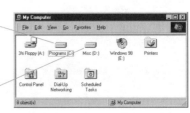

- Drive D: contains the Windows 98 setup files, and other miscellaneous data files. It is about 90% utilised.

While there may be plenty of room at present, adding new applications and using the Internet and e-mail will quickly make inroads. It is well worth exploring ways to make the most of the space, before it becomes an actual problem.

FAT drives

The FAT file system is the default setup for most disk drives, and can be accessed by all operating systems.

A FAT drive uses an IDE or SCSI controller, not a FAT Controller!

Start with the existing setup. The disk is formatted in the standard Windows and MS-DOS manner, as expected when you install Windows 98 over an existing Windows 95, Windows 3.1x or MS-DOS system. This is the FAT (file allocation table) format. With this file system, space is physically divided into 512 byte sectors, but these are managed in groups called allocation units or clusters or sectors. The table contains chains of numbers which identify all the clusters that make up each file. The table has an entry for every cluster, and there is a limit to the number of entries, so larger disks are catered for by setting larger cluster sizes. There's also a limit to the number of clusters allowed. The net effect is to assign cluster sizes as:

Disk size (MB)	Cluster size (KB)
1-15	4 (FAT-12)
16–127	2 (FAT-16)
128-255	4
256–511	8
512–1023	16
1024–2047	32
2048+	Not supported

On average, every file uses only 50% of the final cluster. So half a cluster is wasted per file. The larger the cluster, the greater the waste.

The FAT method was very suitable for diskettes, its original purpose, and for the smaller hard disks, but with larger disks, there are two problems. First, they must be divided into pieces no larger than 2 GB. Second, the cluster methods causes a substantial wastage of disk space.

To see how this happens:

1 Open the C: drive icon in My Computer and click Edit, Select All.

2 Check that you have View All Files set in Folder Options, then right-click the selection and select Properties.

3 Record the current disk usage:

The number of files (6,622).

The data content (461 MB).

Space used (601 MB).

The difference between the data content and the space allocated is the amount of slack space, mainly caused by the large 32 KB cluster size.

To see the capacity of the hard disk:

The Properties for the whole drive show the bytes used but not the actual data size. There may be differences from the previous value. This is a dynamic system, so files are changing as you work with the system.

4 Right-click the C: drive icon on the title bar or in My Computer, and select Properties.

5 Record the total capacity of the drive (1,547 MB).

On the test system disk, there are 6,622 files occupying 601 MB, with 461 MB of data. This is 140 MB of slack space, or 23%. This works out at 21 KB per file.

With one FAT partition, the 1.6 GB drive holds 1,191MB of useful data.

If this were replicated over the remaining space on the drive, the total wasted space would be 356 MB, and net data space of 1191 MB.

In practice, the percentage of waste will vary depending on the proportion of particular file types. Small files such as shortcut links, which average only 300 bytes, cause a relatively high amount of waste. Files allocated in exact multiples of the cluster size have no waste.

It is not possible to avoid all wasted space, but you can reduce the amount by adjusting the configuration of your hard disk in one of the several ways available.

Partitioning

The traditional way to tackle the problem of wasted space is to partition the disk, that is to split it up into smaller parts that each need a smaller cluster size, and hence generate less slack space. This partitioning of the disk is also the method used when the disk is larger than 2 GB, to allow the whole space to be used with FAT.

There may be many options for subdividing the disk, using a mix of sizes. For the test system, there are some natural options such as two or three drives, and others as well:

Disk size	Drives	Cluster size
1,547 MB	1	32 KB
773 MB	2	16 KB
511 MB	3	8 KB
255 MB	6	4 KB
127 MB	12	2 KB

Each reduction in cluster size reduces the overall amount of wasted space. However, increasing the number of drives and drive letters adds complexity since you'll have to organise your applications and data to fit on the D: or the E: drive, etc., rather than allocating everything to the C: drive. You may also find yourself short of space even though there is enough space in total, because the free space is fragmented across several drives.

The default Setup options do not install the Backup program.

Although the examples quote equal sized disks, you can of course partition your drive into a mix of different sizes, to meet particular needs.

The process involved in partitioning the disk can be both time consuming and potentially problematic, since any change to the disk setup effectively deletes all the data on the partitions concerned.

The first requirement is to back up the whole drive, or make sure that you have everything you need to reinstall the operating system and all the applications.

...cont'd

For an easier way to partition the disk, see Partition Magic on page 252.

Then make sure that you have a bootable diskette so that you can start up the PC without relying on the contents of your hard disk, plus the software required to restore the backup. To partition the disk:

1 Boot the PC from diskette and start Fdisk.exe, which you will find on the Startup disk.

2 Reply [N] to the question "Do you wish to enable large disk support", to remain with the FAT file system.

3 If you are sure that you have the backup, type [3] then [1] to delete the existing primary DOS partition.

The DOS partitions are actually Windows 98 partitions also.

4 Type [1] then [1] to create a primary DOS partition, and specify 50% or 33% etc., depending on how many drives you want.

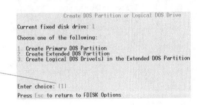

5 Type [1] then [2] to create an extended DOS partition using the rest of disk space.

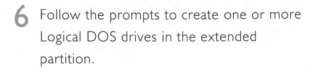

If the disk was already more than 33% or 50% filled, you will have to exclude some of the backup files, and restore them to the D: or E: drive.

6 Follow the prompts to create one or more Logical DOS drives in the extended partition.

7 Reboot the system from diskette and reinstall a Compact version of Windows 98, and restore the backup to the resized C: drive.

Format drive

When you reboot your PC after partitioning, you will find new drive letters for the logical drives. These will follow after the letters for the primary partitions, but before the letters for DVD, CD-ROM or other removable drives such as ZIP or JAZ. In the test case with two logical drives, the new drives are E: and F:, and the CD-ROM becomes the G: drive.

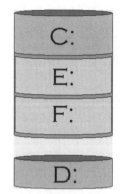

You must run Format and Scandisk for each new partition on the hard disk.

- Primary partition (Disk0)

- Primary (sole) partition (Disk 1).

- Logical partitions (Disk0).

- Renamed CD-ROM drive.

If you partitioned the disk as two drives, you'd have a new E: drive, and the CD-ROM drive would become F:.

The new C: drive will be formatted as part of the setup and restore process, but before you can use the additional disk drives that you have created, they must be formatted. To format the drive:

A Full format for a hard drive does not validate the data areas, unlike the diskette full format.

1 Right-click the new drive and select Format from the context menu.

2 Select Full, enter a label for the disk, and clear the Copy system files box.

3 Click Start, and click OK to confirm that you want to format the drive.

Format will generate the FAT file allocation table for the partition, and create the root folder, and report:

- Total disk space

- System files

- Bad sectors

- Available disk space

- Allocation unit (cluster) size

- Number of units.

For hard disk formats, Format does not scan the drive surface for errors, so it recommends Scandisk to verify the data area.

4 Click Close to end Format, then Click OK.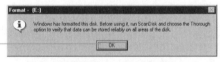

5 Check that the correct drive is selected, and that Thorough is specified. Don't select Automatic fix, so you can see the problems, if any.

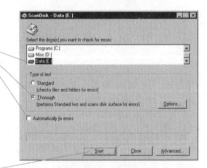

Scandisk provides a summary on completion, similar to the Format report, but now with actual results for any bad areas on the disk.

6 Click Start, and Scandisk checks the partition data area.

7 Follow screen prompts to resolve any problems detected.

8 Review the summary of finds, and then click Close to finish with Scandisk.

Space savings

Splitting the C: drive into two parts reduces the cluster size from 32 KB to 16 KB. The Properties for the drives and contents can be used as before to calculate the space usage.

1   Open drive C:, select all the contents and display the Properties.

2   Record the current disk usage:
The number of files (6,624).
The data content (461 MB).
Space used (525 MB).

3   Display the C: drive properties to note the total capacity (773 MB).

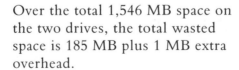

4   Display the E: drive Properties and note the total capacity (773 MB).

With two FAT partitions, the 1.6 GB drive holds 1,361 MB of useful data.

On the test system disk with two partitions, there are 6,624 files occupying 525 MB, with 461 MB of data. This is 64 MB of slack space, or 12%. This works out at 10 KB per file.

Over the total 1,546 MB space on the two drives, the total wasted space is 185 MB plus 1 MB extra overhead.

Adding a second partition has generated 170 MB of extra space, at the expense of some additional complexity in disk management.

...cont'd

To reduce C: below 512 MB, PSP (30 MB) was uninstalled and reinstalled to the E: drive.

Creating three partitions should increase the saving.

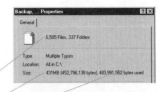

1 Record the C: drive usage:
The number of files (6,505).
The data content (431MB),
Space used (461MB).

2 Display the C: drive properties to note the total capacity (509MB).

3 Record the E: drive usage:
The number of files (120).
The data content (30MB),
Space used (31MB).

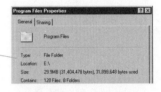

4 Display the E: drive and F: properties to note the total capacities (509MB each).

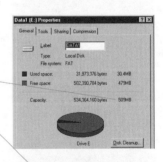

With three partitions, there are 6,625 files occupying 492 MB, with 461 MB of data. This is 31 MB of slack space, or 6%. This works out at 5 KB per file.

With three FAT partitions, the 1.6 GB drive holds 1,436 MB of useful data.

Over the 1,527 MB on the three drives, this gives a total wasted space of 91 MB, plus 20 MB in extra overhead and unused space.

Adding a second partition has generated 245 MB of extra space, compared with the single partition.

Compression

Another way to tackle the problem of wasted space is to Compress the drive. This converts the contents of files using a 'compaction' technique so that they take up less space, but mapping the compressed data into a file space based on the original file size. The system also makes use of the slack space in clusters. The result is that the partition can hold more data, and the effective disk size is increased.

The compression and decompression takes processor resources, but there are several levels of compression, so you can maximise performance or space saving on a file by file basis. You can also choose to compress the free space only, creating an extra drive.

To view the options available:

1 Right-click the drive icon and select Properties, and choose the Compression tab.

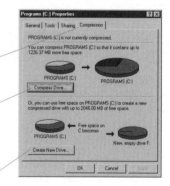

2 Click Compress drive to compress the files in place. This adds up to 1,226 MB extra disk space.

3 Click Create New Drive to prepare the free space to hold compressed files. This increases the available free space from 939 MB to up to 2046 MB.

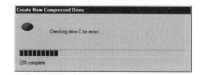

The drive is checked for error. This could take some time. When this completes, the new drive definition is set up and then the details are confirmed.

Note that the drive has been allocated a new drive letter, chosen to follow all existing drive letters, including the removable drives.

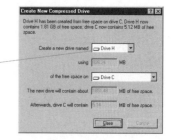

If you convert the whole drive, a second letter is also generated, but this becomes the physical, host drive, and the compressed drive becomes the C: drive.

4 Click Close to end, and you are reminded not to install software or use MS-DOS mode until you've restarted.

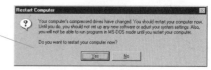

5 Click Yes to restart, and the system checks that you are booting the hard drive. Remove the diskette and retry if necessary.

After restart, you'll see the new drive in My Computer. Right-click the icon and select Properties to view the details.

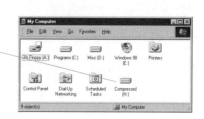

With compression, the 1.6 GB drive holds 2,046 MB of useful data, but this depends on the type of data, and it may be slower.

You'll see from the Compressed tab that the disk space can take several forms:

- UltraPacked files.

- HiPacked files.

- Standard compressed files

- Uncompressed files.

- Free space.

FAT-32 drive

The methods so far have all been traditional, Windows 95 techniques, even though they may use new Windows 98 versions of utilities such as Drivespace. However, there is a technique that is particularly related to Windows 98 that resolves the disk size problem a different way. It increases the size of the entries in the FAT table from 16 bit to 32 bit. This vastly increases the number of clusters that can be handled. The effects are to reduce the size of cluster needed for a given disk capacity, and to increase the maximum capacity supported.

Disk size (GB)	Cluster size (KB)
0.25-0.5	Not supported
0.5–8.0	4
8-16	8
16-32	16
32-2048	32
>2048	Not supported

You can see the benefits that this will provide compared with the FAT setup (referred to as FAT-16), using the FAT-32 info tool from the resource kit. To evaluate FAT-32:

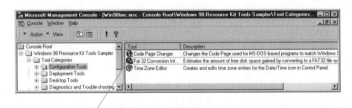

1 Start the FAT-32 Conversion information tool from the Resource Kit folder on the Start menu. Select the drive, and press Scan.

2 The message summarises the findings, in this case 131 MB extra disk space.

3 Press Convert to begin the process, and confirm the drive.

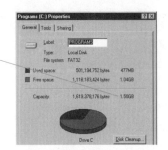

The converter offers you the chance to run Backup before continuing in MS-DOS mode. It runs Scandisk to check the drive, converts the directories and the file allocation table, and updates the partition table and the boot record. Then it restarts Windows 98.

When it restarts, it defragments the drive which will be littered with spare clusters due to the change in cluster size.

4 Record the C: drive usage:
The number of files (6,669).
The data content (458 MB),
Space used (472 MB).

5 Display the C: drive properties to note the total capacity (1,544 MB).

With a FAT-32 partition, the 1.6 GB drive holds 1,513 MB of useful data.

With FAT-32, there are 6,669 files occupying 472 MB, with 458 MB of data. This is 14 MB of slack space, or 3%. This works out at 2 KB per file.

Over the 1,544 MB on the drive, this would give a total wasted space of 31 MB, plus 3 MB extra overhead.

The extra space available under FAT-32 compared with the single partition FAT-16 is 322 MB. Rather more than the estimate provided by the information tool. There are also benefits in large drive support and performance.

PartitionMagic

The best thing about this utility - it makes all the changes you want without having to unload the drive.

Partitioning the hard disk is one of the most difficult tasks, and errors can leave you with an unusable system. To make the task easier you need to add a separately purchased product, such as the PartitionMagic utility.

This does all the types of repartitioning. You can divide your drive, move, shrink or stretch partitions, convert a partition to FAT-32 and even convert it back to FAT-16 (Windows 98 can't do this).

1 Run PM from its folder in the Start menu.

2 Choose one of the wizards to direct you, for example Reclaim wasted space.

You can decide the actions for yourself.

3 Follow the prompts to set up the tasks required.

4 PM may need to switch to MS-DOS to complete the operation.

5 Select Operations, Convert to change the FAT partition to FAT-32.

6 Select Operations, Advanced to view the alternatives available, based on the amount of data.

PM prepares the tasks, then runs them in MS-DOS mode.

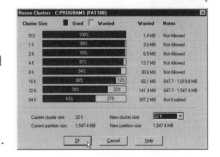

...cont'd

You can run the tools from the Start menu folder entries, or from the Tools menu on the menu bar.

PartitionMagic has a number of other tools to help with tasks related to partitioning, such as:

- Create Rescue Disk (recover from errors).

- DriveMapper (change drive references).

- MagicMover (change drive and folder).

- PartitionInfo (details of disk setup).

- PQBoot (use multiple operating systems).

1 Run DriveMapper to change references to the CD-ROM drive letter from E: to G:, when you have added two extra partitions.

2 Use MagicMover to transfer applications from one drive and folder to a different drive, without having to uninstall and reinstall.

If you need information while using the rescue disk, the second disk contains the data for the Help command.

3 You can create rescue diskettes at Setup, but if you need a new one, PM will rerun that part of Setup.

The MS-DOS version of PM has the same functions as the Windows 98 version.

This disk contains the files needed to boot your PC and run the MS-DOS version of PartitionMagic. This is useful if you find that you cannot access the disk partition with the full version, or if you convert a partition by mistake to a type Windows 98 does not support.

Multiple systems

Windows 98 expects one primary partition on a hard disk, with an optional extended partition. However, the partition table allows up to four primary partitions (or primary and one extended). Only one primary can be active at a time, and it becomes the current C: drive. The other primary drives are hidden from the current operating system.

This allows you to have multiple operating systems on the disk, or multiple installations of the same operating system, each completely separate. You can optionally share data between them, through logical partitions in the extended partition, or via a second hard disk if present.

Other operating systems such as OS/2 allow you to set up multiple primaries and select which one to boot from. You can achieve the same results for Windows 98 systems, using PartitionMagic to create the partitions, and PQBoot to select which partition to boot from. For example, you could divide a 16GB drive into five partitions with three bootable systems, and two data partitions:

BootMagic operates by replacing your master boot record (MBR) with its own version, retaining a backup copy of the original.

- Active primary partition.
- Hidden primary partition.
- Hidden primary partition.
- Extended primary partition.
- Logical data partition.
- Logical data partition.

This is quite an improvement over the OS/2 Boot Manager, since it does not need a primary partition, and it supports the mouse for choosing the system.

You can use PartitionMagic or PQBoot to make any of the primary partitions the active, bootable partition. If you install the BootMagic utility, it creates a menu showing all the operating systems on your PC, so that you can choose one (or accept the default) when you boot your PC. Run the BootMagic Configuration tool to set the delay, and choose the icons for the entries.

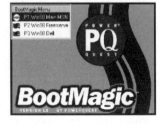

Startup from hard disk

It makes it easier to follow the PC boot process, if you understand the structure of the hard disk

When you switch on the PC, the processor starts the system BIOS code. This runs the POST (power on self test) to make sure the system devices are working correctly.

After POST completes, the BIOS locates the boot drive, using the boot sequence as a guide. Normally this means looking on the floppy disk drive A:, or if there is no disk inserted, looking on the hard disk drive C:.

Using the BIOS Setup program, you can modify the Boot Sequence, e.g. if you have a game that installs from a bootable CD-ROM. You can also specify Quiet Boot, to hide the details, or QuickBoot, to skip the POST checks.

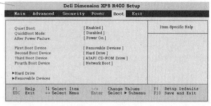

When it has selected the boot drive, the BIOS loads the first physical sector on the disk. If it is a hard disk, this loads the

To get all the setup features your PC must have an ACPI compatible BIOS.

master boot record (MBR) which has the partition table, identifying the active bootable partition. The MBR in turn loads the

boot sector from that partition. For a floppy disk, the first physical sector is the boot sector. It cannot be partitioned and has no MBR.

If you use EZ-Drive you must always start from the hard disk, even if you want to boot from floppy. EZ-Drive adds code in the MBR to overcome the 8 GB, 2 GB, and 512 MB operating system and system BIOS limit on older PCs. This needs to be loaded to make the drive accessible. Then you can press Ctrl to pause and manually select which drive (A: or C:) to boot from.

The boot sector on non-bootable disks contains a program to issue the "Insert a disk and press any key" message.

The boot sector contains a bootstrap loader to read in Io.sys. This checks for the Ctrl key or the boot key (F8) and displays the boot menu, or continues processing the system files. Note that there is no delay or "Starting Windows 98..." message, unlike the Windows 95 startup.

Io.sys processes the Msdos.sys file which specifies the Windows folders and startup options, for example to startup in MS-DOS or Windows.

To make a complete log of the activity during startup, display the Startup menu and choose item two - Logged. This creates a hidden, read-only file named C:\bootlog.txt, with the sequence through Startup and the Windows 98 components and drivers loaded and initialised. This file is very useful when you are trouble shooting startup problems.

Set this option for PCs that are left on for overnight processing or fax receipt etc..

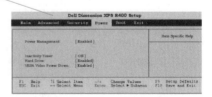

One other item in the BIOS setup program that affects the way the hard disk operates is the Power option. This enables power management for the hard disk, so that you can use the power management features from the display properties to specify the delay period after which the hard drive switches to standby mode. This will reduce power consumption and improve reliability.

Microsoft Office 2000

This chapter reviews the latest version of Microsoft Office, looking at the Web extensions and other new features that complement and extend the Windows 98 environment.

Covers

Chapter Thirteen

Office 2000

These notes are based on the Office 2000 Premium edition. The details for other editions may differ in various aspects.

The premium edition of Office contains these applications:

- Word for Windows 2000 word processor

- Access 2000 database management system

- Excel 2000 spreadsheet application

- Outlook 2000 desktop information manager

- PowerPoint 2000 presentation graphics application

- FrontPage 2000 Web publishing

- PhotoDraw 2000 business graphics software

- Publisher 2000 desktop publishing program

- Office 2000 Tools

- Internet Explorer 5.0

IE5 is already integrated into the Second Edition of Windows 98.

Microsoft Word	Microsoft Access
Microsoft Excel	Microsoft Outlook
Microsoft PowerPoint	Microsoft FrontPage
Microsoft PhotoDraw	Microsoft Publisher
Snapshot Viewer	Microsoft Office Language Settings
Microsoft Photo Editor	Microsoft Office Shortcut Bar
Internet Explorer	NetMeeting

There are also various Office server extensions and Web components, which are particularly useful for corporate and Intranet environments. In fact, all the new products emphasise Internet and Intranet functions to support Web publishing and allow for online real-time collaboration on documents. You can apply the full functions of Office programs in HTML, so you can create documents in Office, transfer them to the Internet, and work on documents received from the Internet – so the Office documents complete the round trip through the Web.

Features that were once restricted to the Web browser, such as Web subscriptions, notifications and Web discussions, can now be used for any office document. You can start an online conference and share any Office document with other on-line users. Office 2000 also integrates e-mail with all its applications.

Office 2000 applications automatically detect and fix critical errors without you having to know about them, by verifying and reinstalling files and registry entries where necessary. There is also a Detect and Repair tool on the Help menu to find problems with non-critical files, such as fonts and templates, and repair them.

The first time you start up your PC each day, the Office 2000 Tune Up wizard runs. This will optimise the Office files on the hard disk to improve performance. You can cancel the wizard at any time. It may run again from time to time, unless you choose to de-select the option.

Office 2000 applications are created in a single executable file that can be used for the US, Europe, Far East, and for the Middle East with its bi-directional languages such as Hebrew and Arabic. This makes it possible for you to change the language of the user interface without affecting the operation of the application. You can also type in multiple languages (if that's the skill that you have), without needing to change the interface, because the applications can detect the language, and use the correct spelling, grammar checking and autocorrection.

Installation

You'll need better than the minimum for Windows 98 to install and use Office 2000 effectively. A Pentium 90 at least, with 32 MB or more is recommended. You'll also require 200MB or more disk space available, for the typical setup.

To install Office 2000:

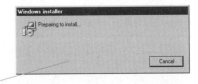

1 Insert the Office 2000 CD into the CD-ROM drive, and the Windows Installer runs.

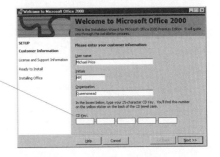

2 Follow the instructions on the screen and enter your details and product code.

3 Accept the terms and conditions when prompted.

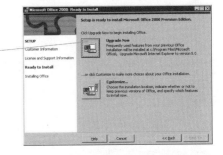

4 Click the Upgrade Now button to start the installation. Setup verifies the tasks and transfers the files needed.

5 Click Yes when prompted, to allow Setup to restart your PC.

After rebooting, Setup will finish updating your registry and the Start menu. It may take up to 15 minutes to finalise the settings. When this completes, Office 2000 is ready to use.

...cont'd

If you want to see what is happening during the installation, you should select the Customise option. You can leave the settings as suggested and still get the default installation, or you can select or deselect items.

1 Press the Customise button, and select the folders for installation.

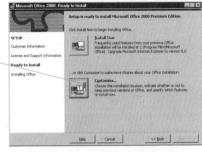

2 Upgrade to Internet Explorer 5.0 if desired. Office 2000 is optimised for this version of the browser.

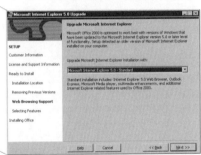

3 Select function. Click the [+] to expand the list.

4 Click an entry and choose to install to disk, run from CD or install on first use.

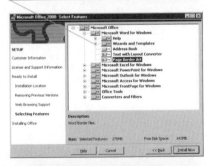

5 Select Install Now and the file transfer and settings proceed as with the Quiet installation. Restart the PC when prompted and allow the installation to complete.

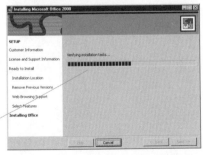

Add/Remove

When you start Office setup from Add/ Remove, it runs in maintenance mode. Note also that AutoRun does not launch the setup program when Office is already installed.

You can uninstall Office 2000 or change your selection of Office functions.

1 Select Start, Settings, Control Panel, and double click Add/Remove Programs.

2 From the Install/Uninstall list select Microsoft Office 2000, and click Add/ Remove. This starts the Windows Installer (the Office 2000 Setup program).

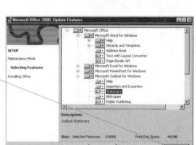

3 Select the appropriate button to repair Office 2000 by reinstalling, or add/ remove features, or remove it completely.

4 Select Update Now to apply the changes. You will need the Office 2000 CD, except for selections that are for Install on first use.

5 You are advised to restart the PC after the processing completes, even if there is no explicit message to do so.

Office 2000 gives you access to all the functions through shortcuts, but only installs the ones you actually use. This avoids unnecessary use of hard disk space, but does mean that you need the Office CD close to hand whenever you use office applications, since it will be needed whenever you select a function for the first time.

You can install Office functions on demand.

For example, the first time you select Snapshot viewer from the Office Tools folder on the Start menu, Windows detects that it is not yet installed.

1 Select Start, Programs, Office Tools, and Snapshot Viewer.

2 This starts the Windows Installer which configures the setup and requests the Office 2000 CD.

3 The installer reads the required files from the CD and transfers them to your hard drive.

4 When all the files have been copied, the Snapshot Viewer is loaded.

5 The next time that you start Snapshot viewer, it loads immediately from the hard disk.

A report snapshot is a file (type .snp) that contains a copy of the pages of an Access report, preserving the two-dimensional layout, graphics, and other embedded objects in the report. You use Access 2000 to create the report snapshot. Snapshot Viewer will allow you to share the report with others who may not have an Access licence.

Office 2000 shortcuts

As is always the case with Office, Microsoft ignores its own good advice about managing entries in the Start menu, and places most of the Office 2000 shortcuts directly into the Programs folder, to mix in with the existing entries. There is one folder, for the Office Tools, and as usual Office puts entries at the top of the first level folder, for creating and opening Office documents.

Outlook Express 5.0 is added with Internet Explorer 5.0, even though Office 2000 contains the fuller function Outlook 2000. However, Outlook Express is useful for Newsgroups.

- Outlook and IE5 icons added to the desktop.

- Office document icons in Start folder

- Office Tools folder.

- Internet Explorer 5 program entry.

- Office applications in Programs folder.

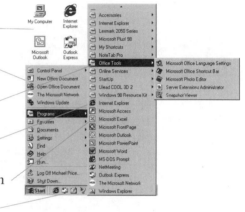

- New Outlook icon on Launchpad, replacing the previous Outlook Express 3.0.

If you open the My Computer folder, you'll find another entry, Web Folders. Here you can create shortcuts to Web folders on the Intranet or the Internet.

You can swap documents between Office 2000 and Office 97 systems without worrying about file formats.

An obvious change that you will find when you create documents is that the icons have been reshaped and recoloured. Even the Word document icon has been changed. You might suspect that this heralds a change in the file formats. In actual fact, the file formats used by Word and most of the applications (with the exception of Access 2000) remain fully compatible with the previous Office 97 formats.

Office assistant

In Office 2000, the Assistant is the main way
of finding help. To ask a question:

1 Select Help (or press the ? button, or press
F1), type your question in the balloon area.
and press Search.

2 If the balloon is not showing, click on the
Assistant to display it.

To get the Help contents and index, you must turn the
Assistant off:

3 Click Options in the
Assistant balloon.

4 On the Options tab, clear
the box saying Use the
Office Assistant. This will
grey out all of the entries
on the panel.

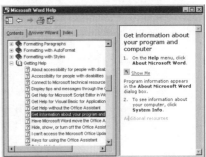

5 Press F1 or click Help,
Word Help to display the
full help.

6 To turn on the Assistant at any time,
click Show the Office Assistant on
the Help menu.

Quick file switching

Office applications can handle multiple files, but in the past this has made it difficult to switch between documents. You had to select the application then select the specific document.

Excel 2000 retains the window within a window approach, but speeds up file switching by putting the document windows on the taskbar. To select a different spreadsheet:

1 Click the document on the taskbar to switch to it.

2 Or press Alt+Tab and select the document from the window list.

Quick file switching in Word 2000 gives you the best of both worlds. One application runs, but the documents open in separate windows with their own controls and toolbars. You can select a specific document from the taskbar, or use Alt+Tab to display the active Window list. This makes it easy to switch between open documents, especially during cut-and-paste or drag-and-drop operations.

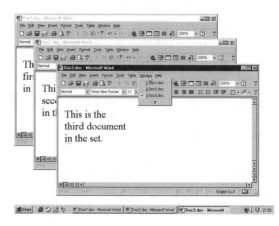

You can still select documents using the MDI methods, such as the Windows menu or Ctrl+F6 to switch files.

Using the Windows menu commands illustrates the new behaviour of menus in Office 2000.

When you first start an Office application such as Word, the menus display basic commands only. As you work, commands that you use most often are stored as personalised settings and displayed on the menus and toolbars.

There are several ways to expand the list of commands:

When you expand one menu, all of the menus are expanded until you choose a command or perform another action.

1 Pause over the menu bar entry for a couple of seconds. Click the double-arrow at the bottom of the menu. Double-click the menu itself.

2 Use a new command, for example click Arrange All.

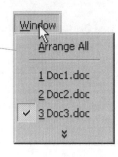

Any command that you select from the expanded menu is added immediately to your personalised version of the menu. If you stop using a command for a while, Word stops showing it on the short version of the menu.

If you prefer, you can specify that Word will always show the full menu lists. To change the setting:

You can also reset your usage data, and switch the pause display on or off.

3 Select Tools, Customise, and the Options tab, and clear the box to stop Menus show recently used commands.

This will also change the menu setting for the other Office 2000 applications.

Collect and paste

You can use the Office Clipboard to collect and paste multiple items from the same or different applications, and paste the collection of copied items. You can copy items from any program that supports copy/cut and paste, but you can only paste items into the main Office applications: Word, Excel, Access, or PowerPoint.

To use the Office clipboard:

1 In Word or other Office application, select, View, Toolbar, Clipboard. This displays the Clipboard toolbar.

2 The buttons are Copy, Paste All, and Clear Clipboard.

3 In any program, mark up an item and copy it to the clipboard by clicking Copy on the clipboard toolbar (collecting the items in the Clipboard).

You will automatically switch to copying and collecting items in the Office Clipboard if you perform any of these actions:

- Copy or cut two different items consecutively in the same program.

- Copy one item, paste the item, and then copy another item in the same program.

- Copying one item twice in succession.

When you're ready to paste the collected items, switch to the Office program that has the target document and paste one or more items into it. You can reuse the items in the clipboard, until you close the Office applications.

You can paste multiple items in the four main Office applications only.

To paste items into an Office application:

1 You can park the clipboard toolbar by dragging and dropping it onto the edge of the window.

2 Place the cursor at the insert point in the document.

3 View the first 50 characters of text, or the type for non-text items, using the icon tip displayed when you pause the mouse pointer over the icon.

4 Click Paste All, or click the individual item that you want to add at that position.

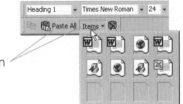

5 If the toolbar is docked, click Paste All, or click Item, and then select the item.

The Office Clipboard is separate from the Windows Clipboard but when you copy multiple items to the Office Clipboard, the latest item is always copied to the Windows Clipboard. Also, when you clear all items from the Office Clipboard, the Windows Clipboard is also cleared.

The Office Clipboard can hold up to 12 items. In an Office application, you will be asked if you want to drop the first item or to cancel copying. With other programs, the new item is copied only to the Windows Clipboard.

The collected items remain on the Office Clipboard until you press Clear Clipboard, or you close all Office programs.

Accessibility

Powerpoint and Excel support zoom by up to 400%. Access only supports zoom for report previews.

To complement the Windows 98 accessibility facilities, Office programs include a variety of features, though the level of support is not consistent throughout the suite of applications.

You can view your documents or worksheets at any magnification up to 500 percent. For example:

1. In the Word Standard toolbar, click the down-arrow on the Zoom button and select a magnification. You can also reduce the page to get an overview.

2. For the best results, select Tools, Options from the menu bar and click the View tab. Select Wrap to window, so you'll see all the text, without affecting page and print layout.

Zoom in on or out of a document

You can "zoom in" to get a close-up view of your document or "zoom out" to see more of the page at a reduced size.

If you're using the Microsoft IntelliMouse pointing device, you can use it to zoom in or out. Just hold down Ctrl as you rotate the wheel forward or back.

In Excel, as well as zooming the sheet, you can enlarge the text in row and column headings and the formula and status bars.

To change the sizes for the one spreadsheet only, select Format, Style, and Modify the Normal style.

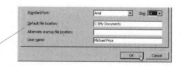

3. In the Excel menu bar click Tools, Options, choose the General tab, set the font and size.

4. You must end Excel and restart to see the effects.

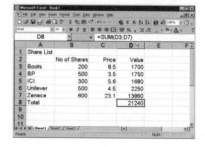

Word 2000

Word 2000 adds ease of use features without losing DOC file compatibility with Word 97.

Since the file format remains compatible with Office 97, the main changes, other than the Web extensions, affect the way you use Word, rather than the end product itself. For example, Click-n-Type allows you to insert text anywhere in the document:

1 Double-click at the point on the page where you want to put text.

2 Note the cursor hinting.

Word shows you what text format will be applied through cursor hinting. It also automatically adds extra lines, tabs, alignment and wrapping as needed. Use this feature to centre titles, to indent paragraphs, or to create a single line of text with multiple formats e.g. left aligned and right aligned sections.

Word also tries to keep you better informed about the fonts you choose, with a WYSIWIG font menu:

3 To change the standard font menu, select Tools, Customise and Options.

4 Click the box to list font names (and sample text) in their own fonts.

This allows you to see what the font looks like before you insert from the drop-down menu on the toolbar, saving time in selecting the right font for your document.

Word and Web

Word 2000 focuses on Web-centred document creation. You can use HTML as your default file format, and use all the functions in Word for printed documents or for Web-based documents, but you can save the document in the standard Word file format without losing any of the text formatting.

Word Themes help you design pages for e-mail or the Web, or just for viewing and printing in Word. These provide coherent backgrounds, picture bullets, fonts, and format. They are shared with the FrontPage 2000 Web site creator, so Web pages created with either application can have a consistent appearance. To select a theme:

1 From Word menu bar select Format, Theme, to show the list of available themes.

2 Select a theme to see a preview of the headings, bullets and type styles it offers.

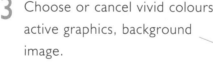

3 Choose or cancel vivid colours, active graphics, background image.

4 Many of the themes are set to install on demand, so you'll need the Office CD.

To install the selected theme and see its preview, click Install.

When you've created your document, preview it using your Web browser from within Word, to see it as others will see it on the Internet.

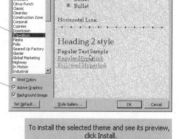

5 Select File from the menu bar, and click Web Page Preview.

...cont'd

Word 2000 contains many new features that help you work with Web pages. It supports frames for Web pages and documents, and offers a frames tool bar to help in creating and modifying frames. For example, to create a table of contents within a frame:

When you create frames and save documents as Web pages, you will generate multiple files since each element in a Web page is a separate file.

1 Click the TOC in Frame button (or select Format, Frames, TOC in Frame). If the document hasn't been saved, you get prompted to do so.

2 The document is divided into two Web frames, with the contents list in the left frame. These are links to the relevant section of the document.

Word 2000 helps in other ways with hyperlinks, jumps and e-mail triggers, and you can create and manipulate these without having to know the HTML jargon.

When you save the document, Word 2000 checks the links and repairs those that aren't working because of moved or missing files.

3 Select Insert on the menu bar and click Hyperlink.

- Enter the text to be displayed as the screen tip.

- Type or select a name, or browse for the file or Web page, or pick an existing bookmark in the document.

- Choose the frame where the linked document appears.

Excel 2000

Excel 2000 supports drag and drop of table data from the browser directly into Excel.

Excel 2000 is designed to be Web-enabled, to provide access to data for anyone with a browser. It can save to or read from HTML files as easily as from the proprietary XLS file format, so Web documents can share the same level of data content as the traditional spreadsheet.

To save a spreadsheet in HTML format:

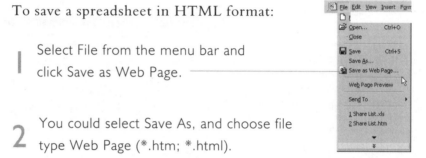

1   Select File from the menu bar and click Save as Web Page.

2   You could select Save As, and choose file type Web Page (*.htm; *.html).

If you use HTML as your default file format for Excel, you have the same functions and capabilities as the standard file format, plus the additional ability to view spreadsheet data in your Web browser.

Although all Web pages have similar file extensions, Office 2000 distinguishes the particular type of document. For example, when you select File, Open in Excel 2000, you may see a variety of HTML files, but the icon explains their roles:

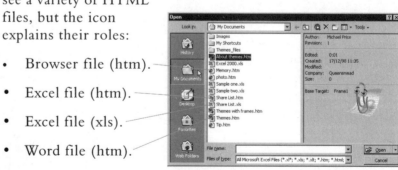

- Browser file (htm).
- Excel file (htm).
- Excel file (xls).
- Word file (htm).

Note the Outlook style bar that provides quick access to the standard locations for documents, on your hard disk or on the Internet or Intranet. You can also select drives and folders from the drop-down box at the top of the screen.

Excel 2000 maintains full read/write compatibility with Excel 97, and many of the enhancements are aimed at improving personal productivity. For example, if you extend an existing list, the List AutoFill feature automatically extends the list's formatting and formulas.

1 Formula and data in columns, formatted.

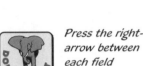

Press the right-arrow between each field entry.

2 Select the next row and start typing the entries.

3 Type the name, then the quantity.

| 7 | Zeneca | 600 | £23.10 £13,860.00 |
| 8 | Booker | | |

AutoFill looks at the preceding cells to determine what formatting and formulas should be extended.

4 Type the price, then press the right-arrow.

| 7 | Zeneca | 600 | £23.10 £13,860.00 |
| 8 | Booker | 3000 | |

| 7 | Zeneca | 600 | £23.10 £13,860.00 |
| 8 | Booker | 3000 | .65 |

5 Field formats and formulae are applied automatically.

| 7 | Zeneca | 600 | £23.10 £13,860.00 |
| 8 | Booker | 3000 | £0.65 £1,950.00 |

Excel also makes it easier to apply formatting. Previous versions used reverse video to indicate a selection, so it was hard to see the styles applied to the selection. Excel 2000 uses light shading instead, so you can apply changes to the selected cells, see the effects, and make adjustments, without having to deselect to view, then reselect to modify the changes.

	A	B	C	D
1		**Share List**		
2		No of Shares	Price	Value
3	Boots	200	£8.50	£1,700.00
4	BP	500	£3.50	£1,750.00
5	ICI	300	£5.60	£1,680.00
6	Unilever	500	£4.50	£2,250.00
7	Zeneca	600	£23.10	£13,860.00
8	Booker	3000	£0.65	£1,950.00

Access 2000

Access is the most powerful of the Office applications, providing sophisticated database functions, and has perhaps been the slowest in adopting the newer Office methods. Access 2000 brings it closer, but the result is that the file format has changed, and is not compatible with Access 97. To compensate for this, Access at last includes the ability to save a database into a previous version, making it possible to share database files in a mixed environment. To save the database:

Select Tools, Database Utilities, Convert Database, To Prior Access Database Version.

The database window makes it clear that you are running a new version, since it not only changes layout, it also includes a new object.

- Database window toolbar.

- Objects bar (back to the vertical).

- A new entry, for Data Access Pages.

- Organise database objects in groups.

Data Access Pages are essentially HTML pages with data binding capabilities. The pages can be run within Access shell or within Internet Explorer 5.0. Unlike forms and reports, data access pages are stored outside the MDB database file, as an HTML file so you can send them to users without Access on their PCs, where they can view the pages in IE5 or Outlook 2000.

Networking Windows

This chapter introduces networks, with emphasis on designing, installing and using a peer-to-peer network using the features supplied in Windows 98.

Covers

Chapter Fourteen

PC networks

If you have more than one PC in your office, you may find yourself wanting to use the devices attached to one PC while working at another PC. For example, you may have specific devices such as a laser printer and a scanner attached to a particular PC.

The other PC may have devices of its own that it can share, or it may be a desktop or laptop PC without any attached peripherals. It could be an older machine that lacks features such as a CD-ROM drive, and may not even be running Windows 98.

In any of these cases, you may wish for a method of linking your PCs together so that they can share each others equipment.

This is exactly what a PC network achieves, but the implications go beyond merely sharing hardware. Because the PCs can access the drives on another PC, they can share data as well as devices.

This makes it possible to maintain consistent information on connected PCs, either by sharing one working copy, or by providing automatic updating when changes are made. This avoids the risk of data files being changed unilaterally and providing conflicting answers.

The connections between the PCs could be created in various ways, depending on their locations and on the type of data sharing you need. For example:

• PC to PC via a modem and telephone line.

• With e-mail and file transfer services.

• Using the Internet and shared Web space.

A network that spreads across separate locations is known as a wide area network or WAN.

• Direct connections using cables and adapter cards.

When you connect two or more PCs together in the same physical location, you create a local area network, or LAN. The connections for the network require both hardware and software components.

The hardware provides the physical path between the PCs and includes:

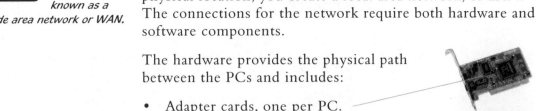

• Adapter cards, one per PC.

• One or more central switch or hub.

• Cables to connect the PCs to the hubs.

The software is required to allow the PCs to communicate across the cables and adapters, and may include:

• Network client software for each PC.

• A network operating system for the controlling PC (if needed).

• Network transport protocols (the language rules for communicating over the network.

Network rules are needed to ensure that the data transfers between PCs are completed, and any errors that may arise are detected and corrected.

All of the necessary components may be found in Windows 98, though for some types of network you may choose to use additional specialised software, to increase security or manage larger numbers of PCs.

Server based LAN

Networks started out in corporate environments, where central control is often demanded.

There are two main ways of organising local area networks. The most common approach is to place all the shared resources on one or more dedicated machines known as servers.

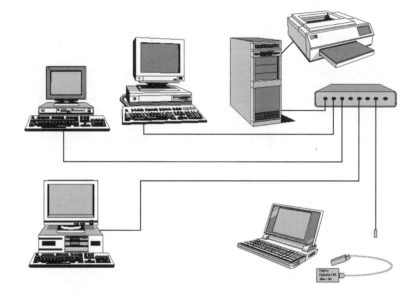

The servers could be PCs or larger computers, running a special purpose network operating system such as Windows NT or Novell Netware. The servers also manage the access facilities permitted for individual users and PCs connected to the network. The PCs may run any operating system that supports the client software needed to communicate with the server system. Windows 98 contains the software needed to communicate with most network systems. Because of the complexity involved and to preserve the security of the system, the server networks usually require a network administrator whose job includes defining new workstations and new users to the system, and managing required changes to access levels and resource allocations.

This is a lot of effort, when all you want is to connect three or four PCs, so a simpler way has been developed.

In a smaller office or home environment, where there are only a small number of PCs, and the security requirements are less rigorous, a simpler network is more appropriate.

Peer to peer LAN

This method allows you to share devices without having to give them up.

The peer-to-peer network provides this by allowing any PC to act as a server. The resource to be shared remains on the original PC, but the PC concerned provides access for other PCs on the network to files, folders, disk drives, printers, fax modems, scanners or CD-ROM drives. Every PC in the network can also function as a client to access resources on the other PCs in the network. The peer-to-peer network PCs share resources without demanding centralised control or administration, since each user in the network acts as the network administrator to assign shared resources and levels of access.

Windows 98 has all the software to support a peer-to-peer network, for server and client aspects, without calling for a high level of technical expertise. By the same token, the security it gives is limited, and may be viewed as voluntary, to stop accidental loss of data, rather than to ensure privacy.

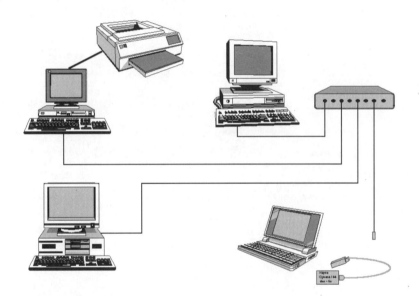

You can start off with a peer-to-peer network, and move to a server-based network by dedicating specific PCs to the server function. Later you could add specialised network software and make these machines into true servers. At the same time, you would be advised to lock these PCs in a server cabinet or room, to add the physical security needed to complement the increased access control that they can provide. You will also want to allocate the task of network administration for the new server-based network.

Planning wires

The effort you should spend in planning your network will be proportional to the number of PCs that will be connected and the number of users that will share access to those PCs. Whether it is a small or large network however, you'll need to consider:

- The resources that need to be shared (files, printers, modems, scanners).

- The volumes of data that may be involved (including printer files, scanner images etc.).

- The number of connections, now and in the future.

- The size in terms of separation between the PCs.

- The software used on the PCs. Older PCs for example may still be running Windows 3.1x or MS-DOS.

- The level of security and control that you want.

In the bus network, PCs are linked in a line - more like a train than a bus:

These will affect the type of network connection you should choose, and whether you'll need a peer-to-peer network or a server-based network.

The simplest way to connect your PCs is using the bus topology where each PC is connected by coaxial cable using a T-piece connector, with 50-ohm terminators at each end. Coaxial cable supports up to 30 PCs, for a total length of up to 185 meters.

This form of network is suitable for small networks, and is easy to set up and to extend, within the limitations noted. There's no problem running the network with some PCs powered off. However, a faulty cable or connector can cause the whole network to fail.

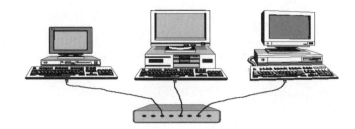

In the star network, PCs are linked to a central point, like spokes on a wheel:

Connecting PCs in a star topology requires a cable from each PC to a central connection device known as a hub.

Hubs can be chosen to handle various numbers of PCs, for example 8, 16 or 24. The cable used is twisted-pair wire rather than coaxial, which is similar to telephone wire, and uses four pairs of wires and RJ-45 connectors that are also similar to some types of telephone connectors. The limit with the star network is that the maximum distance from hub to PC is 100 meters. This supports network speeds up to 10Mbps, unless you choose the higher specification category 5 cable, which supports up to 100Mbps.

With the star network, a defective cable affects only the one PC that it is connected to. On the other hand, the need to run all the cables to one point complicates the wiring. Also, the hub is a critical component. If it fails, the whole network fails.

There are even wireless networks, which use infrared or radio links to eliminate the need for cabling.

Both problems are eased if you use multiple hubs and spread the PCs across them. However, the star network is more expensive than the bus network because of the cost of the hubs and because it requires more cable in total.

There are other types of cabling, including fibre optics, used to connect hubs at very high data rates, and there are many special devices designed to extend the range of a LAN.

Getting help

There is plenty of help available to make it easy for you to design your network, whether you have a small or a large configuration in mind. In the UK for example, you can contact a company such as Black Box, and obtain a comprehensive catalogue with all the networking and communications hardware and supplies you could possibly want. There is technical support available, even if you are not a customer. You can describe your needs and receive advice or even a suggested solution for your requirements.

Call Black Box at 0118965 5000, or visit their Web site http://www. blackbox.co.uk.

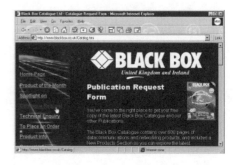

Requested for a design for a network to connect seven users in a small office, with potential for expansion, Black Box provided a range of answers, from the budget, cost-conscious, up to the no-holds barred high speed setup.

The sample network here shows seven client PCs and one server PC, connected at 10Mbps

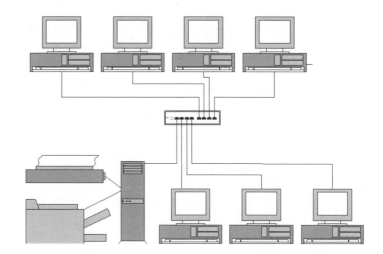

Ballpark cost is £600 for eight users and 10Mbps speed (excluding cabling).

The budget solution suggested included a 10Mbps, 8-port hub, and 10Mbps adapters for the PCs. The network can be extended by adding more hubs, but the speed will be limited to 10Mbps unless all the components are replaced.

You can install dual speed 10/100Mbps adapters and autodetect 10/100Mbps hub. The PCs can then be operated at either 10Mbps or 100Mbps. This is worthwhile if you are working with large files, or sharing video across the network. A second hub will be required to support additional users.

With more users and the high data rate, the network becomes susceptible to collisions between messages. That is, when two or more users transmit data at the same time, the messages interfere with each other, and it becomes necessary to pause and retransmit, in the hope that the network has become clear.

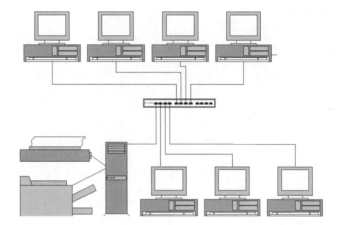

With the addition of a 10/100 Ethernet Switch each user will be on their own 100Mbps segment (separate collision domain). The server runs at 200Mbps full duplex, while the clients run at 100Mbps duplex, to avoid a bottle neck at the server. This switch supports up to 12 users. Additional switches or hubs will be needed for further expansion.

There are many combinations of network components that you may want to consider. You could also investigate items concerned with housing cables and servers, and the hardware and software tools for monitoring and trouble shooting your network.

Adapter cards

When you have decided what type of cabling you will use, you can choose the type of network adapter card needed for each PC, to provide the interface to the network. You must check what type of adapter slots are available on the PCs. There are adapter cards suitable for PCI, ISA, EISA, Vesa local bus, Microchannel, and PC Card (PCMCIA).

For the desktop PCs using the Pentium processor, the preferred choice is PCI, since these offer better performance and are easier to configure than the older ISA that was the previous standard.

For PCs that will be used as servers, use higher function bus-master adapter cards which can handle data even when the main processor is busy.

There are two main varieties of card, distinguished by the type of connector:

- Adapter with RJ-45 connector.

- Adapter with Coax T-connector.

These are available also in the PC card format for mobile PCs.

You may choose an adapter with multiple connection types. This is known as a combo card, and is advised if you plan to start with a bus network but later switch to a star layout.

The wizard may call for the Windows 98 CD-ROM if all the network software is not installed ready.

Install the network card into your PC as advised in the manual supplied for your PC or with the adapter card. When the PC starts, Windows 98 will detect the new hardware, if it is plug and play compatible, and automatically start the Add New Hardware wizard. For adapters that are not plug and play, you can start the wizard from the Control Panel to detect and install your network adapter card. Windows 98 may include a suitable driver for the card, or you may insert the device diskette provided with the card to select the driver that it provides.

Check the setup

After the wizard completes, check the network components that are installed.

Network
Neighborhood

| Right-click the Network Neighbourhood icon on the desktop, or open the Network option in the Control Panel.

- Client for Microsoft Networks or Client for NetWare Networks.

- The network adapter interface.

- The network protocol.

There may be other adapters, for example the dial up adapter used for Internet connection. If there are two or more adapters, the protocols show the names of the adapters to which they are bound.

Check existing devices also, since the network adapter may take over IRQs or other system resources previously assigned to other devices.

You must also check to see if there are any device conflicts with the network adapter.

2 Press Win+Pause/break and click the Device Manager.

3 Expand the Network entry and select the network adapter card.

4 Check that the device is working properly. If the device status shows a problem, select the Resources tab to see the conflicts or other sources of error.

Enable sharing

Before any other PC can share the devices on a networked PC, the PC owner must make the resources available. The first step is to enable sharing:

1 Right-click Network Neighbourhood and open Network Properties.

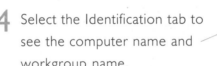

2 Check that Client for Microsoft Networks is selected in the Primary Network Logon box and click the File and Print Sharing button.

3 Select the check boxes to allow access to your files and/or to allow others to print to your printer, and press OK.

You can access resources from PCs in different workgroups, but organising by workgroup makes things easier to find.

4 Select the Identification tab to see the computer name and workgroup name.

The computer name must be unique on the network, up to 15 characters, with no spaces or special characters.

If your network has a small number of users, less than 8 for example, you may prefer all the PCs on the network to have the same workgroup name, so that all the PCs will be listed as members of the same workgroup when viewed in Network Neighborhood.

If you have larger numbers of PCs, you may want to group them by project or particular data needs, and define several workgroups.

...cont'd

Other PCs cannot access your files or printers unless you give permission.

When you have enabled sharing, you can select the specific items that you are willing to share:

1 Right-click the icon for the drive, folder or printer that you wish to share.

2 Select the Sharing entry that was added when you enabled sharing.

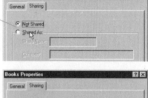

3 Select the check boxes to allow access to your files and/or to allow others to print to your printer, and press OK.

4 Set the access type as read-only or full, and specify the password if desired.

5 If some users have read-only access and others have full access, set the access type by password, and provide two passwords.

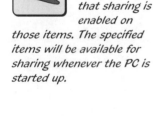

The icons have an overlay, a hand, to show that sharing is enabled on those items. The specified items will be available for sharing whenever the PC is started up.

- Hard disk.

- Folder - open drive to see share icon.

- Diskette drive.

- Zip disk, CD-ROM.

- Printer - open folder to see share icon.

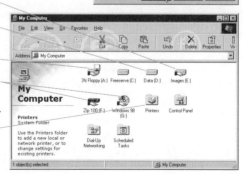

Taking shares

You can explore the shared resources in any workgroup and in any PC on the network.

You can see what resources are available for sharing on your network, through the network neighbourhood:

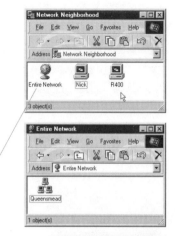

1 Double-click the icon Network Neighbourhood on the desktop to display your workgroup.

2 Double-click Entire Network to display all network workgroups.

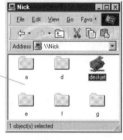

3 Double-click the PC in the workgroup to see the items that it has made available for sharing.

4 To use the printer, it must be defined to your system. Right-click the icon and select Install.

Use Printer Offline allows you to create print jobs when the network is disconnected, for example, on a laptop away from the office.

5 If possible, the printer driver will be copied from the PC owning the printer.

6 The new printer is added to the Printer folder, with an overlay to show that it is elsewhere on the network.

7 Right-click and choose Use Printer Offline, to queue jobs.

You can access the drives and folders from the Network Neighbourhood by double-clicking the icons to open them. You can also address the files by name, using the network address in place of the drive letter, for example:

You still get read-only or full access, as specified by the owner, or based on the password you supply.

D:\HTML files\Voyager.htm is addressed on other PCs as \\Nick\d\HTML files\Voyager.htm.

To make it easier, you can assign a drive letter to a shared folder or drive:

1 Locate the folder in Network Neighbourhood, and right-click the icon.

2 Select the Map Network Drive option on the context menu.

If you don't use the network folder often, click to clear the Reconnect at Logon box. This will speed Windows startup.

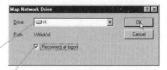

3 Accept the first available letter, as presented, or choose a drive letter from the list.

4 Check this box to specify to connect to this shared folder every time you start Windows.

5 You treat the folder just like a drive. It is even added to My Computer, as a networked drive.
Right-click the drive and select Disconnect to end the mapping.

Security

The main problem in a peer-to-peer network using share level access is the number of passwords that may be needed to control access to resources. The more resources that are available to you, the more passwords you have to remember.

Writing down the passwords is almost as bad as forgetting them. The Windows 98 password caching feature helps by storing passwords in a password file. When you access a password-protected resource for the first time, check the Save This Password in Your Password List option. Your password will be encrypted and then stored in a .PWL file in the Windows folder.

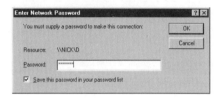

In order for a password list to be created:

• Password caching must be enabled (the default for Windows 98).

• Share-level access must be enabled on the resources that you will be sharing.

• You must connect to the resource using the Map Network Drive option in Windows Explorer, or by typing the path to the network resource on the Run line.

If you connect to the resource from a command line the password will not be added to the password list.

You can view the resources listed, using the Password List editor. You can only display your own list, while logged on to that user name. To install the Password List editor:

Open Add/Remove Programs from Control Panel, select Windows Setup and click the Have Disk button.

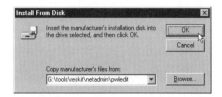

...cont'd

With the password list editor you see the list of resources but not the password itself.

2 Browse to the \Tools\reskit\netadmin\pwledit folder and click OK.

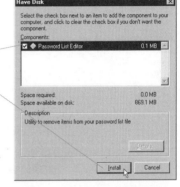

3 Select the Password List editor and click Install.

This will add the utility to the Windows folder and place a shortcut in the System Tools folder in the Start menu.

To run the Password List Editor:

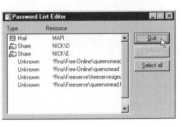

4 Click Start, Programs, Accessories, System Tools, and then click Password List Editor.

You can identify the network resources for which you have either read-only or full password access, but you cannot view the password. If you select an entry and remove it, you will need to enter the password the next time you access that resource.

You can improve the security of your network by limiting the total number of shared folders. By keeping those files that require shared access located in a limited number of folders, you decrease the number of passwords a user has to remember.

Hidden shares are accessed only by users who know the share's name and so can enter it as a path name.

Disable file and print sharing on those computers that do not contain files requiring sharing. This action not only improves security, it also enhances the performance of the computer.

Ending the share name with a dollar sign ($) creates a *hidden share* which cannot be seen by users who are casually browsing your computer across the network.

WinPopup

WinPopup provides a simple method of sending messages across the network.

The network is not just for sharing files and printers. With the network active you can send messages to one PC or to everyone in the workgroup, using the WinPopup utility. You use the same utility to receive messages sent to you from the other PCs on the LAN.

WinPopup is installed automatically with either Microsoft Client for NetWare Networks or Client for Microsoft Networks. It must be running on the target PC when the message is sent, or the message is lost, so it is best to start WinPopup automatically at system startup:

1 Place Winpopup.exe in the Startup folder on each PC that may need to receive messages. To start the program manually, select Win+R, type Winpopup and press Enter.

2 In WinPopup, click Messages, Options to specify choices for how WinPopup will present messages.

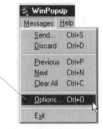

• Play sound on receipt.

• Deselect Stay on top (and minimise the application).

To record the contents of a message in the clipboard, mark up the text, right-click and select Copy. Don't use Ctrl+C - that means Clear All messages.

• Popup on receipt of message.

When a message arrives, the WinPopup window appears over the current application window. You can read your current message, or scroll back and forward through your recent messages, using the arrow buttons. You can Discard messages, but there is no means to save messages, so they will all be lost when you end WinPopup, or shutdown the PC.

You can also use the Net Meeting program to share messages, files and applications across the network.

To send a pop-up message:

1 Select Messages from the WinPopup menu bar, and click Send to display the message creation box.

2 To send a message to a person, click the User or computer option and type the name.

3 To send a message to everyone in the group, click the Workgroup option and type the name.

If the system does not provide a print finished message, perhaps the printer owner can be persuaded to send you that information using WinPopup.

4 Type the text of your message and press OK when you are ready to transmit.

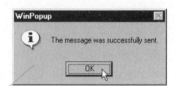

You'll see a response saying that the message has been successfully sent. This does not mean that it has been received or read. Unless WinPopup is running on the target PC or PCs, the message will be lost. You will get no notification of this.

If you are running Netware, and printing to a Netware print server, WinPopup is also used to notify you when printing is complete. There is no notification with the peer-to-peer printer sharing, but you can view the print queue, from the sending PC, the printing PC or from any PC with share access to that particular printer.

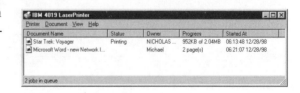

Connecting Two Computers

If there are only two PCs to connect, you do not need a full network setup.

The simplest network consists of two PCs connected to each other. This setup is commonly used in small offices or at home to share a printer or for exchanging files. It is also the setup for connecting a laptop PC to a desktop PC.

Cable

connect

You can buy the required crossover network cable or the file transfer serial or parallel cables, ready configured for use in a two PC network.

There are three connection methods that can be used:

- Coaxial cable and two bus network or combo adapters.

- Crossover twisted-pair cable and two star network adapters.

- Direct Cable Connection using a null modem or parallel port connection cable.

The direct cable connection is slower but uses the existing parallel or serial port. However, with DCC you can connect in to an existing LAN, accessing shared resources on the network from the laptop, through the network adapter of the connected PC.

1 DCC.

2 LAN.

Installing Windows 98

This chapter looks at installing Windows 98 from the CD or from hard disk, and upgrading from Windows 95, Windows 3.1x or MS-DOS systems.

Covers

Chapter Fifteen

Methods of installing

To install Windows 98, you must run the Setup.exe program. There are three ways to start this program, and the method to choose depends on the current configuration of your PC. You can start Setup from:

- Windows 95

- Windows 3.1x (or Windows for Workgroups 3.1x)

- MS-DOS command prompt.

Choose the first option if you are upgrading Windows 95 and you want to retain the existing configuration settings for applications, devices and network connections. This is the quickest and easiest method, and involves the minimum interaction. Most of the information needed for upgrading is taken from your current installation.

If you are upgrading from Window 3.1x, you can start the Setup program from that environment. It will take account of the existing settings and installed applications, and migrate the information into the Windows 98 configuration. There will be more interaction, since you will need to select the Windows 98 components that you want.

If you do not want to pick up any of the settings from your existing Windows environment, you must take the third option and install from MS-DOS. With this method, you will be able to select the installation folder, pick the groups of Windows components, and enter details such as computer name, description and workgroup identifications, and keyboard layout and language support.

If you are planning to install Windows 98 onto a new or reformatted hard disk drive, you must also start Setup from MS-DOS.

You cannot install Windows 98 on a PC running Windows NT or OS/2. However, you can configure the system to dual boot MS-DOS and Windows NT, and run the Windows 98 Setup program from MS-DOS.

New installation

If you buy a new PC with Windows 98, this installation will have been carried out for you by the supplier.

To install Windows 98 onto a new or reformatted hard disk, you must start up the PC using MS-DOS boot disks, or Windows 95 startup disks or the boot disks provided with the Windows 98 upgrade. The following assumes installation from the Windows 98 CD. To begin the setup:

1 Boot the PC from the startup diskette, insert the Windows CD and check that the CD-ROM drive can be accessed.

2 Switch to the CD drive, type Setup, press Enter, then press Enter again for Setup to run routine checks on the system.

Scandisk will find errors, but it does not correct the errors. You will need to fix them using your existing operating system.

3 The MS-DOS version of Scandisk runs, producing a log of the results. Select Exit to continue the setup.

4 Setup initialises your system and copies the files for installing Windows 98 from the CD.

The Windows 98 Setup screen appears. This shows actions and a progress report.

- Information bar

- Five Setup steps

- Time left

- Notes and guidance.

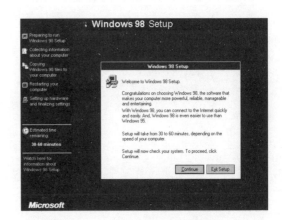

5 Press Continue to run the Setup process.

The setup process

A product key may not be required if you are installing from a LAN server rather than a CD.

In the first stage, Setup prepares the Windows 98 Setup Wizard, displays the Windows 98 Setup screen, creates the Setuplog.txt file in the root of the disk. It identifies the Windows 98 installation drive and the source drive which contains the setup files. It creates a temporary folder called C:\Wininst0.400 and copies Mini.cab, the subset of Windows program files required by Setup. It then extracts all the files in Precopy1.cab and Precopy2.cab to the C:\Wininst0.400 folder. This provides everything needed to run the Setup Wizard.

In the second stage, Setup collects information about your PC, and prepares it for copying the rest of the Windows 98 files.

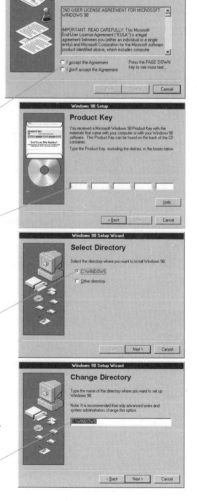

I Read the terms of the Licence Agreement, Page Down to see more, and click here to accept, and press Next.

2 Enter the Product Key to confirm your licence, and press Next to continue.

If possible, stay with the default C:\Windows, since this will match the manuals and avoid confusion.

3 Select the folder for installing Windows 98. If you want a different folder click Other Directory. Press Next.

4 Enter the path for the folder. If it does not currently exist, Setup will create it for you.

You may get a message such as "Disk D: has only 95 MB of free space, You will need 125.5 MB to set up Windows 98". Cancel Setup, clear space on the drive and restart setup.

After you have accepted or selected a folder, Setup checks for installed components and makes sure that there is enough space on the hard disk to install Windows. Then it creates the Windows 98 folder and all the required subfolders.

5 Press Next to see the list of four predefined setup configuration options provided.

Each option includes a set of components chosen to match common situations.

Whichever you choose, if you later want a component that wasn't installed, you can easily add it.

- Most users select this option.

- Users with laptops will need this for the extra comms items.

- For a low disk capacity PC, choose the smallest possible installation of Windows 98.

- Custom allows you to choose exactly which components are installed.

6 Select the option you want, and press Next, and enter your name and company details.

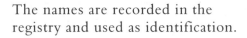

You must enter a Name, but Company is optional.

The names are recorded in the registry and used as identification.

7 You have the chance to amend your predefined components.

Select components

This screen is also displayed when you select the Custom option.

If you selected to Install the most common components, Setup continues the installation. If you selected 'Show me the list of components so I can choose', the Select Components screen is displayed.

To choose which components are installed:

1 Select a component set and click Details.

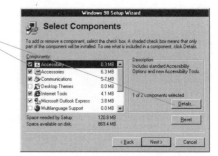

2 Select the individual components, or clear the box for items you don't want, and then click OK.

A shaded box means that only some of the components in the set have been selected.

3 Review the components in each of the categories to make any required changes to the selections.

4 Press Next when you have completed the selection.

Your choice of components will affect the total amount of disk space that Windows 98 requires. This can be much higher than the space used in Windows 95. If you compare the typical option with the custom option with the full set of components selected, the disk space needed is:

You can add or remove any of the components after installation, using the Add/ Remove Programs option in Control Panel.

Chosen Components	Windows 95	Windows 98
Typical Components	64.9 MB	202.1 MB
All Components	101.4 MB	347.0 MB
Typical installed System	88.8 MB	260.0 MB
Backup system files	-	32.0 MB

This table also shows the space required for the installed system, and for the backup operating files if requested.

Identification

The default names suggested are based on your name and company as entered for registration.

When you have selected the components to install, Setup asks you to provide identifications for your PC. These will be used for network or direct cable connection. There are three fields required:

- Computer Name is a unique name on the network. It is up to 15 characters, with no blanks, with alphanumeric characters and some special characters.

- Workgroup name follows the same naming rules as the computer name, and groups PCs to make it more efficient to share information. On a network, it is usually assigned by your network administrator.

- Computer description can be up to 48 characters long, but without commas. It appears as a comment next to the computer name when users browse the network. Typically, it includes department or location details.

Enter valid computer name, workgroup name and computer description details and press Next to continue.

If you plan to share information or devices with another PC, it will be easier if you enter the same name for the Workgroup.

You must also provide your geographical location. This is used during setup to set the region-specific options such as keyboard layout, date and currency format and numbers format. The setting will also be used when you connect to the Internet, to help you obtain the appropriate news, weather and other information from channels and other information Web sites.

2 Select the country or region, for example United Kingdom, and press Next to continue.

The default region is USA, so if you miss out this step you will have problems with your keyboard layout and currency signs.

Startup disk

Setup encourages you to create a Windows 98 Startup Disk, and considers it so important that there is no option to refuse offered at this point. The Startup disk is a bootable system disk which includes a set of MS-DOS mode commands and utilities. It can be used to restart your PC in the event of problems in starting Windows 98, or you can use its diagnostic programs. You probably need several copies of the Startup disks, just in case the disk proves faulty when you do need to use it. You can make more Startup disks after setup, using the Add/Remove Programs option in Control Panel.

You need one 1.44 MB floppy disk or two 1.2 MB floppy disks.

To make the Startup disk during setup:

1. Click Next so that Setup will start copying the required data.

2. Label the disk as Windows 98 Startup and insert it into the diskette drive.

You must let Setup read the first 20% of the data, even if you already have enough copies of the Startup disk. Press Cancel when the Insert Disk message appears.

3. When the Insert Disk message appears, click OK to create the disk.

4. When copying completes, remove the diskette and click OK to continue Setup.

The Startup disk includes a real-mode generic ATAPI driver for IDE CD-ROM drives. Several SCSI drivers are also included on the disk. If these cannot access your CD-ROM when you boot from the Startup disk, you will need to add the device driver supplied with your drive to the Config.sys.

Start Copying Files

│ Click Next to start copying files.

This is the third stage of Setup, which requires no action on your part. Setup begins copying all the Windows 98 files to the folders it has created on your hard disk. You should not interrupt the file copying. If Setup is interrupted during the file-copying phase, Windows 98 may not run when you restart your computer because not all of the necessary files will have been copied. If the copying does get interrupted, you should run Setup from the beginning.

If you started Setup over a network, or from a compact disc, or from a removable hard drive, Setup will also copy the required driver .inf files to access the installation source so that Setup can continue when your PC is restarted.

After Setup finishes copying the Windows 98 files to your hard disk, the fourth stage, restarting your computer, takes place. You are prompted to remove diskettes, if there is a diskette in the drive. Then you receive a message that your PC will be restarted in 15 seconds. You can press the Restart Now button to restart immediately, but Setup will anyway restart automatically.

When the system restarts, the Windows 98 logo displays with the message "Getting ready to start Windows 98 for the first time", and the final stage begins.

Setting up hardware

During this final stage, Setup configures the Control Panel, the programs on the Start menu, Windows Help, MS-DOS program settings, tuning up for application loading, time zone settings and the final system configuration. It may restart the PC once or twice as it detects the attached hardware. There is usually just one action for you to perform.

Since countries may have several time zones, Setup doesn't use your region settings to select the time zone.

Select the time zone for your region.

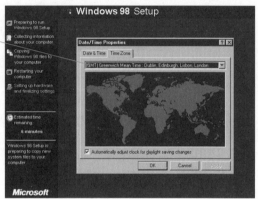

When Setup finishes setting up hardware and configuring settings, it restarts the PC for the final time and asks you to log on. If your PC is connected to the network, you may be asked for a domain name and a network password. After you log on, Setup builds a driver information database, updates system settings and sets up personalised settings such as the settings for Internet Explorer browsing and the Start menu. Then Setup displays the Welcome to Windows 98 screen and you can start using your new system in earnest.

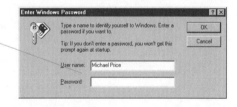

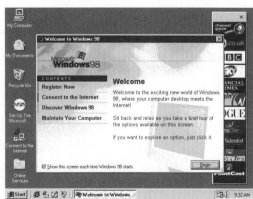

Setup from Windows 95

To speed up the installation, Setup skips the setup choices (Typical, Portable, Compact and Custom). It also skips full hardware detection and configuration, but it does verify the non-plug and play hardware registry settings.

If you have Windows 95 installed on your PC, and you want to upgrade to Windows 98, without changing settings, you start Setup from the Windows 95 user interface. You also use this method when you want to refresh your installed Windows 98 system, or upgrade it with a version at a higher service level. To change the current settings, you should start Setup from MS-DOS as described earlier (starting on page 298).

Setup will replicate the existing set of components and utilities. You can revise the selection after setting up Windows 98, using the Add/Remove Programs in Control Panel.

To start Setup:

1 Insert the Windows 98 CD. Setup starts, and detects that Windows needs upgrading. Press Yes to upgrade.

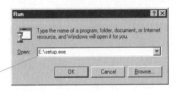

2 If AutoRun is not active, or if you are planning to reinstall Windows 98, select Start, Run, and type E:Setup,exe (where E: is the drive letter for your CD).

The Windows 98 Setup screen appears. This screen is somewhat more graphical in appearance, but contains the same messages and the same stages as the equivalent screen shown when you start Setup from MS-DOS.

From Win95 – stages 1 to 3

In stage one. Setup checks your system and prepares Setup Wizard.

Setup creates the Setuplog.txt file in the root folder and then checks to see if you are running antivirus software that protects the master boot record. If so, Setup asks you to disable the anti-virus software before continuing since it will modify this as part of the installation. You are recommended to close all active Windows applications.

1 Press Alt + Tab to select an application.

2 Save any work in process, and close the application.

3 Repeat for any other active application, then press OK.

In stage two, Setup collects information about your system.

Setup creates C:\Wininst0.400 temporary folder and copies Mini.cab, and extracts the Precopy1.cab and Precopy2.cab files. To continue:

4 Accept the Licence Agreement and press Next.

5 Enter the Product Key and press next. If you make a typing error, you can correct the mistake, without having to retype the correct parts of the code.

Setup runs the protected-mode version of ScanDisk to correct any file system errors. You won't see any Scandisk screens unless an error is found. Setup then checks registry for corruption. If an error is found, Setup prompts you to reboot your computer and run ScanReg in MS-DOS mode.

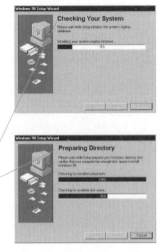

Setup creates the subfolders for Windows 98, making sure that there is enough room on the drive. You cannot choose the Windows folder or drive, since it uses the existing folder.

If you select No, you will not be able to uninstall Windows 98. This is the choice to make when you are simply reinstalling Windows 98.

Setup offers to save your existing Windows 95 system files:

5 Click Yes and press Next to save the current system files in case you need to undo the installation.

Setup locates the files and saves them to Winundo.dat and Winundo.ini, which may take up to 50 MB. They are saved in the root folder unless you have more than one drive, when it lets you choose the drive and folder for the backup.

Setup doesn't ask for computer or workgroup names, it uses the existing values. However, it does ask for the geographical location:

6 Check that the correct country or region is selected and press Next.

Still in stage two, Setup encourages you to create a startup disk.

| Click Next for the Startup disk, whether or not you want one.

The first 20% of the disk contents are read, and then Setup prompts you to insert a diskette.

2 Label the diskette and insert it into the drive, and press OK to create the disk.

In stage three Setup copies Windows 98 files to the hard disk.

3 Just press Cancel if you don't want to create a disk at this time.

4 Click OK and remove the diskette if one was inserted.

5 Click Next to allow Setup to start to copy the Windows 98 files.

Do not interrupt the file copying.

Stage three takes place completely automatically, but you see various informational messages. It shows the time remaining and the progress bar tells you how much copying has been done.

When the files are copied, Setup restarts your PC.

From Win95 – stages 4 and 5

Stage five sets up the hardware, the system and the application settings.

When Setup has copied the Windows 98 files, you are reminded to remove the diskette, if there is still one in the drive, and then you see the 15 second count down to restart. When the system restarts, you see the Windows 98 logo with the "Getting ready to start Windows 98 for the first time" message.

In stage five, Setup modifies the Win.ini, System.ini, and registry files to add the Windows 98-specific settings. It reviews the Autoexec.bat and Config.sys files searching for any incompatible device drivers or TSR (terminate-and-stay-resident) programs, and comments out, using the REM command, any incompatible or unnecessary entries from these files.

The list of incompatible entries is in Setupc.inf file which is in the hidden folder \Windows\Inf. If you find that one of your programs or hardware devices does not run correctly after setting up Windows 98, it may require you to restore entries in Config.sys or Autoexec.bat file, by removing the REM prefix.

Setup will pick up your time zone settings, and your sign-on details and may bypass logon if you had not set a password on your previous system.

Setup detects the hardware you have installed on your computer and configures the Control Panel, Start menu etc.

Setup detects only Plug and Play devices, retaining the existing non-plug and play settings, printer and messaging settings. If you need to add a non-plug and play device, it is best to do this after upgrading, using the Add New Hardware from Control Panel.

When Setup finishes setting up hardware and configuring settings, it restarts your computer and asks you to log on. If your computer is connected to the network, you may be asked for a domain name and a network password. After you log on, Setup builds a driver information database, updates system settings, and sets up personalised settings for Internet Explorer and the Start menu etc., then displays the Welcome screen, ready for you to register your copy of Windows 98.

From Windows 3.1x

You can upgrade to Windows 98 from windows 3.1x, running the setup program from within the Windows 3.1x environment to retain the settings for the hardware and for the installed Windows applications.

Setup from Windows 3.1x is a blend of the two processes already discussed.

| Insert the Windows 98 CD, select File, Run from the Program Manager, type E:\setup.exe and press Enter.

The Windows 98 setup screen is displayed, and Setup proceeds through the same five stages as setup from Windows 95.

- Preparing to run Windows 98 Setup.

- Collecting information about your PC.

- Copying Windows 98 files to your PC.

- Restarting your PC.

Setup from MS-DOS if you want to avoid using the existing settings altogether.

- Setting up hardware and finalizing settings.

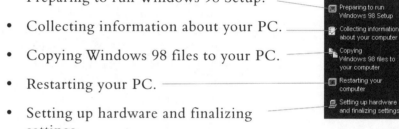

However, with this method, you are given the opportunity to change the target folder for Windows 98. Note that if you choose to install Windows 98 in a new directory, you must reinstall any Windows applications that you want to run under Windows 98.

Setup also offers you a choice of the type of Setup that you want, from the four setup options (typical, portable, compact and custom) as described for setup from MS-DOS.

You can review and revise the selected components during Setup, or later using Add/Remove Programs from control Panel.

The remaining stages follow the pattern for the setup from Windows 95, which ends as usual with starting Windows 98 for the first time, and then displaying the Welcome screen, for you to register, and to view the Windows 98 tutorials.

Contents of startup disk

The Windows 98 startup disk is quite different from the startup disk that was created for Windows 95. It contains the following new functions:

It is worth getting to know the contents of your startup disk so you know how to use it to advantage in an emergency.

```
Microsoft Windows 98 Startup menu

1. Start computer with CD-ROM support.
2. Start computer without CD-ROM support.
3. View the help file.

Enter a choice:1          Time remaining: 29

F5=Safe mode   Shift+F5=Command prompt   Shift+F8=Step-by-step configrmation [N]
```

- Multi-config start menu for booting with or without access to the CD-ROM drive.

- Real-mode IDE CD-ROM support for PCs with an ATAPI IDE CD-ROM drive.

- Real-mode SCSI CD-ROM support for PCs with SCSI CD-ROM drives.

If you skip the Create Startup Disk in Setup, you can create disks later, but you'll need the Windows 98 CD, and the files will not be copied to the hard disk.

- The compressed Edb.cab file with Windows 98 utilities.

- A RAMdrive definition to provide space for the expanded utilities.

- A new extract command (Ext.exe) to extract and expand files from a compressed Cab file.

The files used to create the Startup disk during setup are copied to the \Windows\Command folder for later use.

The startup disk

This contains various CD-ROM device drivers, system startup files, the Edb.cab compressed file, and Windows 98 commands and utilities such as Fdisk.exe, Mode.com, Ramdrive.sys and Sys.com.

The RAMdrive will be assigned the drive letter usually allocated to the CD-ROM, which will be moved on to the next letter.

The Edb.cab file

This is a compressed file which is expanded during startup from diskette into the RAMdrive. The files include the utilities Attrib.exe, Chkdsk.exe, Debug.exe, Edit.com, Ext.exe, Format.com, Help.bat, Mscdex.exe, Restart.com, Scandisk.exe, Sys.com and Uninstal.exe.

Setup from hard disk

Make sure that you have 120 MB disk space in addition to the normal Setup requirements *(typically 195 MB).*

If you have a laptop PC that uses the same disk bay for the diskette drive and the CD-ROM drive, installing from CD can be difficult. One answer is to copy all the setup files to your hard disk before running Setup. This has the additional benefit of speeding up the process. Having the Windows 98 Setup files always available also means you don't have to access the CD when you make changes to the configuration.

To setup from hard disk:

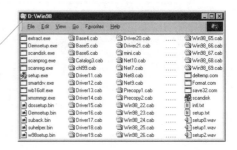

1 Create a storage folder on the hard drive, named for example \Win98.

Add the drive letter if the setup folder is not on the C: drive, e.g. put D:\win98\Setup.exe.

2 Copy all the files in the \Win98 folder on the Windows 98 CD-ROM to the \Win98 folder on the hard disk. You do not need to copy subfolders from the CD folder.

3 Run Setup.exe from Windows 95, Windows 3.1x or MS-DOS as described previously, but specify \win98\setup.exe for the setup program.

Setup proceeds as described for setup from CD-ROM, though it may run faster, depending on the speed difference between hard disk and CD-ROM drive.

When it completes, the source for Windows 98 installation files will be recorded in the registry as the Win98 folder on the hard drive. This allows you to make configuration changes, or add and remove components.

If you install a new device and need files from the Drivers folder, you will have to change the pre-selected address for the installation files.

Plus! 98

This chapter discusses the setup and use of Plus! 98, which makes the PC more efficient and fun to use, with tools, games and desktop themes.

Covers

Chapter Sixteen

Features of Plus! 98

An extra cost add-on with a variety of options, some very useful and some just for fun.

The product, which is a separately purchased component to complement Windows 98, offers the following system utilities, new desktop themes, and computer games:

- **Compressed Folders** save hard disk space by compressing a group of files and folders but allowing them to be processed as if the collection was a normal folder

This is not a replacement for Plus! 95, which has mostly been included into Windows 98.

- **Deluxe CD Player** works with the Internet to access information about the songs and artist on the audio CD being played.

- **Desktop Themes** customises the desktop with various styles including Garfield, and Science Fiction.

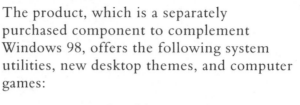

The File Cleaner and Start Menu Cleaner are also referenced by the names of the Windows 98 products that they are designed to enhance i.e. Disk Cleaner and Maintenance Wizard.

- **File Cleaner** extends the Disk Cleaner facilities provided for hard drives in Windows 98.

- **Golf 1998 Lite** offers 9-hole play on an attractive PC golf course.

- **Lose Your Marbles** is a SegaSoft computer game of skill.

- **Start Menu Cleaner** adds functions to the Windows 98 Maintenance Wizard to organise the Start Menu.

- **McAfee VirusScan** software protects your PC system from viruses, and includes six months of updates.

- **Organic Art** provides yet more animated, 3-D screen savers to add to the Windows 98 and the Desktop Themes collections.

These provide sets of wallpaper, cursors, sounds and 3-D screen savers built around a particular topic.

- **Picture It! Express** manipulates and converts images.

- **Spider Solitaire** is an addictive two-deck version of solitaire.

System requirements

Plus! 98 is not advised for Intel 486 PCs.

For the Plus! 98 package Microsoft recommends a higher specification than the base Windows 98 system (see page 14). You should have:

- PC with **Pentium 90** or higher processor.

- **Windows 98** (it won't run on earlier versions of Windows).

- **CD-ROM** or **DVD** drive.

- **16 MB of RAM**: more memory improves performance.

- **100-150 MB** of available hard disk space.

- A **Microsoft mouse** or compatible pointing device.

- **VGA or higher** resolution monitor and video card.

Some features have additional requirements:

- A **16-bit sound board** and speakers or headphones.

- **14,400 baud modem** for Internet connection.

- **Access to the Internet** via an ISP.

Let Windows 98 manage the swap file virtual storage to minimise conflicts, when you are short of disk space.

Some components have greater requirements. For example, the Golf game requires at least a quad speed CD-ROM drive, and a monitor and adapter that is at least SVGA (800 x 600 pixels) and 16-bit hi-colour.

You will find that Microsoft understates the hard disk requirements. Plus! 98 Setup calls for 203 MB when you select all components (the default). Even then, you may find problems. Plus! 98 checks that there is enough space free on your hard disk, but problems can arise if space is unexpectedly used up during installation, for example by increases in the Windows 98 swap file.

To avoid such problems, free extra disk space before starting Setup, or choose the Custom Setup and install the components in several sessions.

Installation

As you'd expect, this product is fully compliant with the Windows 98 guidelines. It uses AutoRun, installs all its folders in a Plus! folder within Program Files, and provides Uninstall and Add/Remove facilities. To install Plus! 98.

I Insert the Plus! 98 CD while Windows 98 is active.

Insert the CD, and double-click the CD icon, if you have turned AutoRun off.

2 The AutoRun screen appears. You can select Browse the CD or Install Plus! 98.

3 Select Browse if you want to see how AutoRun works, and open the AutoRun.inf file.

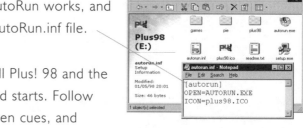

4 Select Install Plus! 98 and the setup wizard starts. Follow the on-screen cues, and supply your name and CD key when requested.

Skip the virus scan offered during setup, if your PC is trouble free.

5 Two Setup Options are offered – Complete to install everything, and Custom to select particular items.

Microsoft suggests the Complete setup, but you can start with a few, and add items at any time.

6 Click Custom to select the items.

There are full versions of Picture It, Golf and Marbles available.

You may have a full version of one of the Plus! 98 items already installed on your system. In that situation, Setup does not select the version on the CD.

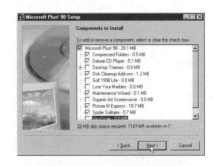

As you select or clear items, the total disk space required is adjusted. The space available value helps you determine if there is a potential problem with disk space.

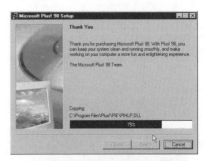

7 When you have completed your selection, press Next then follow the prompts to start copying the files.

8 When all the files are copied, Setup modifies the system settings.

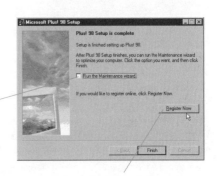

At this point, you can choose whether you want to run the Maintenance wizard, or leave this task until later.

If you are linked to the Internet, or ready to sign on, you can select Register Now to provide your contact details and receive details of any future updates.

When you press Finish, the Setup is completed. You will need to restart the PC if you have installed the Antivirus software, to activate its functions.

Add/Remove Programs

The Golf option only appears if you have already installed this program. It uses the CD for the course scenes.

The next time you insert the Plus! 98 CD and allow the AutoRun program to start up, you will find a different set of options displayed. To make changes to the setup:

1 Select the Add/Remove Programs option to start Setup. The CD key will not be needed.

2 You can Reinstall to replace missing or damaged files, Uninstall to remove components, or Add/Remove to review selections.

Hold the pointer over an item to get a brief description.

3 Select Add/Remove and the list of installed components is displayed. Clear the box to remove an item, or select a box to add an item.

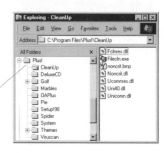

The Disk Cleanup and the Maintenance Wizard shortcuts also appear in the System Tools folder (complete with the Plus! 98 enhancements).

4 Setup proceeds as before, copying or deleting files as appropriate.

You will find all the Plus! 98 programs in subfolders under the \Program Files\Plus!.

The shortcuts are similarly organised, with most of the entries contained in the main Plus! folder, but with separate folders for the Antivirus and the Games shortcuts.

Compressed Folders

You can compress files to transfer them to another drive as backups, or you can keep the compressed folders on the hard drive and delete the original to save space.

There's no Start menu entry for Compressed folders, and no evident program or help file support, but Plus! 98 integrates the compressed folder technology into Windows 98. The change appears as new entries in the context menus for files and folders. To create a compressed folder:

1 Right-click one of the files that will belong to the compressed folder, and select Send To, Compressed Folder.

2 The contents of the file are copied and compressed and a new file is created.

The new file has the same name as the original, but displays a special compressed folder icon. If you have file extensions displayed, you will see that it is type ZIP, and if you switch to the details view, you'll see that it is much smaller.

The compressed folder opens into a new window with no Up button, but otherwise just like any other folder.

You can rename the compressed folder, or move it anywhere on the disk, without affecting the content

3 Double-click the compressed folder to open it, and reveal what appears to be the original file.

Any changes that you make will be lost, even if you save under new file name, unless you also change folders.

You can view or copy this file but you cannot change it since it is expanded as a read-only file in a temporary folder.

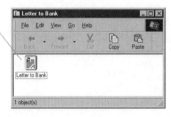

Adding compressed files

Treat the compressed folder as if it is a separate device, rather than a folder.

You can add files to the compressed folder by simply dragging and dropping them onto the ZIP file. They are copied rather than moved.

If you want a compressed version of a whole folder, including any subfolders:

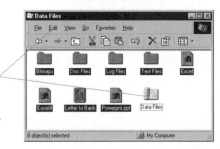

1 Open the folder and right-click an empty area, then select New, Compressed Folder.

2 Rename the new, empty compressed folder.

3 Click Edit from the menu bar, and Select All, then press Ctrl and click the new compressed folder to deselect it.

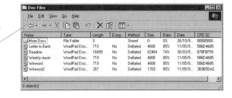

Select View, details to see the compression ratio achieved for the files in the compressed folders. There's also a CRC check number which is used to confirm the integrity of the file.

4 Click and drag the selected files and folders and drop them onto the compressed folder. The files and folder hierarchy will be copied and compressed.

5 Double-click the compressed folder to open it. It will appear like the original, and you can open subfolders by double-clicking them, and navigate the folder levels using the forward and back arrows.

Deluxe CD Player

This replaces the standard CD player from windows 98 and integrates your music with the Internet. To play a CD:

1   Insert the CD. If it is a first time for that CD, click OK to collect details about the disc from the Internet.

If you are not already connected, the sign-on panel for your ISP will be displayed.

2   After a few seconds, the disc and track titles appear on the Player display.

3   Click the Track button to display the list of track titles and duration times.

When the details for a CD have been collected, Deluxe Player remembers them and they will be displayed every time you play that CD, without you needing to connect to the Internet.

You can link to the Internet to find out more about the artist or about similar albums.

4   Click the Internet button to see the options, e.g. More About the artists.

5   The Web site will offer a variety of functions such as sample tracks that you can play on-line.

Desktop Themes

Themes let you change the desktop settings at one place rather than in several, such as Mouse, Display Properties and Sounds.

Desktop themes are a matter of personal preference. Some users like to stay with the bare essentials, an approach that's highly recommended if you have a low power PC or if you have several applications running simultaneously. If you do enjoy themes and have the capacity to spare than Plus! 98 offers a wide range. To select your own favourite:

1 Choose Desktop Themes from the Plus! 98 folder in the Start menu.

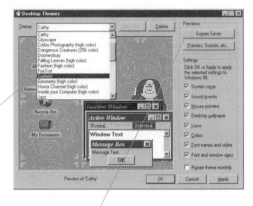

You can also start Desktop Themes from within the Control Panel.

2 Click in the Theme box to select the theme and preview the desktop image.

Many of the Themes require Active Desktop or 16-bit high-colour, sometimes both.

3 Click the Screen Saver or Pointers and Sounds buttons to preview these aspects.

4 Choose which features (e.g. Sounds, Icons, Colours), and press OK.

Click Rotate Themes Monthly to set up regular change using the task scheduler.

5 To reset the desktop and remove the effects, select Desktop Themes, choose Windows Default and then press OK.

Disk Cleaner

This disk cleaner is not automatic like the others, but provides a list of candidate files for you to choose from.

Plus! 98 adds a fifth element to the Windows 98 Disk Cleanup, the Non-critical File Cleanup program from CyberMedia. This will scan your hard drive for groups of files in various categories that are seldom used or just plain invalid, e.g. lost clusters, zero-byte files, or screen savers and help files, and estimates the likelihood that you can safely delete them:

| Run Disk Cleanup from the Plus! folder or the System Tools folder in the Start menu.

2 Select the drive, press OK, click the Non-Critical files box to activate the process and then click OK.

No files are deleted unless you explicitly pick them.

3 Select Yes to confirm the action, and File Cleaner builds a database of files.

4 The colour code list of files on the drive indicate which are likely to be unnecessary.

Red files are essential, Yellow files are important and Green files may be removed, unless you think they are needed. If in doubt, don't delete.

5 Browse the list and click on the files you do not need. Select File, Delete to remove the selected files.

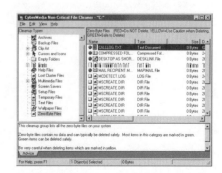

Golf 1998 Lite

If you have only 16 MB of RAM, you can speed up the game by closing all other applications and switching off the Sounds, Shadows and Commentary in Game Preferences.

Golf 1998 Lite needs a higher spec system than Windows 98 or the other Plus! 98 features, in particular calling for a 4x speed CD-ROM drive and a 60 MB swap file. Your computer monitor must be able to support 800 x 600 resolution and 16-bit colour even if you don't normally use those settings for Windows.

During the game, it runs full screen in 800 x 600 display resolution and 16-bit colour, switching modes if necessary. You should avoid changing applications using Alt+Tab while the game is running, or you may encounter video problems.

Before starting Golf, it is recommended that you close other programs, especially network or e-mail programs such as Outlook. To run the game:

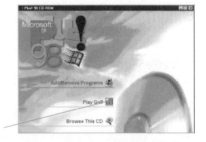

1 Select Golf from the Plus! 98 Games folder in the Start menu, or insert the CD and select Play Golf.

2 There's no information on Golf in the Plus! 98 user guide, since it was a late addition to the package, but clicking the ? button or pressing F1 will display the Player's Guide help manual.

3 Select Options, game preferences to make any required changes to the sound and video parameters, especially on low-spec PCs (see note above).

...cont'd

The first time you play, it creates a player and uses default settings. If you've played before, it uses your most recent settings.

4 Select New Round to pick a course and holes, and to change players and set the weather conditions.

5 Press Quick Start to begin a new game. Each hole starts with a video showing you the layout and the hazards you can expect.

6 When you play a stroke, you get full details of your action and the results, complete with patronising commentary – just like real golf.

7 Press Menu for the options list, to end a game or to reference the manual.

Multiplayer mode via a modem, LAN or Internet is also available in the full version only.

There are two player models and one course in the Lite version. The full product has ten models and four courses.

When you select the Preview button on the start up screen, it connects to the Golf Web site where you can find details of the full version and background details on the golf courses used in the game.

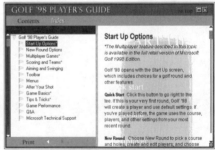

Lose Your Marbles Lite!

A fast, noisy and exciting game in the Tetris category.

The aim of the game is to keep your area as clear as possible, and make your opponent (the computer in this version of the game) fill up his area.

1 Start the game from the Plus! folder and select skill level one to start with.

You can use the mouse but you will find it quicker with the keyboard.

2 The left and right arrow keys move the ring cursor to select a column.

3 The up and down arrow keys slide the selected column, unless it is full in the direction you choose.

Make combos by setting the marbles up so that the new marbles form another group when the first set is removed.

4 The spacebar rotates the centre row to the right, to help you set up groups.

5 To clear the marbles, you have to match three or more in the centre row.

Plus! 98 has the Lite version. The full version has two player mode, works over a LAN, and has bonus marbles and extra levels.

You improve your chances if you transfer marbles to your opponent. The current storage colour is shown to the right of your board. Remove marbles that match that colour to add marbles to your store. Then remove a row of 5 marbles to dump all the stored marbles on your opponent's board.

You win when the computer opponent has no more moves. You lose if your playing area fills with marbles and you have no more moves.

Maintenance Wizard

Plus! 98 adds a new option to the Windows 98 Maintenance Wizard, to perform cleanup on the Start menu.

To add the Start Menu Cleanup to the Maintenance Wizard scheduled task:

I. Select Maintenance Wizard from the Plus! 98 folder or the System Tools folder in the Start menu and choose Change my maintenance schedule.

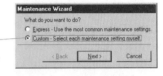

2. Accept Custom to adjust the schedule, rather than accept the defaults, so that you can choose to cleanup the Start menu.

Broken items are shortcuts for which the original program has been moved or deleted.

3. Pick the cleanup options to be applied (remove broken items, reduce levels, remove empty folders) and press OK.

4. The Cleanup option, and any other tasks chosen, are added to Scheduled Tasks.

5. When the task schedule time arrives (or whenever you select to run the job immediately), the Start menu is adjusted as appropriate. For example, the extra level introduced by the Ulead utility is detected and suggested for removal.

The task will run on the schedule selected, and each time you are given the opportunity to review the changes proposed and approve or reject them as you desire.

McAfee VirusScan

You can download a trial version of the McAfee software from the Internet, if you don't have Plus! 98.

Computer viruses are a fact of life, but Microsoft has still chosen not to include any protection from them in the standard Windows 98 package, despite its concentration on Internet access. Plus! 98 does address this issue by including a copy of VirusScan, the McAfee Antivirus product from Network Associates.

VirusScan is a toolkit containing a set of utilities to handle the variety of tasks involved:

- Create a VirusScan emergency disk to start the PC in the event of hard drive problems.

- Scan the hard disk for viruses while the PC is idle (while your screen saver is active).

- Revise VirusScan properties.

- Scan for viruses on demand, in selected files, folders or disks (especially removable ones such as diskettes and Zip disks).

- Revise Vshield properties.

- Scan for viruses on file access and at startup and shutdown.

Vshield is included at Startup and appears as an icon in the system tray. You can also schedule regular disk scans using the Maintenance wizard.

To keep your system safe, you need to update the virus signature files that are used to recognise viruses. The first six months come free with the Plus! 98 package.

...cont'd

When you receive a diskette, or when you download a file from the Internet, Scan to check that there are no infections. To scan a file, folder or disk:

1 Run VirusScan from the Plus! 98 McAfee folder in the Start menu.

VirusScan will carry out a memory scan every time it is started, to make sure that there are no viruses active.

2 Click the types of files to scan, and whether you want to look at subfolders and compressed files.

3 Select Browse to choose the file, folder or drive to scan e.g. the floppy drive.

4 Click Scan Now to scan the selected drive or folder, and any infected files detected will be listed.

VirusScan can repair the damage.

The Help file provides you with information on the actions needed, in the chapter "Respond to a Virus".

You can also Scan a folder or an executable file by right-clicking its icon or a shortcut to it, and then selecting Scan for Viruses. You will start VirusScan, with the file or folder entered, ready for you to press the Scan Now button to complete the task.

Organic Art

1 Select Organic Art from the Plus! 98 folder in Start menu, to open Display Properties at the Screen Saver tab.

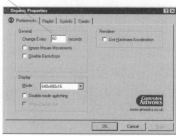

2 Set the delay time, and press Settings to change the time between scene changes or to tailor the playlist.

Problems with 3-D screen savers may apply with Desktop Themes, Organic Art or any other 3-D screen saver.

Take Power Management settings into account when you set the delay. If it is greater than the time after which the monitor powers down, you won't be able to awaken the monitor until the screen saver starts up.

This can cause the PC to lock up.

Avoid having a 3-D screen saver start while you are switched to an MS-DOS full screen session.

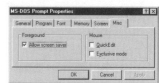

3 Select MS-DOS Properties, Misc, and clear the Allow Screen Saver in Foreground box.

This screen is 2001, one of the many animated 3-D scenes available.

Picture It! Express

This product allows you to manipulate and enhance images such as photos captured by a digital camera or scanner.

1 Select Picture It! Express from the Plus! Folder in the Start menu.

2 Select File, Open and locate an image to process.

3 Drag the image onto the film strip to open it.

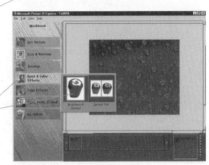

4 Select Paint & colour Effects and then choose Brightness and Contrast.

5 Click Smart Task Fix to let the program recommend the settings.

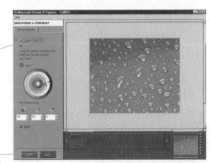

6 Press Done when you are satisfied and then Save, Print & Send.

Picture It! uses its own MIX format, and you should retain this format until you are sure no more changes will be needed. Use standard formats like TIFF or BMP to exchange images.

Spider Solitaire

The objective in Spider Solitaire is to remove all 104 cards (two decks) from the playing area.

At the start of a new game, 54 cards are dealt in ten columns, with the last card on each face up. Move cards until you have lined up a whole suit in order, King to Ace. These are removed, and you continue until all eight sets are removed. To run Spider Solitaire:

1 Select the game from the Plus! 98 Games folder in the Start menu.

The status bar tells you how many rows you have remaining to deal.

2 Click a card and from the bottom of a column and drag it to a free space or onto a card one higher, regardless of suit or colour, on another column.

If you play Spider Solitaire on a multiple monitor system and win a game, the winning sequence runs only when the game is played on the primary monitor.

3 Move a set of cards that are all of the same suit and in order, as if they were one card.

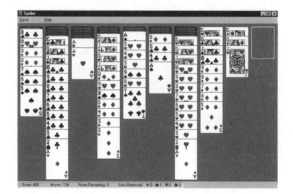

Note that not every game of Spider Solitaire is winnable.

4 When there are no more legal moves to make, click Deal, and the next row of cards is laid. Always check Show An Available Move before you deal.

5 You can Undo a move, but you cannot Undo a deal. You can Save a game and reload it later.

Performance tuning

While Windows 98 provides default settings or self-tuning for system operation, there are tools to allow you to assess the performance for yourself and make changes to improve the speed and responsiveness of your system.

Covers

Chapter Seventeen

Managing resources

Windows 98 is self-checking and self-tuning, to reduce the need for you to adjust the system settings.

Windows 98 is inherently designed for improved performance, since it uses 32-bit device drivers for system components, to take full advantage of the capabilities of the Pentium processor. For example, using 32-bit disk and file drivers allows Windows 98 to bypass the slower system BIOS I/O functions and process in protected mode rather than in real mode. There are a number of functions included to improve performance and resource management such as application launch acceleration, quicker system shutdown and support for ACPI system BIOS features such as OnNow, quiet boot and fast boot.

Windows 98 functions also apply dynamic adjustments to system settings. For example, it uses dynamic sizes for the virtual memory swap file, and for the file, network and CD-ROM caches. These automatically expand or shrink, based on demand for memory from applications and taking account of the current amount of memory physically installed. This means that no adjustments are required when you change the applications installed or when you upgrade the system memory.

Where changes may be needed, Windows 98 provides tools such as the Maintenance Wizard which is used to schedule performance-improving tasks, such as disk defragmentation and disk cleanup, so removing the responsibility from the user to the system.

The system also incorporates self checking mechanisms. For example, the Registry Checker automatically scans the registry for inconsistencies, restoring a previous backup or applying the necessary repairs to the registry if problems are found.

Although the system is designed as far as possible to maintain itself in tune, there are tools provided and others tools separately available that allow you to assess system performance, and if appropriate to apply your own settings and adjustments. Windows 98 can also detect when the device drivers and other components are not providing optimal performance and alert you to the problem.

The majority of program hangs and system crashes in earlier versions of Windows were due to problems in this area: applications failed to find or to release resources, and the system itself was unable to respond due to that very same lack.

The management of system resources is the single most critical aspect of Windows operations. Windows 98 is much more effective at deducing when an application that owned resources no longer needs them. This allows it to clean up orphan resources and reallocate them for use elsewhere in the system. In addition, Windows 98 provides a significant increase in the amount of system resources available to Windows and MS-DOS applications, compared to earlier versions of Windows. Many data structures were moved from the 16-bit GDI (graphics device interface) and User heaps into 32-bit heaps, leaving more room for the remaining data elements.

The table shows the differences in the system limits between Windows 98 and Windows 3.1.

System Resource	Windows 3.1	Windows 98
Windows Menu handles	~299	32 KB
Timers	32	Unlimited
COM and LPT ports	4 per type	Unlimited
Items per list box	8 KB	32 KB
Data per list box	64 KB	Unlimited
Data per edit control	64 KB	Unlimited
Regions	All in 64 KB segment	Unlimited
Physical pens and brushes	All in 64 KB segment	Unlimited
Logical pens and brushes	All in 64 KB segment	All in 64 KB segment
Logical fonts	All in 64 KB segment	750 - 800
Installed fonts	250 - 300 (best case)	1000
Device contexts	200 (best case)	16 KB

The result is that you can rely on more system resources being available for creating windows, using fonts, running more applications simultaneously, or taking advantage of the resource-intensive desktop effects.

Performance report

When you create a new Windows 98 system, or when you install new items of hardware or software (especially items that predate Windows 98 and so may be less than 100% compatible), you should check to see that the system has been set up in an optimal manner. To see if there is any report of performance problems:

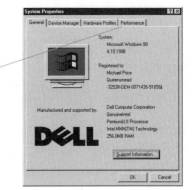

| Click Win+Pause/Break to open System Properties and select the Performance tab.

Windows 98 reports the current performance status of your system:

2 System Resources available – should be 90%+ if you have just started up.

3 File system, and virtual memory type – both should be 32-bit.

4 Performance status report.

If you are using a 16-bit real-mode driver, Windows 98 may switch the file system or the virtual memory to MS-DOS compatibility mode, or even disable the latter. For more information, click an item and then click Details. Any resolution is very much device specific, but you should make every endeavour to obtain drivers that are 32-bit compliant. There may be generic drivers on the Windows 98 CD-ROM, or you may find advice or upgrades at the Web sites for the PC supplier or the component manufacturer.

Hard disk

If your PC was upgraded from Windows 3.1x there may be entries in your Config.sys or Autoexec.bat for Smartdrv.exe or other disk cache utility. If so, these statements should be removed.

Windows 98 provides dynamic disk caching so you do not have to set the size. The purpose of the disk cache is to hold disk data in memory to minimise the amount of physical disk reading required. However, you will find that the hard disk is much more active in Windows 98 than in previous systems.

The reason for the increased disk activity is the amount of paging, the storage of memory data on the hard disk. This is higher in Windows 98 because it aggressively writes the contents of dirty memory pages (pages that contain changes) during system idle time, even if there is no explicit demand for the memory at that time. This means more disk activity during idle-time but faster memory allocations when requests do arrive.

The cache is not the only factor that impinges on file system performance. Swap file I/O operations do not go through the cache. However, if the system begins to page a lot, the disk cache shrinks automatically. A high level of paging may be caused by an application with a working set greater than the amount of physical memory available. If you have this symptom, check that you do not have real-mode drivers, since these exacerbate the problem. Application launch acceleration depends on cluster size. Smaller cluster sizes are better, so the 4 KB cluster size in FAT32 is better than the larger sizes required for FAT16 systems.

There are no explicit settings for cache size, but you can influence it indirectly. To optimise file system disk cache:

1 Select File System from the System Properties, Performance tab and click Hard Disk.

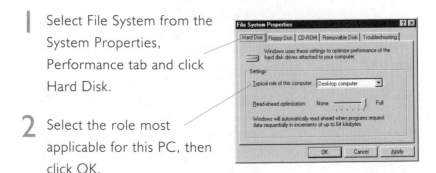

2 Select the role most applicable for this PC, then click OK.

There are three different PC roles and hence three performance profiles defined:

1 The typical applications or network client PC, with adequate memory, and running on power rather than battery.

2 A PC running on battery, or any PC with limited memory, so the disk cache needs to be flushed frequently.

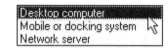

You must restart the PC for changes to take effect.

3 A PC with adequate memory, and with a high level of disk access, or a PC used for file or printer sharing.

The disk performance profile adjusts the values of file system settings in the registry:

PathCache is the size of the cache VFAT uses to save locations of the most recently accessed directory paths (desktop 32 paths, mobile 16 paths, server 64 paths).

NameCache stores the locations of the most recently accessed file names (677, 337 and 2729 locations respectively).

The values to be assigned to each disk profile are stored in the registry under the FS Templates key.

The other hard disk setting provided is readahead optimization. However, you should leave the slider at Full (64 KB read ahead) unless you are extremely constrained for memory.

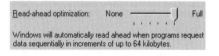

Removable drives

The options for floppy and other removable drives are not very extensive.

1 Select File System from the System Properties, Performance tab and then click Floppy Disk.

2 Select or deselect to search for new diskette.

This option is set on by default, even for desktop machines.

This option directs the floppy disk driver to scan for new drives every time Windows starts. Portable PCs can start with or without a floppy drive. If this applies to you, select to Search, otherwise deselect the option and Windows will start faster, and the floppy driver will use the previous settings for drive information.

Windows 98 also provides an option to improve the performance of removable disks such as ZIP or JAZ, by using write-behind caching. The default is the safety first option to write immediate. To change the setting:

If you switch this on, always wait a few seconds before manually removing a disk. There should be no problem if you use the software Eject option.

3 Select File System from the Performance tab and then Removable Disk.

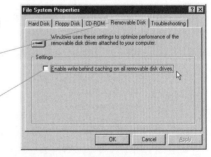

4 Select to Enable write-behind caching on all removable disk drives.

If this option is set, writes are collected and applied as a group. The disk will perform faster, but there is a chance of data loss, for example if a disk is removed too quickly. If problems do arise, you must reselect the option to clear the box and switch off write-caching.

CD-ROM and DVD

This sets the amount of the allocated size to set aside as the cache. Large means 100%.

1 Select File System from the System Properties, Performance tab and then click CD-ROM.

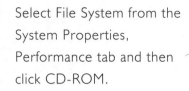

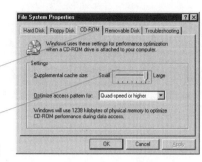

2 Move the slider to Large unless there is a very limited amount of physical memory available.

The access pattern and cache size are allocated by CD-ROM speed.

3 Click the entry that matches the speed of your CD-ROM drive.

4 Click OK and restart the system for the change to take effect.

```
No read-ahead
Single-speed drives
Double-speed drives
Triple-speed drives
Quad-speed or higher
```

The CD-ROM does not share the disk file and network access cache, because the characteristics of the CD-ROM drive are different. This cache can be paged to disk, which reduces the total working set Windows 98 while still providing better CD-ROM performance. It is generally quicker to read data from the cache even when it has been paged to hard disk than to retrieve that data from the CD.

With a typical Windows 98 PC having 32 MB and at least an 8x CD-ROM drive, these options are of academic interest to many users.

Even a small CD-ROM cache makes a substantial difference in performance when information is being streamed from the disc, but the benefit does not change significantly when the cache size is increased. The sizes allocated (Small and Large settings) are:

No read-ahead	64 KB	1088 KB
Single-speed	64 KB	1088 KB
Double-speed	114 KB	1138 KB
Triple-speed	164 KB	1188 KB
Quad-speed	214 KB	1238 KB

The DMA setting does not appear for CD-ROM drives attached through soundcards rather than IDE.

You optimise I/O Transfers by using direct memory access (DMA) with integrated device electronics (IDE) CD-ROM and disk drives. It means that the processor usage during data transfers will be much lower. DMA is enabled by default on modern PCs, but because certain older IDE drives can corrupt data when using DMA, you should approach this option with caution if you have an older PC that has been upgraded to support Windows 98. To enable DMA:

1 Click Win+Pause/Break to open System Properties and select the Device Manager tab.

2 Open the CD-ROM or Disk drives branch, select an IDE device and click Properties.

3 Click the Settings tab and click the DMA box to select it (unless already set).

4 Click OK, and restart the PC for the change to take effect.

This option applies to DVD (digital video/versatile disc) drives connected through IDE, but because they primarily use the Universal Disk Format (UDF) for their file systems, the CD-ROM cache does not apply. Instead, UDF uses the main file system cache (Vcache) and there are no DVD system performance settings for you to change.

Troubleshooting

Turn off aspects of file system operation to help locate the cause of problems.

The File System option provides a set of options for changing file system performance. If you experience strange hardware or software compatibility problems, you can try these options to see if you can isolate the problem. Enabling these file system troubleshooting options will have a serious impact on system performance. Only apply options when so advised by your technical support specialist. To display the list of file system troubleshooting options:

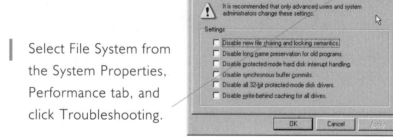

Select File System from the System Properties, Performance tab, and click Troubleshooting.

- Disable new file sharing and locking semantics (for MS-DOS applications with file sharing problems under Windows 98).

- Disable long name preservation for old programs (to run an old application that is not compatible with long file names).

- Disable protected-mode hard disk interrupt handling (for hard disk drives that need to have the BIOS handle interrupts, even though this slows system performance).

- Disable synchronous buffer commits (to allow adequate performance of a defective database application that uses the file commit API incorrectly and excessively).

- Disable all 32-bit protected-mode disk drivers (if the computer does not start because of disk peripheral I/O problems).

- Disable write-behind caching for all drives (if you are running an unstable application, to ensure that no data is lost).

Graphics features can also be switched in and out of play.

You can turn off graphics hardware acceleration features when system performance shows that there are incompatibility problems. Problems can occur when Windows 98 assumes that the display adapter can support functions that are in fact not supported. There will be side effects which could be minor irregularities on screen, or you might have more severe effects, or even system failure.

To change graphics performance settings:

1 Select Graphics from the System Properties, Performance tab.

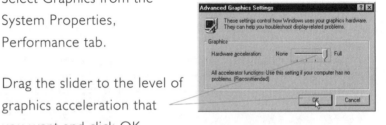

Run the graphics adapter at the highest level that eliminates the errors.

2 Drag the slider to the level of graphics acceleration that you want and click OK.

This option is used to help in problem solving, by eliminating the display adapter as the cause. The slider has four positions:

• The default setting is Full, which is the fastest and the one recommended for most PCs. If your PC has problems and you suspect the graphics adapter, try progressively lower settings to see if the problem is eliminated.

• The first notch down (Most) disables hardware cursor support and can be used to correct mouse pointer problems.

• The next position (Basic) prevents bit block transfers on the display adapter, and disables memory-mapped I/O. It could resolve display errors.

• The lowest position (none) could resolve problems where your PC stops responding to input.

Swap File

Windows 98 allocates virtual memory address space for application programs and data, and allows numerous applications and tasks to operate simultaneously. This could potentially require far more memory than the actual amount installed, so the memory is divided into pages and the working set of currently operational pages is kept in RAM while the rest of the pages are stored on the hard disk until needed. When information is required, Windows 98 copies it back to RAM and if necessary swaps other pages to disk. This all happens in the background, though you may notice the disk activity especially during otherwise idle periods on the PC.

The Windows 98 virtual memory swap file (or paging file) is dynamic, and can shrink or grow based on the demands from the applications and on the available disk space. The dynamic swap file is an efficient method that is not substantially affected by disk fragmentation, though it is important to keep ample free space available on the drive to allow the file to expand when necessary.

The swap file can even be stored on a compressed drive managed by a protected-mode driver such as DriveSpace. This marks the swap file as incompressible and places it as the last file in the sector heap to allow room for the file to shrink and grow as needed.

To view the current settings:

Open System Properties, click the Performance tab, and press the Virtual Memory button.

The default settings show that Windows is managing the virtual memory. There is also a warning message stressing the importance of these settings. However, you can make changes if, for example, you have multiple drives on your PC and want to select a different drive for the swap file.

...cont'd

Run Scandisk and defragment the drive before you assign it for the swap file.

To control the virtual memory swap file settings:

2 Click to specify your own virtual memory settings, and the input fields are revealed.

3 Choose a different drive to see the space available there.

If you set the minimum equal to the maximum, Windows creates the full size at start. This is effectively a permanent swap file.

4 Enter a minimum value and a maximum value.

The swap file could be placed on the drive with the highest performance, or on a drive that has otherwise a low level of activity. For example, one drive could be used for program code and a different drive for virtual memory.

If you set the maximum swap file size to the amount of free space currently on the drive, Windows 98 assumes that it can increase the swap file beyond that size if more free disk space becomes available. To impose a fixed limit on the swap file size, make the limit less than the current maximum as shown.

5 Click Ok, click Yes to the warning message, and restart the PC.

6 You will find the swap file created as Win386.swp on the selected drive.

Network Performance

Windows 98 automatically adjusts system settings to match the network configuration and the application usage. It alters the size of the paging file and cache buffer as memory demands change, and it automatically tunes network time-out values to fit, varying the local area network (LAN) structure. Manual tuning is normally not required or recommended to improve network throughput, but there are a number of ways in which you can help the system to maximise performance:

- Use a 32-bit, protected-mode network client such as the Microsoft Client for NetWare Networks rather than the Virtual Loadable Module (VLM) or NetWare 3.*x* workstation shell (NETX) version of the NetWare client.

- Do not add unnecessary protocols if you already have all the network connections.

- Use the new network driver interface specification (NDIS) version 3.1 or later network adapter drivers provided with Windows 98.

- If your PC has no modem in use, and you do not use Point-to-Point Tunnelling Protocol (PPTP), remove all Dial-Up Networking components.

- Install a new network adapter, preferably PCI, since current adapters have better performance than earlier models and include Plug and Play support.

The following measures can help you obtain the best performance from computers that provide file and printer sharing services:

- Allow Windows 98 to manage the swap file.

- Set the PC role to Network server.

- On a PC running file and printer sharing for NetWare, set the read-only attribute on shared files wherever possible since the network client can take better advantage of file caching with read-only files.

MS-DOS applications

For MS-DOS applications that run in MS-DOS sessions under Windows 98, you should ensure that you are using the features of Windows 98 to handle as much of the processing as possible. Many of the actions needed to achieve this also help with the second requirement, to maximise the amount of conventional memory available to the MS-DOS application.

Consider adding real-mode Autoexec entries to a batch file run when the program starts, so they don't affect the rest of the system.

- Add Himem.sys and Emm386.exe to Config.sys, and load any required real-mode drivers and applications using devicehigh or loadhigh statements.

- Remove as many real-mode drivers and TSRs from Config.sys and Autoexec.bat as possible and use the equivalent protected-mode drivers and applications designed for Windows 98.

- Specify buffershigh, fcbshigh, fileshigh, lastdrivehigh, and stackshigh and the reserved memory that these use will be taken from upper memory.

MS-DOS mode programs lose out on the Windows 98 performance benefits.

- Do not put Smartdrv.exe or other real-mode disk cache programs in Config.sys or Autoexec.bat since Windows 98 handles disk caching, for MS-DOS sessions.

- You may still run the Memmaker.exe program from MS-DOS 6.2x to optimise the loading of real-mode drivers in the upper memory blocks (UMBs). However, this utility is no longer included in the Oldmsdos folder of the Windows 98 CD.

For MS-DOS applications that run in MS-DOS mode, you may still require real-mode disk cache programs. However, these should be added to customised Config and Autoexec files.

You shouldn't expect MS-DOS mode to provide as good performance, since the applications cannot take advantage of Windows 98 protected-mode drivers, Vcache and 32-bit disk access. Since more real-mode device drivers must be loaded, this also reduces the amount of conventional memory available to the application.

Monitoring performance

You can use the System Monitor tool (see page 116) to help resolve performance problems that may arise. However, you need to run the program regularly and learn what sort of charts are typical for your particular system and application usage. If possible, run with the System Monitor window to be always on top.

1 Select System Monitor from System Tools (or add it to your Startup folder).

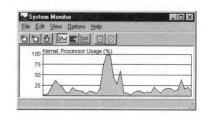

2 Select View, Always on Top and then View, Hide Title Bar. It also hides the menu, toolbar and status bar.

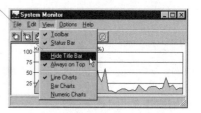

3 Click and drag to move the window out of the way if it obscures part of your application data.

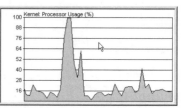

4 Click and drag an edge or corner of the window to resize the window. Even a small window allows you to keep an eye on the progress of the monitored value.

5 To restore the title bar and other items, double-click an empty part of the display, not the chart (that would display the chart options instead).

...cont'd

Run as few applications as possible, and monitor one item or set of items at a time, to avoid interactions.

The items you track when you use System Monitor in troubleshooting performance problems depend on the type of situation you are facing. For example:

- If Kernel: Processor Usage (%) is high even when there are no active applications; check which programs are loaded, using the Tasklist.

- If you suspect an application does not release memory blocks, monitor Kernel: Threads. You should be able to detect if the application starts threads without reclaiming them. Windows 98 will remove them when the application closes, so you can stop and restart an application that has this problem.

To display the Tasklist, press the keys Ctrl+Alt+Del once only.
Press Cancel to return to the applications.

- High levels of activity with Memory Manager: Discards and Memory Manager: Page-outs, indicate a need for more physical memory.

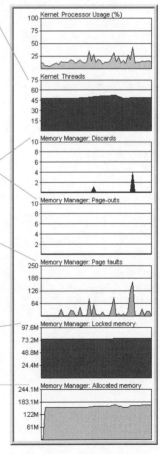

- If Memory Manager: Page faults are high, the applications being used might need more physical memory (or run fewer simultaneously).

- If Memory Manager: Locked memory statistics are continually a large portion of the Memory Manager: Allocated memory value, you may be running an application that locks memory (makes it non-pagable) unnecessarily.

Walign and WinAlign

You cannot realign files such as antivirus utilities that check their own validity before running.

The Winalign.exe and Walign.exe tools optimise the performance of program executable code. Windows 98 Setup installs the Walign.exe tool, and it is used to optimise Microsoft Office programs. The Winalign.exe tool is included in the Windows 98 Resource Kit, and it is used to optimise other programs.

Both operate by writing file sections to start on a 4 KB boundary and updating the section table and file headers to indicate that the file is now aligned. With files aligned in this way, the Windows 98 CacheMap feature can map directly to sections in the cache memory. This can result in significant performance increases and in freeing more memory.

To align the binary program files in the Paint Shop Pro folder for example:

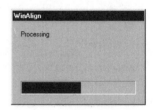

1 Start an MS-DOS prompt, switch to the folder containing Winalign, e.g. C:\Progra~1\Win98rk\Powertoy.

2 Run Winalign, with the PSP folder as the parameter e.g. Winalign c:\progra~1\Paints~1 -X

You can revert to the original files, if required. Run Winalign -R and it uses the log entries to restore files to their original, unaligned state.

Winalign.exe creates and updates a record in the registry to track the changes made to all of the files it has aligned. The registry key is HKEY_LOCAL_MACHINE \software\microsoft\windows\currentversion\winalign.

3 View the registry entry.

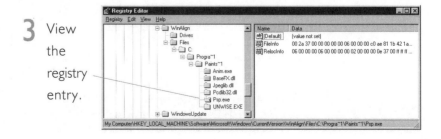

The Registry

This chapter looks at the structure of the registry, the way Windows uses it, how to backup and restore the entries, and some of changes you can apply with its Editor.

Covers

Chapter Eighteen

Registry files

The registry is the central point of storage and reference for all hardware, software, network and communications settings, and for the personal preferences that you have chosen. Even when the equipment details are obtained dynamically, from plug and play or PC card devices, the data is stored in the registry.

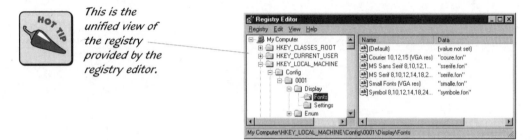

This is the unified view of the registry provided by the registry editor.

The result is that the registry files form a relatively large database, typically 4 MB, which is heavily accessed by applications and system functions. To provide the necessary performance it is organised in a hierarchical structure.

Windows 98 uses the registry to help allocate and manage resources such as interrupt requests (IRQs), I/O addresses and direct memory accesses (DMAs). It is analogous to the INI files used in Windows 3.1x, but with the addition of nested keys and support for binary data as well as character strings. The older 16-bit programs still use INI files, but Windows 98 transfers the settings to the registry.

Registry services use less real-mode and protected-mode memory, and have better caching support. This dramatically improves the time used to look up values in the registry. The 64 KB registry key size limit in Windows 95 has been removed in Windows 98. This allows for more applications with shared dynamic link libraries (DLLs).

Windows 98 provides many ways for viewing and updating the information in the registry. Because it is crucial to system operation, Windows 98 automatically backs-up up the registry and repairs or restores it when needed.

Although the registry is logically one data store, physically it consists of two or three different files, to provide flexibility and allow for networks and multiple users.

To locate the files:

These files are Hidden as well as Read-only, so you must select Show All Files in Folder Options to see them.

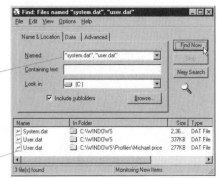

1 Press Win+F and Find "System.dat", "User.dat" on the C: drive.

2 You may find several versions of the User.dat file.

System.dat is always in the Windows folder, and holds the PC-specific information: hardware parameters, plug and play data and application software settings.

With the User.dat in a central server, you can log on to any PC on the LAN and still have your own setup and authorities.

User.dat contains the user-specific information: logon name, desktop settings and Start menu settings. Setup puts User.dat in the Windows folder, but if user profiles are enabled, users will have their own copy of User.dat in the Profiles folder, or on a central network server.

The use of separate registry files allows multiple users to share PCs, yet retain their own logon name, user profile, and personal authorities and permissions.

A third file Policy.pol may exist on a network system, to override settings in the two DAT files, and so enforce company or departmental standards, or to hold additional data specific to the network or company environment. This file is not a mandatory component, and so will not appear in every Windows 98 installation.

The Policies approach makes it easy for the network administrator to manage all the users defined for a local area network, to establish standards and to apply the level of control that the company considers appropriate.

Registry structure

The Registry Editor displays the contents of the registry database in six root keys with a hierarchical Explorer style display. The root key names begin with "HKEY_", standing for Handle, and each HKEY contains subkeys, which themselves may contain subkeys or data names and values.

- Root key.

- Subkey.

- Subsubkey.

- Data name.

- Data value.

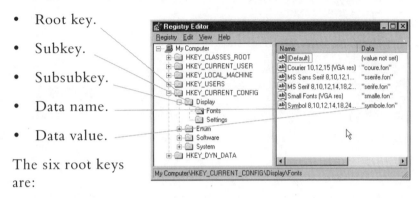

The six root keys are:

Some of these root keys are actually aliases for branches within the other roots, so programs can reference current values.

HKEY_LOCAL_MACHINE contains the hardware installed and the software settings. On a multiple configuration PC, for example a laptop with a docking station, it has a configuration branch for each hardware profile.

HKEY_CURRENT_CONFIG points to the branch of the HKEY_LOCAL_MACHINE\Config that contains the data for the current hardware configuration (active profile).

HKEY_DYN_DATA holds dynamic data stored in RAM which may change as devices are added to or removed. It is used by the Device Manager and System Monitor.

HKEY_CLASSES_ROOT points to the \Software\Classes branch of the KEY_LOCAL_MACHINE and describes software settings related to OLE and file associations, used for drag-and-drop operations, and Windows 98 shortcuts.

HKEY_USERS contains generic and user-specific data about the users who log on to the PC, with application defaults and desktop layouts (user profiles).

HKEY_CURRENT_USER points to the current user profile, the branch of HKEY_USERS for the logged on user.

...cont'd

Any change that you make to the system is reflected in an update to the data values in particular subkeys associated with the item you have reconfigured.

Wallpaper holds the file name, and the TileWallpaper and WallpaperStyle values specify the tile, centre and stretch options.

1 Open Display Properties and select Clouds as your desktop background.

2 The Wallpaper data values in the Current User Panel Desktop show the new settings.

The keys and value sets are initialised by setup programs, and modified by the various Properties options available. Registry values may be added or updated whenever you:

- Install or reconfigure Windows applications.

- Run the Add New Hardware option or other hardware setup programs.

- Access Windows Update to add fixes and changes to Windows 98.

- Customise the desktop, the settings are added to the registry.

- Add or remove a Plug and Play device.

The Editor does not provide any form of content or context validation.

- Install or remove a PC Card device.

- Run the System Configuration utility, or TweakUI.

- Customise the desktop or the display.

Keys and data values can also be added and changed by hand, using the Registry Editor (Regedit.exe).

Registry Editor

Registry Editor is a very powerful utility, mainly intended for use by specialist PC and network support staff. It will make any change you want, but the user support functions are very basic – it applies the changes without checking that they are valid or appropriate. The updates happen immediately, and are written into the System.dat or User.dat file on disk. The effects may also be immediate. However, it may be necessary to prompt the system into rereading the data, either by pressing F5 to refresh the display and other settings, or by restarting Windows completely.

To run the editor:

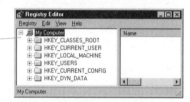

1. Select Start, Run (or press Win+R), type regedit, press OK.

2. Click [+] to expand branches, and scroll the lists of subkeys.

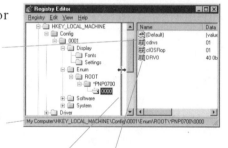

The values of the selected or active key appear in the right pane of the Registry Editor window.

3. The status bar shows the fully qualified name.

4. Drag the divider to the right or left to change the page sizes.

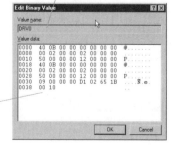

5. Double-click a value to view or change its contents.

...cont'd

Registry Editor does not have an Undo function. All changes are written directly to the disk.

To add a new entry to the registry:

1 Highlight the entry point branch and right-click the Values pane.

2 Select the type of entry – a new key, or a data value.

3 Type the name for the item and press Enter (or click elsewhere on the pane).

4 To initialise a new data value, double-click the name.

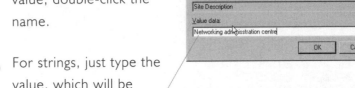

5 For strings, just type the value, which will be enclosed in quotes and stored in the registry.

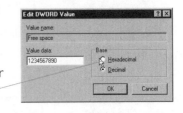

6 For a double word, select hex or decimal, and enter the value.

Dwords are displayed in hex and in decimal on the values pane.

7 For a binary value, enter a sequence of hex digits, up to 16 KB in length.

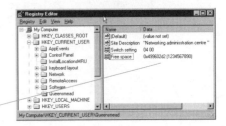

8 The data values will be shown on the pane.

Finding entries

Registry Editor does not search for binary or Dword values. Export the Registry to a REG text file to search in these data types.

You can search for particular entries by names or string values:

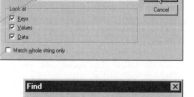

1 Select Edit, Find (or press Ctrl+F) and type all or part of the text string item.

2 Specify where to look (keys, values or data) if possible.

The registry is searched forwards from the selected key. The first item that matches is displayed.

You may see the same entry more than once, for example in HKEY_CURRENT_ USER and HKEY_USERS, because of the root key aliases.

3 Select Edit, Find next (or press F3) to search for the subsequent matches.

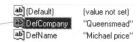

The Editor lets you know if there are no further matches in the registry.

If you wish to remove an entry from the registry, locate it as above, and then:

4 Select the entry, and select Delete from the shortcut menu.

All lower level entries will also be removed. There is no checking. You may prefer to rename the entry, and check that there are no side effects. Avoid using names that could relate to a valid system function. To rename an entry:

5 Select the entry, and then select Rename from the shortcut menu.

Registry Checker

Registry Checker runs automatically each time you start the PC, and scans the registry for inconsistent structures. If no problem is found, Registry Checker makes one backup for each day. Registry Checker also compacts the registry when necessary to remove space.

Each new backup replaces the oldest CAB file, so the file names are recycled.

If a problem is found, Registry Checker can restore the registry from a good backup copy from one of up to five compressed backups in the \Windows\Sysbackup folder. It attempts to fix the registry if a valid backup cannot be found.

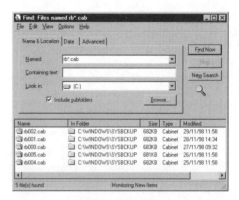

To run Registry Checker after startup:

You can also press Win+R, then type Scanregw.exe, and click OK to start the program.

1 Run System Information from the System Tools folder.

2 Select Tools from the menu bar and then click Registry Checker.

3 If there are no errors, select No to a new backup to finish.

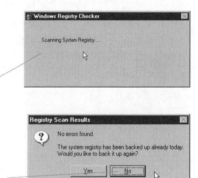

Scanregw detects when optimization is required, and sets a signal for the next startup.

If it detects a problem with the registry, Scanregw starts the MS-DOS mode Scanreg.exe, which prompts you to restart the PC to fix the problem. ScanReg restores the registry from a known good backup, or, if no backups are available, it repairs the current registry by removing the invalid entries.

Backup and restore

You can also create a backup from MS-DOS mode, running Scanreg /backup.

If you have changed the registry or system files, and want a new backup without waiting for next day's automatic copy:

1 Start Registry Checker from System Information and allow it to check your files.

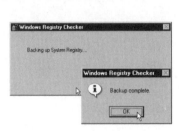

2 If there are no errors, choose Yes to create a new backup.

3 The new backup is prepared and added to the Sysbackup folder, using the next filename.

If the registry structure is sound but you want to revert to a previous backup, perhaps to remove some unwanted changes, you need to manually restore from a backup:

Started means that the file has successfully started Windows 98, and is a known good file.

1 Select Start, Shutdown, Restart in MS-DOS mode, press OK. At the MS-DOS mode prompt, enter Scanreg /restore.

2 Select a working cab backup file that meets your needs.

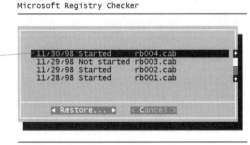

Select a cab to restore from.

You can change the number of backups from the default of five, using the INI file.

3 When the system files are restored, click Restart.

The Registry Checker scan and backup tools use the Scanreg.ini file for configuration details.

The Registry Checker creates compressed backup files, typically 25% of the working size. However, the registry can be exported in a plain text format, with file type REG. The plain text version contains all the keys, names and values, stored in sequence. The file size is somewhat larger than the working registry, and there are around 100,000 lines of data. It can be used as a backup and to search for binary or double word entries.

You can also export individual branches, and these can be used to add or remove particular registry definitions without having to restore the whole registry, and as a precaution prior to deleting entries.

To export a REG file using Registry Editor:

1 Run Registry Editor, and select the branch or subkey that you want to export.

2 Select Registry from the menu bar, and click Export Registry File.

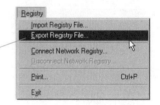

3 Select the folder, enter the file name and click Save.

4 View the contents using Notepad (or Wordpad for large REG files).

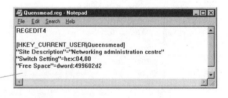

You can import a REG file by double clicking on the file icon.

To import a REG file that you previously exported or that has been prepared for you by your technical specialist:

5 Select Edit, Import Registry file, and select the REG file.

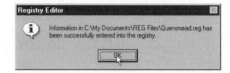

Real mode registry

You can replace or rebuild your registry, even if Windows won't start. Use the Registry Editor, but run it in MS-DOS mode.

The Registry Editor program can run in real-mode MS-DOS as well as under Windows. If Windows won't start, boot your PC from the emergency disk into MS-DOS mode. Access the Registry Editor from the Windows startup disk or from the Windows folder, and run the editor using its command line interface. Check out the facilities while your system is working, so that you will know what to do in an emergency:

1 Select Start, Shutdown and Restart in MS-DOS mode, or boot the PC from your emergency startup disk.

2 At the MS-DOS prompt, enter Regedit, without parameters, to display a help screen showing the functions offered.

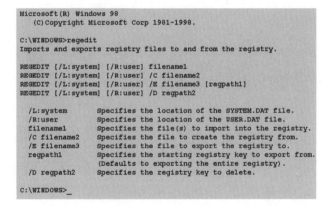

You must use the MS-DOS aliases for the names of folders and files.

Regedit allows you to specify the locations of the registry files, the names of the import or export REG files and the address of the subkey branch. You can import or export the whole registry or the specified subkey, or delete the subkey.

To add the contents of a REG file into the registry:

3 At the MS-DOS mode prompt, enter a command such as regedit c:\mydocu~1\regfil~1\quensm~1.reg

Plug and Play

Everything that the system needs to know about your hardware is stored in the registry, allowing you to add and remove plug and play devices without having to reconfigure the system.

Although Windows 98 and the registry support plug and play operation, for full function your PC must have a plug and play system BIOS, and the devices likewise must be compliant. Installing new devices happens transparently, without any need for card jumper settings, or software settings. Devices can even be added while the system is active.

The registry provides the foundation for this since it contains all the hardware information to allow Windows 98 to automatically configure the hardware device, or to assist you in setting it up.

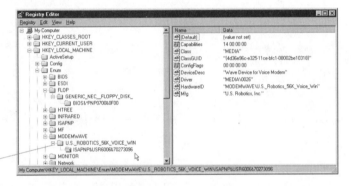

This branch of the registry shows some of the details recorded for the USRobotics voice modem.

Windows 98 uses the device ID to search the INF files for that device. It then creates an entry in the HKEY_LOCAL_MACHINE key and copies information from the INF file into the Enum keys. Enum refers to the Windows 98 enumeration process that checks the hardware device. The registry entries define the allocation of system resource, the device status and configuration information.

If you have several different setups, for example with a mobile PC that sometimes uses a docking bay, you may have several separate hardware profiles defined, and Windows will select the appropriate one at startup time, based on the hardware detected.

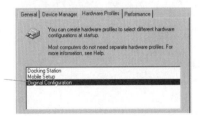

User Profiles

When you allow several users to share the same PC, by default they all share the same desktop, Start menu and display settings. However, some will want different folder views and desktop layout, which could mean that the setup always needs adjustment.

Users

Passwords

The first time you click on this icon the wizard runs to enable multiuser support.

The Users option in the Control Panel resolves the problem by allowing you to define user profiles:

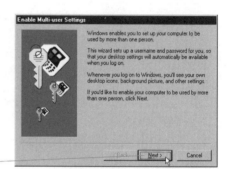

I Open the Control Panel from Settings and double-click the Users option, then click Next.

If you have previously logged on using that name it will remember and prompt for your password (even if set to null).

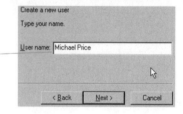

2 Enter the user name and supply a password if required.

3 Select the items you want to personalise, choosing from:

Desktop

Start menu

Favorites

Web pages

My Documents

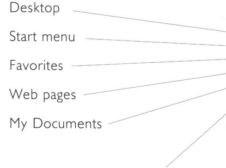

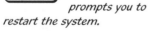

Windows copies or creates your User folders and then prompts you to restart the system.

4 Choose to copy the items, or create a new set of user folders for these items.

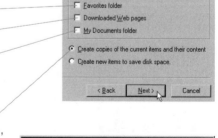

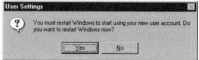

...cont'd

When the system reboots you see the new multiuser logon panel.

User Profiles are part of Password but have no real security features.

I Select the user name and enter the password if required.

The first time you log on with a particular name, the profile is created, settings are personalised and shortcuts are set up.

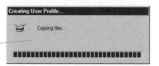

2 Open Control Panel from Settings and double-click Passwords.

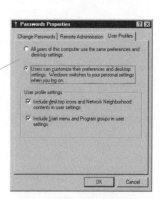

You will see that the User Profiles option has now been enabled. However, although included in the Passwords option, User Profiles does not provide any security features. Any user can sign on and add, remove or modify profiles.

To add a new user:

3 Open Users from Control Panel. This time the user list is displayed.

4 Click New User, enter the name and password and profile settings.

5 Select any user profile and click the Set Password or the Change Settings button to make any required adjustments.

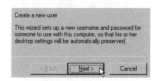

Troubleshooting

When problems arise with the registry, Windows can usually detect the cause and take the necessary action, or issue a message telling you what needs to be done.

When Windows 98 starts up, the first step is to read the registry system information, so problems here will prevent Windows initialising. If there are problems accessing the registry, you may get one of these error messages:

- Windows encountered an error accessing the system Registry. Windows will restart and repair the system Registry for you now.

- Windows 98 will restart your PC and run the Registry Checker in MS-DOS mode (Scanreg.exe) to fix the problem.

When you start Windows 98, you receive the following error message:

- Windows was unable to process the registry. This may be fixed by rebooting to Command Prompt Only and running SCANREG /FIX. Otherwise there may not be enough conventional memory to properly load the registry.

If this message appears after you run ScanReg /Fix, then you need to free up conventional memory in your PC.

You may also encounter errors when you use Add/Remove Programs to remove an application:

For example, if you delete the Paint Shop Pro folder, you'll lose Unwise.exe, and you'll have to remove the reference by hand.

- An error occurred while trying to remove <Appname>. Uninstallation has been cancelled.

This can happen if you manually delete the application folder and remove the uninstall program. To remove the invalid entry from the Install/Uninstall list:

1 Run Regedit.exe and navigate to HKEY_LOCAL_MACHINE \Software\Microsoft\Windows\CurrentVersion\Uninstall.

2 Locate the <Appname> entry and delete that subkey.

Easy double-click

When you understand the registry editor and checker, you can afford to take advantage of some of the so-called registry hacks to add useful features to your setup.

Windows 98 provides many tools for changing and customising the system. If the standard tools don't have the function you want, you'll probably find it in one of the tools provided in the resource kit sampler. However, there are some changes that can only be made through the registry. Make a backup or export the branch concerned before applying any of these changes.

The first suggestion is making double-clicks easier.

Some members of your family may find it difficult to master the double-click. You can change the delay in Mouse Properties, but it is not just a matter of timing. If the mouse pointer moves slightly between clicks, Windows interprets this as a really small move instead of a double-click. You can change the sensitivity for this interpretation:

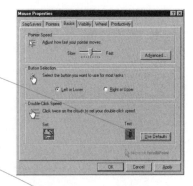

If you have enabled multiple users, you need to log on as the specific user.

1 Log on to Windows as the user with the concern over double-click.

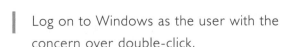

2 Run Regedit.exe and expand the branch HKEY_CURRENT_USER \Control Panel\Desktop.

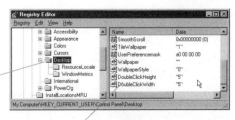

Start at 5 x 5 pixels, but you may need to experiment with the number to suit the user.

3 Create two new string values called DoubleClickHeight and DoubleClickWidth and initialise each of them as 5.

4 Select Registry, Exit. Logoff and logon again as the same user, and try double-clicking.

Registration data

You may want to change the registration data if you pass your PC on to someone else.

You might start by making sure that the registry gets your name right. The user name and company are provided during the initial Windows installation. To see the entries:

1 Press Win+Pause/Break to open SystemProperties, and view the General tab entries.

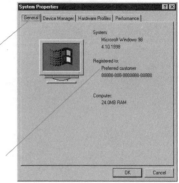

You may have a mis-type perhaps dating back to your original Windows 3.1x installation, or you may have the Preferred customer entry that some manufacturers seem to delight in. With Registry Editor, you can change the values.

2 Run Regedit.exe and expand the branch HKEY_LOCAL_MACHINE\Software\Microsoft \Windows\Current-Version.

This data is loaded when System Properties runs, so there is no need to restart the system.

3 Locate the values RegisteredOwner and RegisteredOrganization and modify them as required.

4 Select Registry, Exit and Open the System Properties again to check that the changes have been applied.

Change aliases

Treat this idea with some caution. Installing new applications to Program Files could create confusion between the alias PROGRA~1 assigned at Setup, and the alias PROGRAMF that the new rule implies.

As discussed on page 68, Windows 98 allocates MS-DOS aliases for long file names using an algorithm. It takes the first six valid characters, adds a tilde and then a numeric counter, even if there would be no duplicates within the folder.

With a Registry change, you can modify the rule so that the first eight valid characters are selected for the first occurrence. The tilde and counter method will only be used for the second and subsequent duplicate alias.

| Run Regedit.exe and expand the branch HKEY_LOCAL_MACHINE\System\CurrentControlSet \Control\FileSystem.

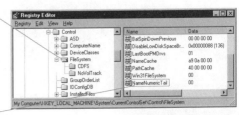

2 Create a new binary value and name it NameNumericTail and set its value to 00.

This change affects the machine definition so a complete restart is needed.

3 Click Start, Shutdown, Restart, OK. This will reload the definitions for the current machine.

4 To see the change, create a new folder, right-click, and select New to add two new Wordpad files

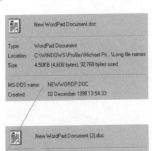

5 Right-click each file and select Properties, General to see the MS-DOS names. Only the second file has a tilde and counter.

Start menu sequence

When applications add entries to the Start menu, they initially appear at the end of the folder list. When Windows 98 restarts however, they are moved to their alphabetic position in the list. When you add entries using the Start menu options in Settings, the items are sorted right away.

You can change this by simply dragging menu items to a new position in the list. However, this will inhibit Windows 98 from sorting the folder for future changes.

1 Add Regedit to the System Tools folder on the Start menu. It appears in the middle of the list, in alphabetical sort sequence.

2 Click and drag the entry to the top of the list, and drop it into its new position.

3 Add an entry for Msconfig.exe. It appears at the end of the list and does not get sorted.

Windows 98 stores the sort order of the Start menu in HKEY_CURRENT_USER\Software\Microsoft\Windows \CurrentVersion\Explorer\MenuOrder\StartMenu with Menu subkeys and Order values for each subfolder.

- Menu Order.
- Start Menu.
- Subfolder.
- Menu.
- Order values.

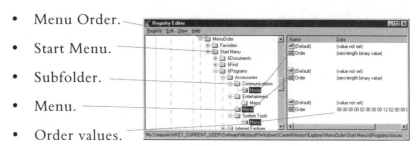

In this case, they will all be set to (zero length binary) except for the System Tools folder which has a binary string defining the sequence of the entries in the folder.

To save the sort sequence, so that you can restore it later if the menu accidentally gets rearranged:

4 Select the MenuOrder\StartMenu key, and click Registry, Export registry file, to create a REG plain text backup file.

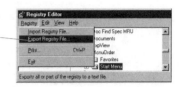

Don't try to edit these strings to revise the sort order. It is much easier and safer to rearrange the entries with drag and drop.

To restore the default Windows 98 sort action for a particular folder:

5 Select the MenuOrder\StartMenu key, locate the folder, and select its Order value. Press Del. Press Yes to confirm.

To restore sorting for all subfolders in the Start menu:

6 Select the MenuOrder\StartMenu key, and press Del to delete the whole sub branch. Press Yes to confirm.

The next time you start the system, the menu items in the selected folder or in the whole Start menu will be back to their normal sequence.

Note that there are similar Menu and Order entries for the Favorites folder and subfolders, so you can use similar procedures to sequence or restore these also.

Preview bitmaps

Folders full of bitmaps are not very exciting, but you can brighten them up if you tell Windows 98 to display a miniature version of the contents of each BMP file, instead of the icon from the associated viewer program.

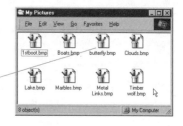

Thumbnail view (see page 65) provides an alternative, but must be applied to individual folders.

To change the default action for bitmaps:

1 Run Regedit.exe and expand the branch HKEY_CLASSES_ROOT\Paint.Picture\DefaultIcon

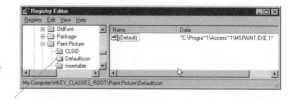

This is an example where it would be very useful to Export the branch to a REG file, so that the change can be reversed if you change your mind later.

2 Set its default value to "%1" (you don't have to type the quotes).

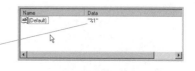

3 Exit Registry, and restart Windows, for example by logging off then logging on again.

4 Open a folder containing bitmaps, and they appear in miniature as the icon for the file. If you view the folder in small icon or list form, the preview is even smaller.

Index

D

Z